# Information Systems Development for Decentralized Organizations

**IFIP – The International Federation for Information Processing**

IFIP was founded in 1960 under the auspices of UNESCO, following the First World Computer Congress held in Paris the previous year. An umbrella organization for societies working in information processing, IFIP's aim is two-fold: to support information processing within its member countries and to encourage technology transfer to developing nations. As its mission statement clearly states,

> IFIP's mission is to be the leading, truly international, apolitical organization which encourages and assists in the development, exploitation and application of information technology for the benefit of all people.

IFIP is a non-profitmaking organization, run almost solely by 2500 volunteers. It operates through a number of technical committees, which organize events and publications. IFIP's events range from an international congress to local seminars, but the most important are:

- the IFIP World Computer Congress, held every second year;
- open conferences;
- working conferences.

The flagship event is the IFIP World Computer Congress, at which both invited and contributed papers are presented. Contributed papers are rigorously refereed and the rejection rate is high.

As with the Congress, participation in the open conferences is open to all and papers may be invited or submitted. Again, submitted papers are stringently refereed.

The working conferences are structured differently. They are usually run by a working group and attendance is small and by invitation only. Their purpose is to create an atmosphere conducive to innovation and development. Refereeing is less rigorous and papers are subjected to extensive group discussion.

Publications arising from IFIP events vary. The papers presented at the IFIP World Computer Congress and at open conferences are published as conference proceedings, while the results of the working conferences are often published as collections of selected and edited papers.

Any national society whose primary activity is in information may apply to become a full member of IFIP, although full membership is restricted to one society per country. Full members are entitled to vote at the annual General Assembly, National societies preferring a less committed involvement may apply for associate or corresponding membership. Associate members enjoy the same benefits as full members, but without voting rights. Corresponding members are not represented in IFIP bodies. Affiliated membership is open to non-national societies, and individual and honorary membership schemes are also offered.

# Information Systems Development for Decentralized Organizations

## Proceedings of the IFIP working conference on information systems development for decentralized organizations, 1995

Edited by

**Arne Sölvberg, John Krogstie and Anne Helga Seltveit**

*Information Systems Group*
*The University of Trondheim*
*Norway*

SPRINGER-SCIENCE+BUSINESS MEDIA, B.V.

First edition 1995


Originally published by Chapman & Hall in 1995

ISBN 978-1-4757-5491-9 ISBN 978-0-387-34871-1 (eBook)
DOI 10.1007/978-0-387-34871-1



A catalogue record for this book is available from the British Library

∞ Printed on permanent acid-free text paper, manufactured in accordance with ANSI/NISO Z39.48-1992 and ANSI/NISO Z39.48-1984 (Permanence of Paper).

# CONTENTS

**Editor's Preface** vii

**Officers, Program Committee Members and Additional Referees** xi

1 Exotica/FMQM: a persistent message-based architecture for distributed workflow management
*G. Alonso, D. Agrawal, C. Mohan, R. Gunthor, A. El Abbadi and M. Kanmath* 1

2 Usability of some workflow products in an inter-organizational setting
*J. Juopperi, A. Lehtola, O. Pihlajamaa, A. Sladek and J. Veijnalainen* 19

3 The systems integration architecture: an agile information infrastructure
*J.J. Mills, R. Elmasri, K. Khan, S. Miriyala and K. Subramanian* 35

4 Message flow control
*A.T.M. Aerts, W. Hofman and L.J. Somers* 51

5 A light weight name service and its use within a collaborative editor
*J.-C. Lugeon and F. Pacull* 67

6 Organizational management system in a hetrogeneous environment: a WWW case study
*A. Silva, J. Borbinha and J. Delgado* 84

7 A federated information system for quality management processes
*P. Peters, P. Szczurko, M. Jarke and M. Jeusfeld* 100

8 A support environment for the disclosure of heterogeneous systems documentation
*D. Fijma, T.F. Verhoef and G.M. Wijers* 118

9 Modelling business relationships in a non-centralized systems environment
*I.G. Macdonald and R.A. Veryard* 133

10 Realization of a decentralized IS-strategy
*K. Axelsson* 168

11 A software process model for business reengineering
*A.T. Berztiss and J.A. Bubenko* 184

12 Coupling process models and business rules
*P. McBrien and A.H. Seltveit* 201

13 Discussants comments on the ten main papers 219

14 Panel: The future of business meetings – possibilities and problems of computer support
*Chair: J. Haake* 239

15 Panel: Organisations' IT competence: the limiting factor?
*Chair: N. Høeg* 241

**Index of contributors** 243

**Keyword index** 244

# Editors' Preface

## ISDO'95: AN EXPERIMENT IN USING WWW

The ISDO'95 conference is about information systems development in decentralized and distributed organizations. We felt that it would be in the spirit of the conference to use computers to support the highly distributed process of paper reviewing. We wanted to take our own medicine so to say. Our approach and our experiences are described in the last part of this short introduction to the conference.

## Information systems for decentralized organizations

Organizational efficiency in enterprises and public administration depends increasingly on the ability to support organizations which operate in networks of decentralized, autonomous units. Most of the routine tasks have already been thoroughly automated, in factories as well as in offices. Further improvement of organizational productivity depends on our ability to give adequate support to knowledge workers in organizations, and to make it easier to rapidly change information systems when organizational change is wanted.

Technological change enables increased organizational effectiveness and efficiency. Human factors are of key importance as well as our ability to implement organizational structures that take advantage of the enabling information technologies.

There are many relevant issues some of which are:

- Information systems for business process re-engineering.
- Information systems for supporting cooperation between organizations.
- IS support for improving the work flow in organizations.
- Information resource management.
- Methods and tools for decentralized information systems engineering.

## The papers and the discussants

IFIP Working Conferences tend to be focused on limited subject areas. The number and contents of the papers submitted reflect on the level of activity in the research community, in universities and research institutes. The selected papers were thoroughly discussed at the conference. A discussant was appointed for every paper, and prepared a critique for the author to respond to at the conference. Most of the discussants' contributions are published at the end of the book. Three panel sessions on appropriate themes were arranged. Position papers are published at the end of the book as well.

## THE PAPER REVIEW PROCESS

The preparation of a professional conference often involve a large set of widely distributed people. In the ISDO'95 conference, being no exception, the members of the program-committee of the conference were situated on four different continents, and the prospective contributers on five.

To coordinate those involve in such an event, interchange of paper using ordinary mail is still largely used and is an important factor when it comes to time-use and cost. For a typical professional conference, the following normally takes place:

- Call for papers is distributed widely using both paper and electronic means
- Contributers prepare paper-copies of their manuscripts and send these often in the last minute using express mail to the program organizers.
- Papers and review-forms are sent by ordinary mail to program committee members for review.
- Reviews are sent to the organizing committee by mail, fax, or sometimes by email.
- Notification about the decision is sent by email or ordinary mail to the contributers.
- A camera ready copy is prepared and sent by ordinary mail to the organizing committee, which collects the papers and send them to the publisher. This creates a paper proceedings which is returned to the organizing committee in time for the conference.
- Information about the conference is sent by email or ordinary mail to prospective participants. In the last years it has also been usual to have this kind of information available on WWW.

As we see, although some of the tasks are supported by electronic communication, many still basically utilize the postal services.

In connection with the preparation of the conference we set up an experiment to test a scenario that in principle can be used to get rid of the paper altogether, and at least should be able to minimize the use of the postal services applying standard communication technology.

### Scenario

First of all, it was obvious for us that we would have to be able to support both the standard way of working as described above in addition to a completely electronic one, since not all prospective contributers would be linked to the Internet and not even all the program committee members were. Based on current experience with the use of Internet, we went in addition for a contingency approach, making it possible to do the same thing in several ways in case some of the underlying technology would be temporarily unavailable.

The paperless scenario is as follows:

- Call for papers is distributed actively via mail and news, and passively via WWW. It is possible for people to use WWW to issue interest in the conference.
- Contributers can submit papers by using ftp and use mail or WWW to tell the organizers about this. A notification of the reception of papers is sent by email.
- Information about how to access the papers they are to review is given to the program committee members who themselves access and print out the papers, either using ftp or

WWW. Reviews are given electronically, preferably by WWW or alternatively by email. The reviewers are able to update and print out their reviews on WWW until a given date.
- Notification about the result is given out by email, and CRC's to be prepared by the authors of accepted papers is issued using ftp.
- Finally, the accepted papers are made available on WWW, and call for participation distributed via email.

The last point was not carried through, since it was already arranged for traditional publication of the proceedings, but the system that was made support this. We note that other conference-series support this part of the cycle (e.g. ICCI). Several of the CRCs *were* issued electronically because it was the most convenient for the authors.

## Preparation and description of the system

We prepared a set of directories on the ftp-server of the UNIX-network of our university. In addition was a WWW-server established running on the same machine as the local Ingres-server. Ingres was used to contain the necessary data about papers and reviews. Links between WWW and Ingres was coded in C. The WWW-server contained in addition to standard information about the conference, functionality for the reception of reviews.

In addition to this, a back-end system to be used towards the same data-base to input and update data about papers, persons, and reviews was prepared.

As part of the CFP, detailed guidelines for the use of the ftp-server were issued, and the format (Postscript according to Adobe DCS) that we would accept was specified.

All program committee members were given a password to use on the web-server, and those who had explicitly agreed to use it was highly advised to test it out thoroughly before the review-process started. The reviewing on WWW was arranged so that when entering the personal password, a HTML page was created according to the papers that the PC-member was meant to review and if he or she had already reviewed them or not. Electronic papers were also available on ftp. If the paper was available in electronic format, the paper could be retrieved, and printed out by the PC-member. If the paper was not reviewed yet, a form that was made dynamically based on the database contents was created for this paper, into which the review could be entered and submitted. After submitting, the reviewer could return to his overview page (which now would be updated) and enter the review of another paper, or alternatively delete, update, or print the entered reviews.

One important aspect with a system of this kind is security. Papers under consideration and reviews should not be available for anyone but the program and organizing committees, and then on a need to know basis.

This was addressed by making the directory where papers were submitted unreadable, and by having an automatic mechanism for removing the paper from the ftp-server when it was transferred. As for the reviews, we found it sufficient to use a simple password-scheme.

## Experience

Below is some of the experience we made with the system.

- Reception of papers: About 2/3 of the papers were received by ftp. Most of these could be printed unproblematically. The papers were written in diverse text-editors and formats such as latex, framemaker, Word, Ami Pro, and Word Perfect, using Apple Macintosh, Unix workstations, and Windows PC's, and we experienced that postscript is not always Postscript. In most cases, it was simple to get the files printed (i.e. removing the C-D in the start of postscript-files made in Word), but in a few cases it was necessary to get assistance from the local Postscript-experts.
- Distribution of papers: We expected that down-loading the postscript-files using WWW could take some time. The experiences were very different from place to place. Whereas some seemed to have large problems down-loading the files (according to the time outs reported in the error-log) others reported that this was not problematic.
- Entering of reviews: A majority of the reviews were submitted by email, but also quite a few came by the WWW-interface. We had to close this interface down one and a half week before the program-committee meeting though, because of traveling, thus email (or fax) was the only opportunity for late-comers. In addition did we experience an error that was difficult to trace right before the deadline for reviews.
- No security violations were detected, and very few were attempted.

In addition to this, email has been used extensively within the program and organizing committee, as it normally is.

## Conclusion

All in all, the use of the system meant more and not less work for the organizing committee. This was partly because of the novelty of the solution using a newly developed system, and because we had to support several formats.

For contributers, we expect that this way of submitting papers generally should be an advantage. For the program committee this can also be so when it comes to the convenience of entering reviews, but since the organizing committee in any case has to print out the paper to check that this can be done, and the program committee member in most cases also would print out the paper to take it home and read it, it would all in all be more time-efficient to send paper to the PC-members by ordinary mail in the first place, at least as long as the response time on internet across the globe is as it is.

To those who would like to do something similar we have the following advice:

- Have a stable environment.
- Be prepared for trouble and have a contingency approach.
- Have the system properly tested, especially by the program committee, and find out how it is best for the individual PC-member to work.
- If you accept postscript papers, have experts on the format available to help you in case of trouble.

May 1995

Arne Sølvberg
John Krogstie
Anne Helga Seltveit

# Officers, Program Committee Members and Additional Referees

**General Conference Chair:**

Keith Jeffery, Rutherford Appleton Laboratory, UK

**Program Committee Chair:**

Arne Sølvberg, NTH, Norway

**Program Committee:**

| | | | |
|---|---|---|---|
| Rudolf Andersen | Norway | Patrizia Asirelli | Italy |
| Martin Bever | Germany | Sjaak Brinkkemper | The Netherlands |
| Janis Bubenko | Sweden | Panos Constatopoulos | Greece |
| Georg Doukidis | Greece | Peter Egloff | Germany |
| Maria Grazia Fugini | Italy | Ted Goranson | USA |
| Alex Gray | UK | Sol Greenspan | USA |
| Matthias Jarke | Germany | John Kalmus | UK |
| Dimitris Karagiannis | Austria | Gerhard Klett | Germany |
| Michel Leonard | Switzerland | Eva Lindencrona | Sweden |
| Fred Lochovsky | Hong Kong | Peri Loucopoulos | Great Britain |
| Erich Neuhold | Germany | Antoni Olive | Spain |
| Maria Orlowska | Australia | Mike Papazoglou | Australia |
| Barbara Pernici | Italy | Colin Potts | USA |
| Colette Rolland | France | Gunter Schlageter | Germany |
| Costantino Thanos | Italy | Yannis Vassiliou | Greece |
| Anthony I. Wasserman | USA | Richard Welke | USA |

**Program Coordinator:**

John Krogstie, NTH, Norway

**Organizing chair:**

Anne Helga Seltveit, NTH Norway

**Additional Referees:**

A. Bapat
T. Berkel
P. Buhrmann
A. Delis
R. Engmann
P. Fankhauser
C. Ferguson
G. Gable
G. Grosz
F. Harmsen
R. Heite
S. Joosten
T. Knopik
K. Klement
A. Laribi
F. Mazzanti
I. Mistrik
R. Muhlberger
O. Parchet
A. Scherer
G. Scholz
F. Semmak
M. Straube
F. Turini
W. Wilkes
M. Zimmermann
R. L. W. van de Weg

# 1

# Exotica/FMQM: A Persistent Message-Based Architecture for Distributed Workflow Management

*G. Alonso, C. Mohan, R. Günthör*
*IBM Almaden Research Center*
*650 Harry Road, San Jose, CA 95120, USA.*
*E-mail:* {gustavoa,rgunther,mohan}@almaden.ibm.com
*D. Agrawal, A. El Abbadi*
*Computer Science Department, UC Santa Barbara,*
*Santa Barbara, CA 93106, USA.*
*E-mail:* {agrawal,amr}@cs.ucsb.edu
*M. Kamath*
*Computer Science Department, UM at Amherst,*
*Amherst, MA 01003, USA.*
*E-mail:* kamath@cs.umass.edu

**Abstract**

In the past few years there has been an increasing interest in workflow applications as a way of supporting complex business processes in modern corporations. Given the nature of the environment and the technology involved, workflow applications are inherently distributed and pose many interesting challenges to the system designer. In most cases, a client/server architecture is used in which knowledge about the processes being executed is centralized in one node to facilitate monitoring, auditing, and to simplify synchronization. In this paper, we explore a novel distributed architecture, Exotica/FMQM, for workflow systems in which the need for such a centralized database is eliminated. Instead, we use persistent messages as the means to store the information relevant to the execution of a business process. Our approach is to completely distribute the execution of a process so individual nodes are independent. The advantages of this approach are increased resilience to failures and greater scalability and flexibility of the system configuration.

**Keywords**

Workflow Management Systems, Distributed Systems, reliability, scalability.

# 1 INTRODUCTION

Business processes within large organizations often involve a large number of resources, people and tools distributed over a wide geographic area (in what follows, the word *process* refers to a business process, or workflow, rather than to the conventional operating system process). *Workflow management systems* are used to automate the coordination of all these diverse elements thereby increasing the efficiency of the corporation and its ability to monitor its activities. In designing such systems there is a trend towards client/server architectures in which a dedicated server provides most of the functionality of the system while the computing potential at the clients is barely used. There are a number of reasons for this choice: lightweight clients, centralize monitoring and auditing, simpler synchronization mechanisms, and overall design simplicity. However, an architecture based on a centralized server is vulnerable to server failures and offers limited scalability due to the potential performance bottleneck caused by the centralized server. Hence, client/server architectures may not be the most appropriate approach in certain applications. In particular, it is not clear how this kind of systems will scale to hundreds of thousands of business processes or will be able to provide the high availability required in mission critical applications. In this paper, we explore a fully distributed workflow system and discuss the trade-offs of our approach with respect to a centralized architecture. The key idea of our approach is to eliminate the need for a centralized database by using persistent messages. We use the *workflow reference model* proposed by the Workflow Management Coalition [Hollinsworth, 1994] to guarantee the generality of the results. The Workflow Management Coalition is formed by a group of vendors setting standards for the interoperability of their systems. Our immediate research, however, has been centered around FlowMark [IBM, 1995d], [IBM, 1995a], [IBM, 1995b], [IBM, 1995c], [Leymann and Altenhuber, 1994], [Leymann and Roller, 1994], IBM's workflow product, and MQI [IBM, 1993], [Mohan and Dievendorff, 1994], an IBM defined API for persistent messaging, along with *MQSeries*, a family of products that supports MQI. This has allowed us to check our assumptions and results against a real system and real customer requirements. Both FlowMark and MQI follow closely standards in their respective areas, making the issues discussed in this paper pertinent to workflow management systems in general.

The system we have designed, *Exotica/FMQM**, FlowMark on Message Queue Manager, is a distributed workflow system in which a set of autonomous nodes cooperate to complete the execution of a process. Each node functions independently of the rest of the system, the only interaction between nodes is through persistent messages informing that the execution of a step of the process has been completed, thus avoiding the performance bottleneck of having to communicate with the server during the execution of a process. Moreover, the resulting architecture is more resilient to failures since the crash of a single node does not stop the execution of all active processes. Our main contributions are to present a distributed architecture for workflow management using a persistent message passing system and provide an in-depth analysis of the impact a fully distributed architecture has on the workflow model.

*IBM Almaden Research Center's Exotica project aims at incorporating advanced transaction management capabilities in IBM's products and prototypes. Exotica also involves IBM groups in Hursley (U.K.), Böblingen (Germany), and Vienna (Austria).

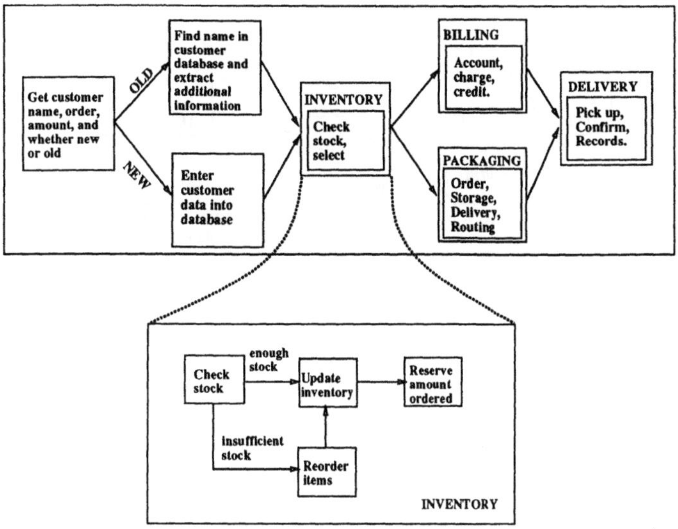


**Figure 1** A business process example.

The paper is organized as follows: in the next section, we describe the model proposed by the Workflow Management Coalition and some of the particular details of FlowMark, as well as a generic persistent message mechanism. In Section 3, we present a novel architecture for workflow systems based on persistent message passing. Section 4 discusses practical aspects of the implementation and the impact of distribution on the overall model. In Section 5 we briefly discuss related work. Section 6 concludes the paper.

# 2 BACKGROUND: WORKFLOW AND PERSISTENT MESSAGING

To establish a common notation, in this section we will present the reference model of the Workflow Management Coalition as well as a generic persistent message mechanism. To further focus the discussion and cover some implementation details, FlowMark is also briefly described.

## 2.1 Workflow Systems

The work taking place in large organizations is often referred to as *business processes*. A business process is "a procedure where documents, information or tasks are passed between participants according to defined sets of rules to achieve, or contribute to, an overall business goal" [Hollinsworth, 1994]. Figure 1 shows an example of a nested business process [García-Molina et al., 1990]. In the context of information systems, these business processes need a suitable representation. This representation is called a *workflow*. Hence, a *workflow management system*, WFMS, is "a system that completely defines, manages

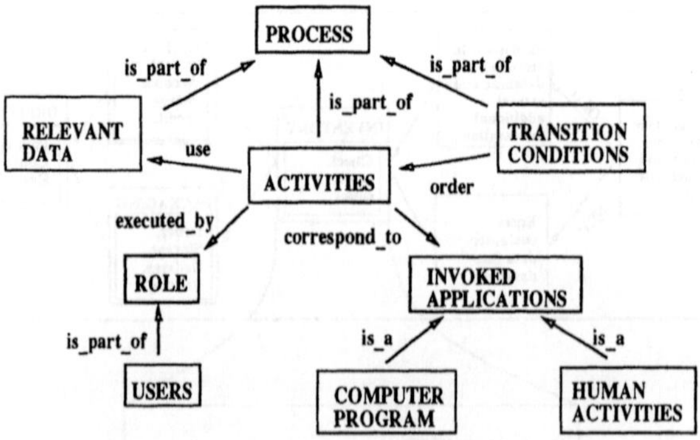


**Figure 2** Elements of the Workflow Model.

and executes workflows through the execution of software whose order of execution is driven by a computer representation of the workflow logic" [Hollinsworth, 1994].

In more concrete terms, the task of the WFMS is to schedule the execution of activities. In scheduling these activities, the WFMS determines what to execute next, locates the tools associated with each activity, transfers information from activity to activity, assigns activities to users, checks the timeliness of the execution, monitors the overall progress and determines when the process has been completed successfully.

## 2.2 Workflow Model

To perform its task, the WFMS needs to be supplied with a description of the business process. This is a workflow model. The Workflow Management Coalition has proposed the following meta-model [Hollinsworth, 1994]. A business process is represented as a *process* with a name, version number, start and termination conditions and additional data for security, audit and control. A process consists of *activities* and *relevant data.* Each step within a process is an *activity,* which has a name, a type, pre- and post-conditions and scheduling constraints. It also has a *role* and one *invoked application* associated with it. The *role* determines who will execute the activity. The *invoked application* is the tool to be used in the execution, which may range from computer programs to human activities with no specific tool, e.g., a meeting. Furthermore, activities use *relevant data* defined as the data passed to and produced by the activities. Relevant data includes name and type, as well as the path specifying the activities that have access to it. The flow of control within a process - what to execute next - is determined by *transition conditions,* usually boolean expressions based on relevant data. The users of the system are represented in terms of *roles.* Invoked applications have a name, type, execution parameters and, in the case of programs, a location or access path. All these elements and their relationships are shown in Figure 2, which is our own interpretation of the reference model [Hollinsworth, 1994].

## 2.3 Navigation and Execution in FlowMark

The reference model does not provide implementation details. To discuss how a process is actually executed we need to resort to an existing system. We use FlowMark since its model closely follows the reference model of the Workflow Management Coalition. In FlowMark, omitting users and invoked applications, an activity has the following concepts associated with it:

- **Flow of Control**: specified by *control connectors* between activities, is the order in which these activities have to be executed. This corresponds to the *transition conditions* of the reference model.
- **Input Container**: a sequence of typed variables and structures which are used as input to the invoked application.
- **Output Container**: a sequence of typed variables and structures in which the output of the invoked application is stored.
- **Flow of Data**: specified through *data connectors* between activities, is a series of mappings between output data containers and input data containers to allow activities exchange information. The data containers and the flow of data form the *relevant data* mentioned the reference model.
- **Start Condition**, that must be met before the activity is actually scheduled. If the condition can never be met, then the activity is marked as having actually terminated. The start condition is a boolean expression involving the states of the incoming control connectors. It corresponds to the pre-condition of the *activity* in the reference model.
- **Exit Condition**, that must be met before an activity is considered to have completed. If the exit condition is not met, then the activity will be rescheduled for execution. It corresponds to the post-condition of the *activity* in the reference model.

Navigation in FlowMark takes place through the data and control connectors. Control connectors determine the flow of control within the process. A control connector between two activities, $t_1$ and $t_2$, implies that $t_2$ can only start execution after $t_1$ has terminated. Thus, when $t_1$ terminates, $t_2$ must be notified of the fact - note that the user written code for $t_2$ does not get executed at this point, the notification is internal to FlowMark. On the other hand, if $t_1$ is never going to be executed, $t_2$ must also be notified of that fact. The notification will be done by $t_1$ upon termination or when it is marked as finished because it will not be executed. The process by which activities that will never execute are marked off is known as *dead path elimination* [IBM, 1995a], [IBM, 1995b], [Walk, 1993].

Each control connector has a state. Before the activity from where it originates finishes, the control connector is *unevaluated.* Once the activity terminates, the control connector is evaluated and its state is set to TRUE or FALSE. The evaluation involves checking whether the *transition condition* for the connector is true or false. Such transition conditions are boolean expressions involving data returned by activities in the output containers.

Similar to the flow of control, FlowMark lets the user define the flow of data in a given process. The flow of data is expressed via data connectors. Each data connector is a mapping between the output container of an activity and the input container of another. To avoid race conditions, the data flow must follow the ordering imposed by the control flow, except for the fact that an activity can have a data connector between

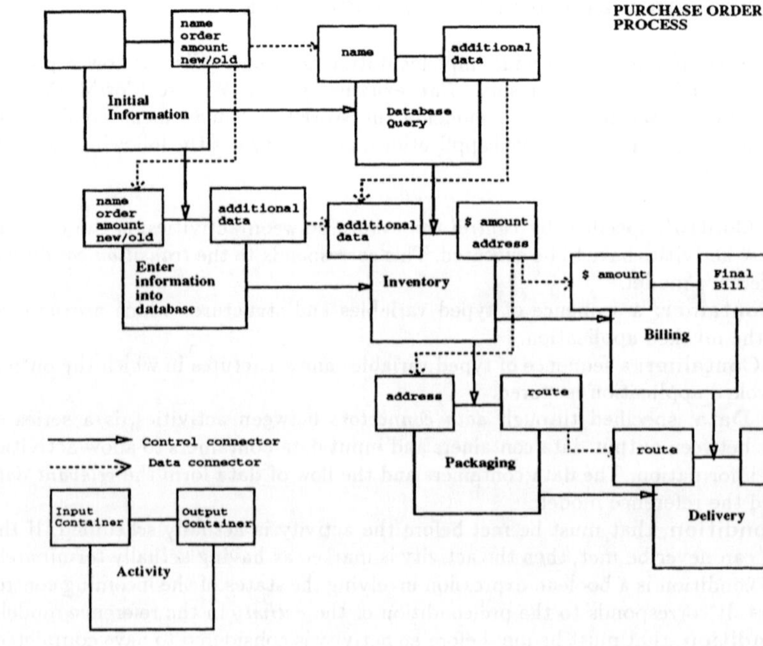


**Figure 3** The example of Figure 1 formalized using FlowMark concepts.

its output container and its input container to provide feedback information in loops. Figure 3 illustrates the purchasing example discussed earlier in the context of FlowMark and illustrates the usage of the FlowMark entities discussed above. Finally, processes are independent entities, i.e., there are no inter-process dependencies.

## 2.4 The Architecture of FlowMark

FlowMark runs across different platforms (AIX, OS/2, Windows) and supports distribution of most of its components. However, in its current version, persistent data resides in a single database server, ObjectStore. This has facilitated the design of the overall system, but introduces a single point of failure in the architecture. As far as we know, most existing systems are also based on a centralized database and, hence, suffer from the same problem. Besides the database server, FlowMark is organized into three other components: *FlowMark Server*, *Runtime Client* and *Buildtime Client*. These correspond to the three functionalities mentioned in the reference model [Hollinsworth, 1994]: Buildtime Client for build-time functions, Runtime Client for run-time interactions, and FlowMark Server for run-time control. A FlowMark system can have several of these components executing at the same time. A FlowMark server is connected as a client to a database. FlowMark servers can reside in remote hosts other than the one where the database is located. Communication between the server and the clients takes place through TCP/IP, NetBIOS or APPC, depending on the platform.

Navigation, as explained above, takes place in the FlowMark server. The creation and definition of processes is done using the GUI interface provided by the buildtime clients. Finally, users and programs interact with the server through the runtime clients. There can be several clients, both buildtime and runtime, attached to a server.

## 2.5 Persistent Messages

In the past few years, there has been a growing interest in message passing/queuing [Mohan and Dievendorff, 1994]. In general, many applications require a communication mechanism that hides the complexities of the underlying system and allows communications across heterogeneous platforms and independently of the protocol used. These services are, preferably, connectionless and accessible through API calls. The most common mechanism is to provide a local queue where applications can place and retrieve messages. Once left in the local queue, the communication system will take care of delivering it to the appropriate queue in a remote machine. This has the advantage of being protocol independent since the application just uses queues. Moreover, these queues can be made persistent so messages survive crashes, making asynchronous communication possible between applications that run at different points in time. There are even some standarization efforts underway lead by the *Message Oriented Middleware Association*, MOMA. Numerous products exist: DEC's *MessageQ*, Transarc's *Recoverable Queuing Services*, Novell's *Tuxedo/Q*, and IBM's MQSeries, to name a few. The type of features provided by these products is very suitable for connecting highly distributed applications, therefore we will rely on the features they provide.

We base our design on a generic queue system with the following characteristics. Nodes will communicate via recoverable queues, i.e., once a message is placed on a queue and the corresponding transaction is committed it becomes persistent until it is retrieved. Each queue is associated with one node in the system. Messages are added and retrieved from a queue using *PUT* and *GET* calls, which can be issued both on local and remote queues. GET calls can access any message in a queue, not necessarily only the first message in the queue. Finally, it is possible to browse through a queue without actually retrieving any messages. A key aspect of the messaging system is its ability to support transactional semantics for both PUT and GET calls. We will use this property to ensure that messages do not get lost when failures or crashes occur.

# 3 THE DISTRIBUTED ARCHITECTURE OF EXOTICA/FMQM

In this section, we describe a distributed architecture for a workflow management system with high reliability and scalability. We refer to this system as *Exotica/FMQM* - FlowMark on Message Queue Manager.

## 3.1 Motivation

As we have already pointed out, the centralized database needs to be replaced in the new architecture, both to eliminate it as a single point of failure and a bottleneck. In a workflow system, the execution of a business process is analogous to a distributed computation. That is, each node executes its part of the job and synchronizes with other nodes by communicating over a network. However, in our case we cannot afford node or communication failures affecting the work in the entire system. One more restriction is that the nodes, the runtime clients, must be kept simple since they probably will run in low-end machines like PCs or laptops, which rules out the possibility of providing each node with full database functionality. To overcome these limitations, we propose to use a persistent message mechanism and a minimal amount of persistent storage at each node. The communication layer is used as persistent storage to maintain workflow related information. The storage at each node is used to recover from failures. Moreover, we have tried to minimize the need for storage outside of message queues at each node so it can be easily implemented in files.

With this approach, a process is executed in a truly distributed fashion, with each node holding only the information it needs to perform its part of the workflow. Failures can only lead to blocking behavior on the activities that are being executed at the failed node but single failures do not prevent other nodes from working on different parts of the same processes or in completely different processes.

For notational purposes, a process refers to the representation of a business process. There can be many instances of the same process running concurrently, these are called process instances. Note that some of the information stored at each node will relate to the process - static information - while other parts will relate to process instances - runtime information.

## 3.2 Process Definition and Binding

According to the reference model, all the procedures related to defining a process are performed in the *Buildtime Client*, an independent module that provides a graphical user interface to perform all these tasks. The equivalent to the Buildtime Client in Exotica/FMQM is any node that has the appropriate user interface and can check the process definition for inconsistencies and errors. We will refer to this node as the *process definition node.* The nodes where the process instances are executed are the *runtime nodes.* For simplicity, we will refer to them simply as nodes.

Once a process has been defined, this definition is compiled to determine the information relevant to each node, binding activities to the nodes where they will be performed. At each node, there is a *node manager* in charge of communicating with the process definition node. The node manager maintains a *process table* on a per process basis, which contains the static information related to the execution of instances of each process. During the execution of process instances, communication between nodes takes place through queues. At each node there will be a queue for messages related to all the instances of the same process. Queues are named with the process id and the node id. Hence, each process table corresponds to a queue, and both correspond to a single process. Each node is interested in the part of the process that it will have to execute. Therefore, the process definition node sends to each involved node's manager only the information pertaining to the activities that will execute at that node. The node manager, upon receiving the information from the process definition node, creates the process table.

Once a node manager has all the static information stored in the process table, it starts a thread that will be in charge of coordinating the execution of instances as they arrive at the node. We will refer to this as the *process thread.* The first task of the process thread is to create the queue where the messages from other nodes will be received. A process thread examines the queue for incoming messages and decides when an activity is ready for execution. When this happens, an *activity thread* is started to manage the execution of the activity.

The process table is a list of what to do to execute the activities that correspond to the node. Hence, it is organized according to these activities. Without getting into details of how its implementation could be optimized, the process table has an entry for each activity in the following form:

- Process identifier.
- Activity identifier.
- List of incoming control connectors, plus the corresponding starting condition.
- List of outgoing control connectors, plus the associated queue where the result of the evaluation of the connector is reported. For instance: $t_4, Q_{D,0}, CONDITION$ represents activity $t_4$, of process 0, located in node D, and accessible through a queue named $Q_{D,0}$. $CONDITION$ is a transition condition, i.e., a boolean expression used to decide whether to follow or not the path marked by the connector.
- Exit condition, which is a boolean function of the values found among the output data.
- Incoming data connector, plus the filtering information to select the relevant data. For instance, $t_1, FILTER$. $FILTER$ specifies which is the relevant data out of all the data received. Since many activities may read data from the same output data container, each one of them needs a mapping to extract only the relevant data. The filter specifies this mapping.
- Outgoing data connector, which specifies the receiving activity and the queue where this has to be reported. For instance, $t_4, Q_{D,0}$.
- Input data template, where the type of the input data is specified.
- Output data template, where the type of the output data is specified.

To summarize, what we have described so far is the per-process data structures, queue, threads and algorithms at each node. The sequence of events is as follows: a user first creates a process. The process is compiled in the process definition node. After compilation, the process is divided in several parts and each part is distributed to an appropriate node. The division of the process into parts will be based on the users associated with the different nodes and the roles associated with the different activities in the process. Upon receiving its part of the process, a node creates a process table to store this information and starts a process thread to handle the execution of instances of such process. Finally, the process thread creates a queue for communicating with other nodes all information relevant to instances of the process. Figure 4 shows all these components and their interactions. Specific examples of process tables are shown in Figure 5.

## 3.3 Process execution

During execution, the information regarding the process instances will be stored in an *instance table* handled by the activity threads. These threads are responsible for the execution of individual activities within an instance. All PUT and GET calls are executed within transactions, i.e., their effects are not permanent until the transaction commits.

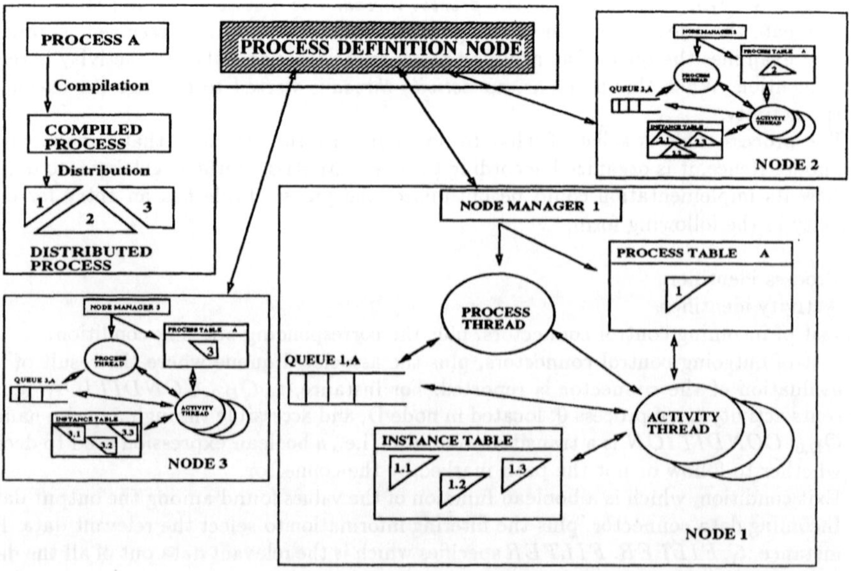


**Figure 4** Distribution of a process among several nodes with three active instances.

When a process instance is started, for all starting activities of that instance - those without predecessors, i.e., without incoming control connectors - messages are sent to the nodes where the activities are located. This is done by PUTting the messages in the appropriate queues. In a node receiving that message, the sequence of activities that take place is as follows. The process thread scans the queue periodically, looking for new messages. If there is a triggering facility in the queue system it can be used to receive messages more efficiently. When it finds a new message, it browses through it - without retrieving it from the queue, this is important in case of failures - and spawns an activity thread. The activity thread first checks the process table to find the data pertaining to that activity. With this data it creates an entry for that activity in the instance table where it will record the progress of the activity. It then checks the start condition of the activity. If it cannot be evaluated, because not all incoming control connectors have been evaluated, it makes a note in the instance table about what control connector has been evaluated - the one to which the message received corresponds - and goes to sleep until the process thread awakens it again with new messages.

If the start condition is false, then the activity is considered terminated. Dead-path elimination messages are sent along the outgoing control connectors - PUT calls to the corresponding queues - the entry is removed from the instance table and the messages corresponding to this activity are retrieved from the process queue - with a GET call. All the operations performed upon termination of the activity are one atomic action. This can be accomplished by using the transactional properties of the GET and PUT calls.

If the start condition evaluates to true, then the corresponding application is invoked, passing to it the data in the input template. When the application terminates, it returns an output data template which is stored in the instance table. Then the activity thread evaluates the exit condition of the activity. If it is false, the application is invoked again. If it is true, the activity is considered terminated. Upon successful termination, the outgoing control connectors' CONDITIONs are evaluated and messages are sent to the appropriate nodes with PUT calls to their queues. The output data template is sent to the nodes specified in the process table as outgoing data connectors. Then the entry is removed from the instance table and all messages corresponding to the activity are retrieved from the process queue. Note that each message corresponds to one activity, once the activity successfully terminates there is no need to keep the messages. These operations are performed as an atomic transaction as explained above.

Note that some of the messages received by a node may correspond to data templates sent by other nodes. In this case, the activity thread uses the FILTER specified in the process table for that data connector to extract the relevant information. This information is then stored in the instance table, in the input data template entry for that activity.

The instance table contains runtime information concerning the evolution of activities as different instances are executed. It has the following structure:

- Process and instance identifiers.
- Activity identifier.
- Input data, the actual values for the input data. This will be gradually filled as the data becomes available - as messages containing the data arrive.
- Output data, the actual values of the output data. This is what will be sent to all activities specified in the outgoing data connectors.
- Status of the activity: *inactive*, *in execution*, *executed*, *terminated.*
- Start condition, to store the partial results necessary to evaluate the start condition. As messages are received, the different parts of the boolean expression are evaluated.

The instance table is stored in memory, there is no need to keep it in stable storage. The process table, however, needs to be in stable storage to allow proper recovery after failures. We will elaborate more on these points in the discussion.

## 3.4 Example

To better illustrate the above concepts, the example described in the initial sections can be adapted to the new notation. Assume that there are four nodes, $A$, $B$, $C$, and $D$, involved in the processing of a purchase order. The process table for this process at each node is shown in Figure 5. For simplicity, we have omitted in this figure the CONDITION of the control connectors, the exit conditions of the activities, and the FILTER of the incoming data connectors.

Note that in the process table, the information is expressed in terms of actual queues. The notation used is as follows. $T2Q_{A,0}$ - outgoing control connector of node A - means that there is a control connector between $T_1$ and $T_2$ for process 0, i.e., node $A$ upon completing the execution of activity $T_1$, must notify the node who "owns" activity $T_2$. This can be found in the queue name, $Q_{A,0}$, which specifies that such node is $A$, reachable through queue $Q_{A,0}$. This queue name will be the one used in PUT calls.

As an example of what happens during runtime, assume activity $T_4$ is executing at node $B$. When this activity terminates, let's assume it is successful, its activity thread has to

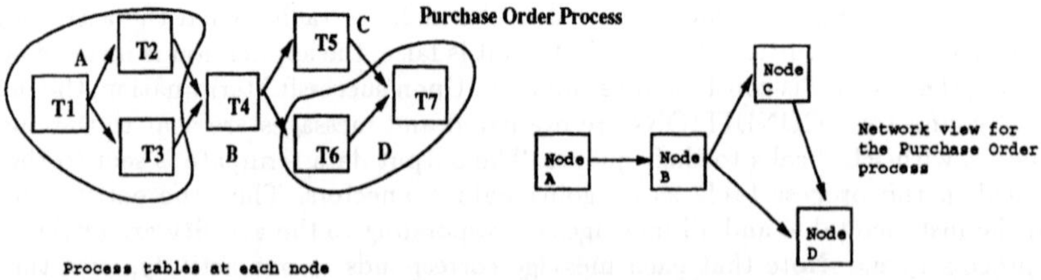


Process tables at each node

Node A — Process Table

| Proc. | Act. | In.CC | Out.CC | Exit | In.DC | Out.DC | I/Data | O/Data |
|---|---|---|---|---|---|---|---|---|
| P0 | T1 | – | T2QA0 T3QA0 | – | – | – | – | name order amount new/old |
| P0 | T2 | T1QA0 | T4QB0 | – | T1QA0 | T4QB0 | name | – |
| P0 | T3 | T1QA0 | T4QB0 | – | T1QA0 | T4QB0 | name order amount n/old | addit. info. |

Node B — Process Table

| Proc. | Act. | In.CC | Out.CC | Exit | In.DC | Out.DC | I/Data | O/Data |
|---|---|---|---|---|---|---|---|---|
| P0 | T4 | T2QA0 T3QA0 | T5QC0 T6QD0 | – | T2QA0 T3QA0 | T5QC0 T6QD0 | add. info. | $amount address |

Node C — Process Table

| Proc. | Act. | In.CC | Out.CC | Exit | In.DC | Out.DC | I/Data | O/Data |
|---|---|---|---|---|---|---|---|---|
| P0 | T5 | T4QB0 | T7QD0 | – | T4QB0 | T7QD0 | $amount | Final bill |

Node D — Process Table

| Proc. | Act. | In.CC | Out.CC | Exit | In.DC | Out.DC | I/Data | O/Data |
|---|---|---|---|---|---|---|---|---|
| P0 | T6 | T4QB0 | T7QD0 | – | T4QB0 | T7QD0 | address | route |
| P0 | T7 | T5QC0 T6QD0 | – | – | T6QD0 | – | route | |

**Figure 5** The example of Figure 1 distributed among four nodes and their corresponding process tables.

send the output data template along the outgoing data connectors, and notify about the termination along the outgoing control connectors. All this is done with PUT calls. For the control connectors, it will look in the *Out.CC* column of its process table for activity $T_4$. There it finds the name of the next activities, $T_5$ and $T_6$, and the queues to which it has to send the messages, $Q_{C,0}$ and $Q_{D,0}$. Hence, it will perform one PUT call to each of these queues. For the data connectors, the mechanism is similar. In the column *Out.DC* of the $T_4$ entry in the process table of node $B$, there are two activities indicated, $T_5$ and $T_6$, and their queues, $Q_{C,0}$ and $Q_{D,0}$. The output data template is sent to those nodes by PUTting it in their queues.

## 4 DISCUSSION

In distributing the execution of a process completely, we had to make certain assumptions that are not necessary in a client/server architecture. For instance, with a centralized server each process has an owner, who can start process instances, abort their execution, and is notified of their termination. When the process is distributed among many nodes, the notion of a process owner is much less obvious. For simplicity, we assume that a process instance starts by executing an activity that triggers the execution of all starting activities of the process instance. This is similar to the notion of "process owner", in the sense that the user assigned to the starting activity is the one who can effectively start an instance of the process. Similarly, a process instance is deemed terminated when all of its activities have terminated or have been marked as such by dead path elimination. In a client/server architecture all this information is centralized in the database, and hence checking for the process instance termination event is simple. In a distributed system, where the status of each activity is stored in a different node, process termination could raise some complicated issues similar to those of snapshots and termination detection [Chandy and Lamport, 1985], [Misra, 1983]. To avoid such complexity, we assume that all processes have a *terminal* activity such that when this activity terminates, or it is marked as terminated, the process has also terminated. This terminal activity is unique within a process and follows all other activities in that process. For notification purposes, this activity will have to contain information about the user that needs to be notified of the termination of the process instance. Similar problems arise for auditing and monitoring the system.

Another interesting aspect of the distributed architecture is the management of worklists. Worklists are lists of workitems belonging to one user. In a centralized system, this is very easy to maintain since users only need to logon to the central server to retrieve their worklist. Once retrieved, the server can update it by sending the updates to the runtime client where the user is currently logged on. Moreover, an activity may appear on several worklists simultaneously, but only one user will be allowed to execute it. The synchronization problem of ensuring that only one user actually executes the activity is solved by having the server select the user who contacts it first. These two features are complex to implement in a fully distributed environment since activities are associated with nodes. The use of remote GET helps to allow an activity to appear in several worklists. Nodes will be notified that messages are in a queue, rather than getting the message themselves. The first node to GET the message from that queue will be the one to which the activity is assigned. Other nodes trying to GET the message will find that it has already been retrieved from the queue and therefore discard the activity.

To achieve resilience to failures we use transactional PUT and GET calls, plus the ability to browse a queue without retrieving messages. When a message is received regarding an activity, it is not retrieved from the queue until the activity has terminated. In other words, messages are kept until they are not needed anymore, and they are removed in an atomic operation. In this way, in case of failures which result in the loss of the instance table, a recovering node will restart the process thread which will find the messages still intact in the queue and, based on them, spawn again the appropriate activity threads which will reconstruct the instance table. This is the reason why instance tables do not need to be stored in stable storage and why process tables should be kept in stable storage. For the sake of completeness, it must be mentioned that an audit log is necessary to keep track of which activities have completed execution and to store messages, in case the user decides to restart a finished activity. This audit log can be another queue, checkpointed every so often.

Persistent messages may be too expensive in same cases. A system designer should consider to use both *persistent* and *non-persistent* messages. Persistent messages survive crash failures whereas non-persistent messages are lost when a crash occurs. Communications between the process definition node and other nodes, for instance, can take place through non-persistent messages. The same can be said about other operations such as monitoring or auditing.

There are several aspects to the algorithms and mechanisms presented above that are crucial to the implementation of Exotica/FMQM. To provide a generic approach we have enumerated the features of the persistent message passing layer that are necessary in this implementation. Obviously, we do not expect to find all of these features in every message passing system. Therefore, in a real implementation, there are some trade-offs to be considered. For instance, IBM's MQI does not support remote GET calls and this complicates worklist management. Some other systems, like DEC's MessageQ, may provide only limited transactional semantics which would require the handling of messages in a different way to avoid data loss due to failures. Transarc's RQS, for instance, does not support non-persistent messages which does not allow one to tune performance by using non-persistent messages in cases where there is no risk of data loss. In general, each implementation will have to deal with a different set of issues depending on the particular system being used.

# 5 RELATED WORK

The concept of workflow management has been around for a number of years. Only recently, however, the technology required to implement suitable systems has been available. Today there are more than 70 products that claim to be workflow solutions [Frye, 1994]. Standarization efforts are underway to guarantee a common reference model across all workflow products and platforms. The Workflow Management Coalition has recently published the *Workflow Reference Model* [Hollinsworth, 1994], along with other documents, in which the basic components of a workflow management system are outlined and described.

There are many areas that have influenced or are related to workflow management. Document management, for instance, is concerned with the lifecycle of electronic documents. These systems can be traced back to early systems like TLA [Tsichritzis, 1982] where *form procedures* were proposed to organize the flow of forms. Electronic mail systems [Goldberg et al., 1992], [Malone et al., 1987], which provide means to distribute information among individuals. Office automation systems such as DOMINO, where the control and data flow in an office is controlled by a mediator that controls the execution of *office procedures* [Kreifelts and Woetzel, 1986], [Kreifelts et al., 1991]. Transaction based applications, like the model based on extended nested sagas [García-Molina et al., 1990] for coordinating multi-transaction activities, or the ConTract model, which provides reliable control flow between transactional activities [Waechter and Reuter, 1992]. Most of these early efforts were limited in their scope and did not address business processes in their full generality. More recently, several high level designs have been proposed for modeling and managing business processes [Tomlison et al., 1993], [McCarthy and Sarin, 1993], [Medina-Mora et al., 1993], [Sheth, 1994], but most of them are centralized and fail to address issues such as high availability, failure resilience or scalability. Moreover, they tend to be transactional in nature and too centered around databases, which contrast with the reference model created by software vendors [Hollinsworth, 1994]. Barbara et al. [Barbara et al., 1994] proposed INCAS for distributed workflow management. In this model, each execution of a process is associated with an *Information Carrier*, which is an object that contains all the necessary information for the execution as well as propagation of the object among the relevant processing nodes. In [Dayal et al., 1990] and [Dayal et al., 1991], a specification language and a transactional model for organizing long running activities is developed. Although intended for workflow systems, the primary emphasis is on long running activities in a transactional framework using triggers and nested transactions. The authors present a preliminary design using recoverable queues, which have similar semantics to the message queue interface (MQI) used in this paper.

# 6 CONCLUSIONS

Exotica/FMQM's architecture has two concrete goals. The first is to study the effects of complete decentralization on the design of a workflow product. The second is to analyze the feasibility of replacing a centralized database by persistent messaging. Both goals are of interest in workflow environments but they are broad enough to provide some insight in other areas. In particular, complete decentralization such as that achieved by Exotica/FMQM turns out to have implications that affect not only the underlying architecture but also the expressiveness of a business process, which suggests the importance of using models with enough expressiveness but no *a priori* assumptions about the system.

The gains obtained from using Exotica/FMQM's architecture are a greater resilience to failures, scalability, and the possibility of dynamically configuring the system as processes evolve. Since there is no centralized server, there are neither bottlenecks nor single points of failure. Node failures will stop the execution of process instances that use that node, but will not prevent other process instances from being executed at other nodes. The price for all this is more complex algorithms for navigation. Our conclusion is that for small or mid-sized business environments, a centralized architecture will probably suffice. However, for large or very large business environments, a distributed one provides much more flexibility and eliminates bottlenecks, thus appearing as a more promising venue for implementation.

Future work includes using two phase commit protocols to integrate legacy applications, using logs for monitoring workflow processes, and exploiting non-persistent messages to improve performance. In general, message systems are designed for messages to be consumed fast. In our system, messages may remain in a queue for a long time and indexes on message header contents may be needed to help performance. Some extensions to the message system are necessary to provide an appropriate functionality.

# ACKNOWLEDGEMENTS

This work was done while Divyakant Agrawal and Amr El Abbadi were on sabbatical at IBM Almaden and Mohan Kamath was visiting IBM Almaden. This work is partially supported by funds from IBM Hursley (Networking Software Division) and IBM Vienna (Software Solutions Division). Even though we refer to specific IBM products in this paper, no conclusions should be drawn about future IBM product plans based on this paper's contents. The opinions expressed here are our own.

## REFERENCES


Barbara, D., Mehrota, S., and Rusinkiewicz, M. (1994). INCAS: A Computation Model for Dynamic Workflows in Autonomous Distributed Environments. Technical report, Matsushita Information Technology Laboratory.

Chandy, K. and Lamport, L. (1985). Distributed Snapshots: determining Global States of Distributed Systems. *ACM Transactions on Computer Systems*, 3(1):63–75.

Dayal, U., Hsu, M., and Ladin, R. (1990). Organizing Long-running Activities with Triggers and Transactions. In *Proceedings of ACM SIGMOD 1990 International Conference on Management of Data*, pages 204–214.

Dayal, U., Hsu, M., and Ladin, R. (1991). A Transaction Model for Long-running Activities. In *Proceedings of the Sixteenth International Conference on Very Large Databases*, pages 113–122.

Frye, C. (1994). Move to Workflow Provokes Business Process Scrutiny. *Software Magazine*, pages 77–89.

García-Molina, H., Gawlick, D., Klein, J., Kleissner, K., and Salem, K. (1990). Coordinating Multi-transaction Activities. Technical Report CS-TR-247-90, Department of Computer Science, Princeton University.

Goldberg, Y., Safran, M., and Shapiro, E. (1992). Active Mail - A Framework for Implementing Groupware. In *Proc. of the Conference on Computer-Supported Cooperative Work (CSCW)*, pages 281–288, Toronto, Canada.

Hollinsworth, D. (1994). The workflow reference model. Technical Report TC00-1003, Workflow Management Coalition. Accessible via: http://www.aiai.ed.ac.uk/WfMC/.

IBM (1993). *Message Queue Interface: Technical Reference*. IBM. Document No. SC33-0850-01.

IBM (1995a). *FlowMark - Managing Your Workflow, Version 2.1*. IBM. Document No. SH19-8243-00.

IBM (1995b). *FlowMark - Modeling Workflow, Version 2.1*. IBM. Document No. SH19-8241-00.

IBM (1995c). *FlowMark - Programming Guide, Version 2.1*. IBM. Document No. SH19-8240-00.

IBM (1995d). *FlowMark for OS/2: Installation and Maintenance*. IBM. Document No. SH19-8244-00.

Kreifelts, T., Hinrichs, E., Klein, K., Seuffert, P., and Woetzel, G. (1991). Experiences with the DOMINO Office Procedure System. In *Proceedings ECSCW '91*, pages 117–130. Amsterdam.

Kreifelts, T. and Woetzel, G. (1986). Distribution and Exception Handling in an Office Procedure System. In *Office Systems: Methods and Tools, Proc. IFIP WG 8.4 Work. Conf. on Methods and Tools for Office Systems*, pages 197–208. October, 22-24, Pisa, Italy.

Leymann, F. and Altenhuber, W. (1994). Managing Business Processes as an Information Resource. *IBM Systems Journal*, 33(2):326–348.

Leymann, F. and Roller, D. (1994). Business Processes Management with FlowMark. In *Proc. 39th IEEE Computer Society Int'l Conference (CompCon), Digest of Papers*, pages 230–233, San Francisco, California. IEEE.

Malone, T., Grant, K., Lai, K., Rao, R., and Rosenblitt, D. (1987). Semistructured Messages Are Surprisingly Useful for Computer-Supported Coordination. *ACM Trans-*

*actions on Office Information Systems*, 5(2):115–131.
McCarthy, D. and Sarin, S. (1993). Workflow and Transactions in InConcert. *Bulletin of the Technical Committee on Data Engineering*, 16(2). IEEE Computer Society.
Medina-Mora, R., Wong, H., and Flores, P. (1993). ActionWorkflow as the Enterprise Integration Technology. *Bulletin of the Technical Committee on Data Engineering*, 16(2). IEEE Computer Society.
Misra, J. (1983). Detecting termination of distributed Computations Using Markers. In *ACM Proceedings of the Symposium on Principles od Distributed Computing*, pages 290–294.
Mohan, C. and Dievendorff, R. (1994). Recent Work on Distributed Commit Protocols, and Recoverable Messaging and Queuing. *Bulletin of the Technical Committee on Data Engineering*, 17(1):22–28. IEEE Computer Society.
Sheth, A. (1994). On Multi-system Applications and Transactional Workflows, Bellcore's projects PROMP and METEOR. Collection of papers and reports from Bellcore.
Tomlison, C., Attie, P., Cannata, P., Meredith, G., Sheth, A., Singh, M., and Woelk, D. (1993). Workflow Support in Carnot. *Bulletin of the Technical Committee on Data Engineering*, 16(2). IEEE Computer Society.
Tsichritzis, D. (1982). Form Management. *Communications of the ACM*, 25(7):453–478.
Waechter, H. and Reuter, A. (1992). The ConTract Model. In Elmagarmid, A., editor, *Database Transaction Models for Advanced Applications*, chapter 7, pages 219–263. Morgan Kaufmann Publishers, San Mateo.
Walk, K. (1993). Workflow Management Concepts, a White Paper. Technical report, IBM Vienna Software Development Laboratory, Austria.

## BIOGRAPHY

- **Gustavo Alonso** is a Senior Research Associate in the database group of the Information Systems Institute at ETH Zürich in Switzerland. Previously, he was a Visiting Scientist at IBM Almaden Research Center, where he participated in the Exotica project working on advanced transaction models and workflow management systems. His research interests are in transaction processing, advanced database applications and distributed systems. He received an engineering degree in Telecommunications from ETSIT, Madrid Technical University, in 1989, and his MS and PhD degress in computer science from the University of California at Santa Barbara, in 1992 and 1994, respectively.
- **Divyakant Agrawal** received his Ph.D. in computer science in 1987 from State University of New York at Stony Brook. He is currently an Associate Professor of computer science at the University of California at Santa Barbara. His research interests are in databases and distributed systems and has served on several program committees of international conferences, symposia, and workshops on database and distributed systems. He has over 60 publications in refereed journals and conferences. Dr. Agrawal recently has been involved with several large projects dealing with scientific and spatial data. As co-PI on the Amazonia project funded by NASA, Dr. Agrawal and his colleagues have developed efficient mechanisms for retrieving data scattered over heterogeneous information repositories. As co-PI on the Alexandria project (Digital Library) funded by NSF/ARPA/NASA, he in collaboration with his colleagues is involved in developing

a distributed library for map and image data. His current research interests are in the area of content-based retrieval of image data and multidimensional index structures.

- **Amr El Abbadi** received his Ph.D. in Computer Science from Cornell University. In August 1987 he joined the Department of Computer Science at the University of California, Santa Barbara, where he is currently an Associate Professor. His research interests are in the fields of fault-tolerant distributed systems and databases. He has designed several protocols for highly available fault-tolerant systems. He has also been involved in designing systems and database support for geographic information systems and collaborative environments. Recently, he has been involved in The Alexandria Digital Library project, whose goal is to design a distributed spatial digital library. He was ACM lecturer for 1991-92, and is currently the area editor for Information Systems: An International Journal.
- **C. Mohan** is a Research Staff Member at IBM's Almaden Research Center since 1981 and is a member of the IBM Academy of Technology. He is currently leading the Exotica project on workflow systems. He is a designer and an implementor of R*, Starburst and DB2/6000. He is the primary inventor of the ARIES family of locking and recovery algorithms, and the industry-standard Presumed Abort commit protocol. His research ideas are incorporated in numerous products (e.g., DB2 Family, S/390 Parallel Sysplex Coupling Facility, MQSeries, ADSM). Mohan has received 5 IBM Outstanding Innovation Awards, and is an inventor on 14 issued and 13 pending patents. He was the Program Chair of the 1987 International Workshop on High Performance Transaction Systems and a Program Vice-Chair of the 1994 International Conference on Data Engineering. He will be the Americas Program Chair for the 1996 International Conference on Very Large Data Bases. He is an editor of VLDB Journal. Mohan has a PhD from University of Texas at Austin and a BTech from IIT Madras.
- **Roger Günthör** received a Dipl. Inform. in computer science from University of Stuttgart in 1990. Afterwards, he became a Ph.D. candidate at the IPVR at the University of Stuttgart. His thesis about reliable base services for long-lived activities was written in the context of the ConTracts project. In August 1994, he joined the Exotica group at the IBM Almaden Research Center. His areas of interest include transaction processing, extended transaction models, workflow management, scheduling, temporal logic, and client/server technologies.
- **Mohan Kamath** is a PhD candidate in the Department of Computer Science at the University of Massachusetts, Amherst. After receiving his undergraduate degree in engineering from India, he received a Master's degree in Computer Integrated Manufacturing and Design from the University of Maryland, College Park and a Master's degree in Computer Science from the University of Massachusetts, Amherst. His research interests include transaction processing, workflow management, mobile computing and multimedia database systems.

2

# Usability of Some Workflow Products in an Inter-organizational Setting*

*J. Juopperi, A. Lehtola, O. Pihlajamaa, A. Sladek, J. Veijalainen*
*VTT Information Technology, Multimedia Systems*
*P.O.Box 1203, FIN-02044 VTT, Finland.*
*Telephone: +358-0-4565953. Fax +358-0-4567028.*
*Email: {jari.juopperi,aarno.lehtola,olli.pihlajamaa, jari.veijalainen,aija.sladek}@vtt.fi*

**Abstract**

Workflow techniques have gained plenty of attention lately as a means to support business process re-engineering. One has also argued that they are an important asset when integrating legacy systems within an organization. In the following, their applicability in an inter-organizational setting will be evaluated. This is done by grasping requirements of three different inter-organizational applications and relating them with the facilities offered by some existing workflow products, notably IBM FlowMark, Staffware, and TeamFlow. The reference architecture and terminology used in comparisons is that of the Workflow Management Coalition. The focus in this context is on specification needs deducible from the applications and the corresponding support by the products. Further point of interest is the applicability of the products as an integrating facility of legacy systems within and between organizations. A third point of interest is the support for advanced transactional properties which is of prime importance in the light of the application analysis in these environments. The overall conclusion is that the products analysed lack many of the advanced transactional features and specification facilities needed in inter-organizational environments, though some products will have more of them in their future versions.

**Keywords**

Workflow, workflow tools, computer supported cooperative work, business process re-engineering

---

*This work was done in the ESPRIT LTR project TransCoop (EP8012) which is partially funded by the European Commission. The partners of TransCoop are GMD (Germany), University of Twente (The Netherlands) and VTT (Finland).

# 1 INTRODUCTION

Workflow techniques were first developed for and used in distributed project management systems. The background were big government funded software projects in USA in the seventies [Gru94]. Currently, they are seen as the key technique to facilitate business process re-engineering, because they support process-oriented work-groups. The tools needed are part of a new set of products and resources for solving business problems [Loc94].

We are here interested especially in inter- and intra-organizational workflows and systems which could support them. Such workflows span between autonomous organizations and fairly autonomous* organizational units. These workflows might be fully automated, in which case no human beings are involved in the execution of the steps (or activities, see below the terminology), or they might contain manual steps. In both cases, correctness of the workflow process definitions, recovery from all kinds of errors, as well as intra-instance and inter-instance concurrency are important issues which should evidently be addressed by the supporting systems. Below we will show, based on three real-world cases, that these *transactional system requirements* are really adequate. We will also discuss other system requirements deducible from the cases and evaluate three products against all the requirements so gained. The cases are the PortNet system used by Finnish ports and the National Board of Navigation (NBN)†, the 101-service provided by Telecom Finland, and a software error reporting system used by the Valmet Corporation. The analysed products are Flowmark by IBM, Staffware by Staffware PLC and TeamFlow by ICL Personal Systems.

The workflow field is immature, which is also reflected in the lack of widely accepted common terminology. In this context we will apply the architectural approach (see figure 1) and terminology defined by the Workflow Management Coalition (WfMC) [Wor94]. The WfMC reference model distinguishes between manual and computerized parts in (business) processes. From the modeling point of view, the phases identified are the *process definition* and the subsequent *instantiation* of the process definition, again and again, to perform the actual work. It is foreseen that the process definitions will be modified from time to time. In this terminology, *a process* is a finite collection of manual or computerized *activities* organized to accomplish some business process. *Workflow activities* (processes etc.) are computerized steps, whereas *manual activities* (processes etc.) are non-computerized steps. Each performs a piece of work.

From the point of view of the global process definition, semantics of an activity are indivisible and well-defined. At the other level of the process definition, e.g. within the local environment, however, there maybe a complete process definition again, which corresponds to the activity. In this case it is called *sub process.*

There is no much related work known to us where application analysis, the WfMC reference model and products would have been brought into relation with each other in the way we have done it here. There is, however, a lot of work done in other contexts towards advanced workflow concepts.

Klein [Kle91] has shown that most known *transaction dependencies*, which seem to be

*In this context we do not handle further the definition of autonomy and its consequences. The interested reader is urged to consult e.g. [Vei90, VEH92, Vei92, Vei93]

†We use below also the Finnish acronym MKH

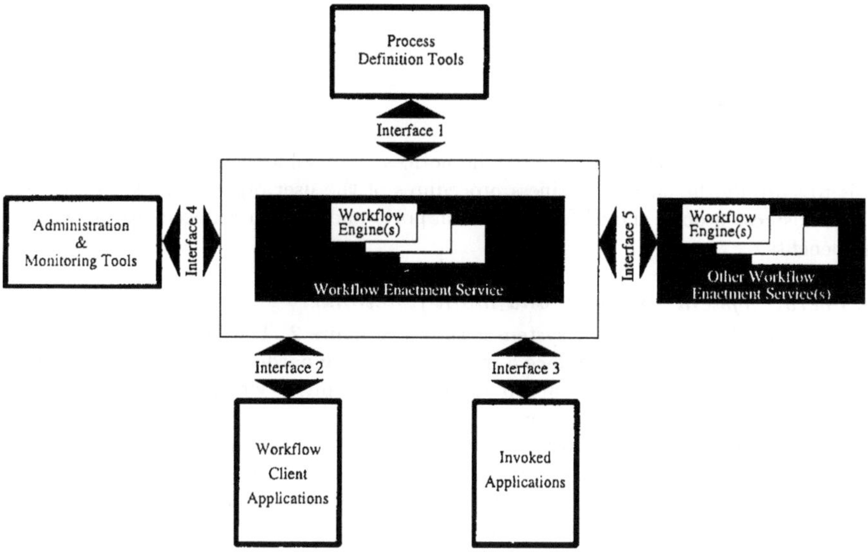


**Figure 1 The WfMC reference model**

important in the light of our application analysis, can be represented already by Create-, Finish-, Commit-, Abort-, Compensation- and Weak Commit dependency.

In general, if the integrity constraints on the persistent data do span multiple systems, then concurrent workflows may interfere with each others in an undesirable manner and thereby there is a need to control concurrent workflows. One of the most relevant contribution towards this end is the concept of*transactional workflows*[GH94] which include a workflow specification language and which explicitly address the problems of concurrent workflows. The *Contract Model* [Wäc91, WR92] introduces a control mechanism over so-called ACID transactions [GR93] by invariant predicates which can be specified to hold across tasks, and which prevent possible interference of concurrent workflows. In the approach presented in [BDS+93] a workflow specification model [ASSR93, SR93] and an open nested transaction model [WS92] is combined. In their approach the workflow enactment service above would enforce termination dependencies and the control and data flow dependencies within a workflow definition. The semantic transaction management component they propose would manage the compensation dependencies, and the dependencies between incompatible tasks of different workflows to ensure multi-system consistency.

*Transaction metamodels* provide a common framework within which one can specify and reason about the nature of interactions between transactions in a particular model. ACTA [CR90b, CR90a, PC94] allows one to specify transaction dependencies as well as the so-called conflict relations of operations.

The rest of this paper is organized as follows. In Section 2, the requirements from the applications and literature are discussed. In Section 3, we relate the requirements with the three products and analyse their deficiencies. Section 4 concludes the paper.

# 2 CASE STUDIES

## 2.1 The PortNet case

PortNet [Tra94] is an EDI system to handle notices of vessel arrivals and departures. Its goal is to simplify the current business procedures of the user organizations, to create a uniform business process model for all Finnish ports and to gain reduced cost as well as other benefits.

### *The overall system structure and main functions*

The environment of the PortNet system is shown in figure 2. The information exchange between various parties (the interface 5 in figure 1) is standardized partly through a few EDIFACT message types. Those parts of the process definition which go beyond the data formats are given in natural language.

When a foreign ship visits a port, various activities must be carried out by a number of commercial and administrative organizations. For example, the ship arrival must be declared to the customs, the information concerning the arrival date and the ship itself must be recorded into various databases, navigation of the ship and other services must be ordered etc. The activities related to the ship departure include the recording of information concerning the departure date, navigation and other services, calculating the duration of the stay of the ship and the related cost etc. Next we outline the processing of the arrival of a ship.

There are essentially seven types of actors involved in the arrival of a ship: a ship, an agent, a stevedoring company, customs, a port, the National Board of Navigation (NBN) and a sea pilot station. An agent is a company which organizes the handling and further delivery of the cargo of the ship. The National Board of Navigation is an authority which controls the traffic near the coast of Finland.

The process definition describing the arrival of a ship is instantiated when a local agent receives a manifest concerning the arrival of ship from a foreign agent. When this happens, the local agent informs the selected stevedoring company, customs and the local port about the forthcoming arrival of the ship. The local agent also stores the received service order into a service database. Finally, the local agent creates an advanced arrival notice (AAN) and sends it to the port and the NBN. The AAN contains detailed technical information about the ship, e.g, name, radio call sign, length, width, machine power etc.

When the local port receives the AAN from the agent or from the NBN, the contents of the AAN is stored into a database and the local service companies are requested to prepare to handle the ship. When the NBN receives the AAN from the agent, it transmits the AAN to the appropriate sea pilot station so that a pilot can be reserved to navigate the ship to the port.

The agent may receive further notification from the foreign agent from time to time because the information contained in each notification is only an estimation and may have to be refined repeatedly. For example, the exact date of arrival of a ship is affected by many unpredictable factors, such as the weather conditions on the sea, the possible delay in the intermediate ports, etc. As the exact arriving date draws closer, the information will become more accurate.

When the ship arrives at the port, the actual arrival time (ATA) is stored into the local

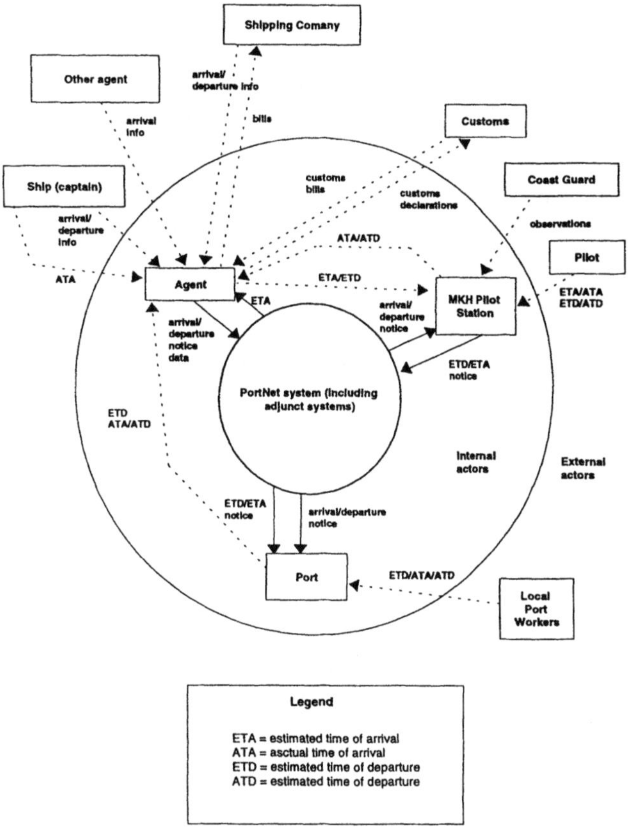


**Figure 2 Handling a ship visit: environment diagram**

database and the NBN is informed about it. The agent asks the ATA (currently by phone) and then creates a Final Arrival Notice (FAN), stores the real arrival date of the vessel into the database and sends the FAN to the port and to the NBN. It is required that this process finishes no later than three days after the arrival of the ship.

## *Observations from the application*

Next we summarize the characteristic features of the PortNet case. First, the processes in the environment are complicated in structure and span several organizations. This requires the interface 5 in figure 1 to be carefully designed and the overall process definition must span several organizations. Second, the processes have a long duration, as the ships move slowly; at the same time, also deadlines are needed, so the enactment service must support workflows with long duration and deadlines. Third, the environment is heterogeneous in many respects (different kind of processes at different participants, very different equipment, manually mediated information flows, like captain confirming the order of a sea pilot by phone or an agent asking information) and includes many autonomous participants. These aspects must be taken into consideration when the process definition tools and workflow engines are designed to interoperate.

Fourth, the environment shows clearly the need of a hierarchy of the processes; The port bases its functioning on the information of the ship arrivals and departures, but the small piece of information telling that the ship is coming/leaving starts a big internal process within the harbour. The same applies to other participants. Finally, a ship may call off its visit to a particular harbour and go to another, e.g. due to ice barriers or storms. This causes the need to reverse some activities already done in harbour. In transactional sense one needs compensation.

The PortNet case would require the process definition tools to allow the creation of definitions which contain both manual and computerised activities. They should also support hierarchical definition of the workflow processes. This is needed to help a process modeller to use top-down approach and to promote reusability.

Due to the hierarchical nature of processes tools should support the description of two kinds of activities: *basic activities* and *process activities.* Basic activities are leaf-level activities that are not structured but the activities where the actual work is done. Process activities are executable workflow processes used as subprocesses.

The support for *transactional properties* is needed for correct and reliable execution of workflow process instances. Workflow tools should also support different subsets of traditional transactional properties for different activities and processes. The required set of supported properties varied from empty to full ACID-properties[GR93]. For example, the AID-properties were needed for some activities, such as "Checking, approving and sending the notice" performed by the Agent. On the other hand, the Agent's activity "Checking minimal data requirements" had no transactional properties and it could be interrupted at any time. At the upper levels, the AD-properties were required for the inter-organizational scenario, "Handle a ship visit" (see PortNet case 2.1).

*Support for long-living process instances* is also needed. For example, the execution of the whole PortNet inter-organizational process can take up to two months. During the execution time, other process instances may need the partial results. Thus a workflow management system should export the updates of a workflow process instance before its completion. *Backward* and *forward recovery* is needed in case of failures.

*Activity assignment* should be allowed to single users, to roles and even to organizations. In some cases assignment must be dynamic and thus it must be solved at run time.

A workflow management system should offer three basic operations for the control of workflow process activity instances: `Begin` which starts an execution of the activity instance, `Release` which finishes an execution of the activity instance and `Cancel` that cancels an execution of the activity instance because of a semantic failure or an user initiated cancel operation.

Describing the different options of control flow (sequential/parallel execution of the activities, splitting/joining the threads, time dependencies between activities, etc.) is a tricky problem. One has found it useful to use *dependencies* between activities to express them. Ordering dependencies form the basis of the control flow definition (routing) of the workflow process. In addition to *serial dependency*: `Release` $\mathcal{A} \rightarrow$ `Begin` $\mathcal{B}$[‡] many other *ordering dependencies* between the activities $\mathcal{A}$ and $\mathcal{B}$ and their basic operations should

‡The execution of $\mathcal{B}$ will be started after the execution of $\mathcal{A}$ has been successfully finished, i.e. released.

be supported by the workflow tools: `Cancel` $\mathcal{A} \rightarrow$ `Begin` $\mathcal{B}$, `Release` $\mathcal{A} \rightarrow$ `Release` $\mathcal{B}$, `Release` $\mathcal{A} \rightarrow$ `Cancel` $\mathcal{B}$, `Cancel` $\mathcal{A} \rightarrow$ `Release` $\mathcal{B}$, and `Cancel` $\mathcal{A} \rightarrow$ `Cancel` $\mathcal{B}$. These dependencies, especially the serial dependency, often contain some *transition condition* that sets a criterium for moving control from one activity to the subsequent one. The transition conditions together with the dependencies form a *rules-based routing* (conditional routing) that enables one or more control flow paths (from multiple possibilities) to be followed (*OR-Split*) depending on the criteria (e.g. a value of variable or a result derived from some complex calculation).

The support for *Parallel routing* is needed to describe concurrently executing activities. In order to achieve parallel routing control flows should be able to split to many parallel threads (*AND-Split*) and later converge into a single thread again. At least two different kinds of converging is needed: *AND-join* for synchronising all the converging threads before control is moved forward and *OR-join* for asynchronous converging. In some cases more advanced rules might be needed for the synchronization (e.g. the control can be moved forward when certain number of converging control flows have been synchronized.)

The workflow process definition should also explicitly specify the *data flow* between the activities.

## 2.2 The Intelligent Networks case

The term "intelligent networks" (IN) refers to an architectural and functional concept which is intended to ease the introduction of new telecommunication services. Traditionally telecommunication services have been built directly on the hardware of a switch with proprietary tools. This approach is very expensive; it takes several years to specify, develop, test and deploy new services. The crux of the IN approach is that it offers a standardised environment where the software controlling the basic switch functionality is separated from the software which controls the call progression.

### *The 101-service of Telecom Finland*

Telecom Finland is a Finnish network operator and telecommunications service provider with a turnover of ca. FIM 5 billion/year and 6500 employees. Besides the conventional telephone services (local calls, long distance calls, international calls) and telephone services based on the cellular systems technology (GSM, NMT-900, NMT-450), it offers more complex services based on the modern IN switches. Freephone, virtual private network and conference calling are some examples of the services based on the modern switching technology.

The purpose of the 101-service is to make it easy for a customer to direct all his long distance telephone calls to the network of Telecom Finland. In principle this is a very simple service but due to the company organisation and actors beyond the control of the company there are many difficult questions related to the process which realizes the service.

When a customer wants to make a long distance telephone call in Finland, he must either implicitly or explicitly select the operator which arranges the connection from the switch of the local operator to the destination. If the customer does not care which company arranges the long distance connection then he only selects the dialling code and the local telephone number as usual. The operator responsible for the long distance connection is then randomly selected among the operators which provide long distance services in this particular geographical area. If, however, the customer wants to govern the selection of the long distance operator, then he must give an operator code before the dialling. To use a certain long distance operator by default, the customer must sign an agreement with the operator. The 101-service is a way to initiate the service agreement process with Telecom Finland.

### *An overview of the analysis*

Five different actors are involved in the realization of the 101-service. *A customer* is a private person who wants to direct all his long distance calls to the network of Telecom Finland. *A business unit* is the part of the organisation of Telecom Finland which offers the 101-service to customers. There exists exactly one business unit which offers this kind of service to private persons. *An operations centre* manages all the long distance calls related issues of some geographic area. Telecom Finland has several operations centres around the country. *A customer centre* is responsible for both technical and administrative issues related to local calls in a geographic area. While there are several customer centres around Finland, the customer centres and operations centres do not necessarily reside in same places. The services of a *local telephone company* are needed if the customer lives in an area where Telecom Finland does not offer local telephone services.

A customer initiates the service process by making a telephone call. An officer of the business unit receives the order and feeds it into an information system. After the check of the customer's credit information, a written agreement is sent to the customer and the operations centre is requested to establish the connection. When the connection is established the customer centre sends a notification to the business unit which in turn informs the customer about the connection. The long distance telephone calls of the customer are then automatically directed to the network of Telecom Finland.

The main tasks of the regional customer centre is to determine the organisation which is responsible for the local telephone service in the area where the customer lives and to order the physical connection from an appropriate organisation. If Telecom Finland takes care of the local service then the connection order is done via a database. If the local services are provided by another company, a standardised fax message is used to order the new routing of connection.

Several database are used in the production of 101-service. The business unit stores administrative information about the customer in the customer database. The business unit also initially adds the customer to the billing database. The customer centre stores technical user agreement information in the database containing user related technical information. Finally, the operation centre stores records of actual calls in a database which is used as a basis for billing. All the mentioned databases are managed by different database management systems.

Several key observations were made of the environment of 101-service:

- The organisation of Telecom Finland is inherently distributed and heterogeneous. Computers and databases are used extensively.
- The organisation of Telecom Finland must satisfy two kinds of needs:
  - the needs emerging from the customer service and
  - the needs emerging from the management of large and very complex technical systems.

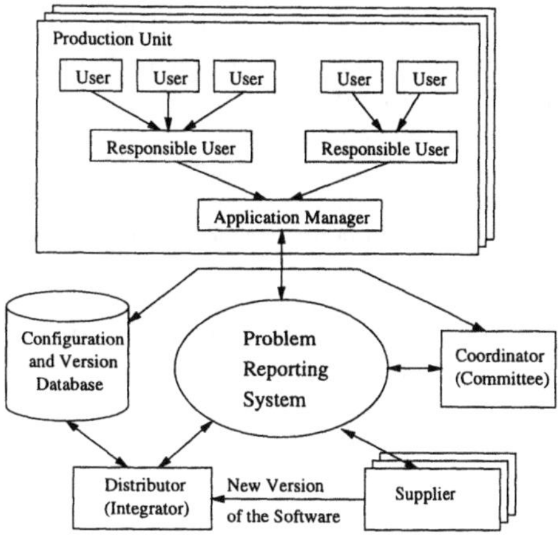


**Figure 3 Problem Reporting at Valmet**

- The 101-service contains both manual and computerised steps.
- The quality of the 101-service depends very much on how the company manages to co-ordinate and control the various workflows occurring in the service production process.
- There exists actors which can not be steered by Telecom Finland, i.e., the local telephone companies.

The detailed analysis of the 101-service introduced three principal requirements for the workflow tools. First, the formalism which is used to describe the workflow process definitions should allow one to express temporal constraints. Second, there should exist tools which allow the simulation of the process definitions. Simulations should produce information which helps one to predict the time consumed by process instances. Finally, the workflow engine should support the control of process instances by offering the possibility to get snapshots of these instances.

## 2.3 Problem reporting system of Valmet Corporation

Valmet Corporation is one of the biggest paper mill machinery producers in the world. It has production units in many countries in Europe and in the USA. Valmet has developed a problem reporting system to help corporate wide maintenance of certain central legacy systems of the production units. The problem reporting system helps in getting the faults reported quickly to relevant parties and in having standardised processes for repair. It keeps track of the problem frequencies and of the performance of the software suppliers.

### *The overall system structure and functions*

The problem reporting system embeds a workflow definition between many organizations including production units of Valmet, the corporate level management of Valmet, software suppliers, and a software distributor. Next we outline the interorganizational process definitions. Within each organization there is a local process definition that might be rather complicated. The overall system is depicted in Figure 3, where the rectangles illustrate actors and the arrows data flows.

In the production units each software system has a *responsible user*, who may be able to solve solve some of the problems other users report. Unsolvable problems get forwarded to the *application manager* of the production unit, who can insert a new problem report to the problem reporting system or make searches to find if there are already solutions available.

The problem reporting system is implemented on top of Lotus Notes ((tm) Lotus Development Corp.). Each problem report corresponds to a form, that contains a reporting area for users (application managers), an answering area for suppliers, a common commenting area. Each form contains also the following data:

- Author identity code
- Target software identification (also version number)
- Data access rights for actors
- Status of processing (reported, received, under work, done, distributed, approved, frozen, cancelled)
- Report class (software fault, change request, development inquiry, other report)
- History of status changes
- Performance information

A new report on the help desk first gets the status *reported.* In case of *software faults* and *change requests* the processing includes a series of actions. The main actors here are the reporting application manager, the *supplier* of the software and the *distributor.* The flow is controlled by setting different statuses to the form depending on its processing phase. Other parties can follow how the case develops on the bulletin board. In case of other types of reports, the system serves as a discussion forum.

The report category *software fault* has two subcategories: *fatal* and *operational limitation.* The former subcategory means that the software cannot be used at all, while the latter rather poses constraints on the use of the software. Faults are usually supposed to be repaired in 3 to 5 days depending on the software component. The report category *change request* is used when the coverage by the maintenance agreements is not evident. The report category *development inquiry* contains cases that need cooperative planning. This category contains development initiatives and specification of new versions, and the corresponding processing is cooperative planning with concurrent access to the report by several authors.

The *supplier* has partial access to the corporate level help desk and is responsible for finding from it the relevant reports. After noticing a new *software fault* report (status to *received*) the supplier is supposed to give an initial response containing first hand estimates on the correction time and possible temporary workarounds. This must be done within 24 hours. The supplier is also supposed to provide a correction plan. After the initial response, the status is set to *under work.* After the supplier has shipped the corrected version of the software to the distributor, the supplier changes the status to *done.* The *distributor* gets the fixed version from the supplier and installs and tests it in those production units that want to have it. The distributor maintains and utilises the configuration and version database, that is used to track the corporate wide installations. This database is also used for compatibility considerations. After the distributor has delivered the software to the appropriate production units, the distributor sets the status to *distributed.* The unit that initiated the whole process sets the status to *approved* after it has found the result acceptable.

All areas on a report are readable to all parties except the measuring area which is visible to Valmet personnel only. All parties can write to the common commenting area where each comment is automatically attached with authentication, date and time. Measuring area is visible to Valmet personnel and contains performance indexes to be used to evaluate the behaviour of the suppliers.

On the corporate level there is the *coordinator* (possibly a group of technical managers and consultants) that makes strategic guidelines and decisions on the software architectures and components. The coordinator helps to solve cases where the troubles cannot be clearly localised to a single system. For instance, troubles in interfacing two systems with each other might require solutions at both ends, not only at one end.

### *Analysis of the system*

The underlying bulletin board metaphor provides weak support for workflow thinking. Processing of a workflow is mainly based on the use of the statuses in the reports. It is up to the users to interpret and set the statuses in a proper way. In the future, mechanisms for controlling the status changes should be added. The control conventions are well defined in the handling of software fault and change request reports. Development inquiries, and other reports do not have so clear conventions. In those cases the system functions as a discussion forum and processing becomes cooperative authoring. For instance, the cooperative planning process of a new software version needs support for concurrent access of the shared reports by many actors.

The system involves many autonomous organizations. The approach so-far has been to publicly announce reports to all users. Also competing suppliers can see each others faults. This arrangement works in favour of Valmet. In more general cases of interorganizational workflows data hiding and autonomy considerations ought to be considered. The transaction support within the report database could be made better as the current system maintains only one copy of the data and lets the actors do destructive changes to this data.

The overall response time of the system depends on how active the users are in reading the reports. There is a need to give the system a more active role. For example, it could alarm the responsible actors for delays in processing. This self monitoring could be combined with forecasting capabilities to estimate durations of process instances. In order to give a more active role to the system it might be good to integrate message exchange (e.g. electronic mail) functions to it.

## 3 SUMMARY OF THE MAJOR SHORTCOMINGS IN THE CURRENT WORKFLOW PRODUCTS

**Inadequacy for inter-organisational workflows.** Although in some cases high-end workflow products (e.g. FlowMark) might be suited for defining workflows that take place in many organisations, none of the products can deal with wide range of heterogeneity and autonomy issues in in this kind of system. (This is also true in enterprise-wide systems.)

**Lacking standards.** Although workflow products provide many ways to integrate external applications and documents, they lack standard interfaces that would support interoperability among workflow management systems and third party software. The standards to be developed by the Workflow Management Coalition will help to overcome this problem.

**Business process analysis and re-engineering.** Workflow products usually do not include tools for BPA and BPR for the basis of the workflow process definition. Moreover, although there is a great variety of separate BPA/BPR-tools the definitions can not be exchanged between them and workflow products.

**Inadequate support for testing, debugging and analysis of the scenario definitions.** Most of the products enable manual experimenting of the scenario definition before putting it into the production use. However, certain correctness aspects (e.g. the correct termination of the workflow process in all possible cases) can not be tested automatically. Workflow products also usually lack simulation tools.

**Missing advanced monitoring tools.** While most of the workflow products provide some kind of audit trail and status reporting, only few of them can produce more advanced reports that would e.g. reveal the efficiency of the system and possible bottlenecks in it, thus supporting continuous enhancing of the system.

**Inadequate of totally missing definition of the transactional properties.** None of the products we know enables the definition of some or all of the traditional ACID properties for an activity or a group of activities.

Moreover, none of the products contains backward recovery by compensation. Neither do current products have a possibility to define contingency activities for alternative execution after a scenario instance is cancelled or cannot be executed for some other reason.

Managing shared resources also has serious shortcomings. In some products some of these shortcomings are solved by preventing the concurrent access of data items and document files related to the certain workflow process instance. Other products leave this problem to the application programmer. Even less is offered by the workflow systems if one needs to control the correctness of the data retrieved from the external data storages that are used concurrently by many workflow process instances (or even by several different workflow management systems). This means that none of the programs we know enable to define all the shared data and its visibility. All this leads also to inadequate support for co-operative workflow applications.

**Inadequate definition of inter-activity and inter-process dependencies.** Only few workflow products enable the definition of advanced dependencies above the serial dependency (`Release` $\mathcal{A} \rightarrow$ `Begin` $\mathcal{B}$) between the activities while many other types of dependencies might be needed (e.g. `Cancel` $\mathcal{A} \rightarrow$ `Begin` $\mathcal{B}$ and `Release` $\mathcal{A} \rightarrow$ `Cancel` $\mathcal{B}$.

**Dynamic and ad hoc features.** Typically ad hoc workflows, modifying the rules or data of the scenario instance in the execution and other features empowering the end users are lacking from the workflow systems aimed to production type tasks. However, there are growing number of products including this kinds of features in their functionality.

## 4 CONCLUSION

In this paper, we have studied three inter-organizational workflow applications, deduced requirements from them and compared the requirements with tools and properties offered by some commercial workflow products. We have concentrated ourselves mainly on aspects like workflow definition tools and advanced transactional properties which seem to be of prime importance in these environments. The comparisons show that the chosen products do not support many features needed in these environments. Especially lacking are the advanced transactional properties and specification facilities which could be used in interorganizational environments.

We have applied the conceptual framework and reference architecture defined by the Workflow Management Coalition. We have found them valuable in assessing the products and applications. Further work needs to be done, however, before they can be used to solve real problems of interoperability.

The results also show that further research is needed to better understand the transactional requirements and their implications in the autonomous workflow environments like those handled here. The process definition tools should support pre-analysis of the transactional properties. What those properties are, is for further study.

**Acknowledgements** We are grateful to the "TransCoop people" at GMD-IPSI in Darmstadt and at University of Twente in Enschede for clarifying discussions during the application analysis.

We thank PortNet consortium and especially Ms. Ina Mickelsson and Mrs. Eija Berg for mediating information about the system. We also thank Dr. Olli Martikainen, Vice President (R&D) as well as Mr. Panu Hämäläinen and Mr. Atte Nikkanen of Finnish Telecom for releasing information concerning the 101-service and supporting our work. We further thank Mr. Hakan West, Vice President (Systems & Procedures) and Mr. Tuomo Raitanen of Valmet Corporation.

We also thank Mr. Esko Uotila from ICL Personal Systems for kindly providing us the TeamFlow software. We are also grateful to Dr. Frank Leymann and Mr. Harri Puhilas from IBM for interesting discussions and material concerning the FlowMark product. Finally, we thank Mr. Kai Vehmersalo from WorkFlow Oy for information about Staffware product.

## REFERENCES

[ASSR93] M. Attie, M. Singh, A. Sheth, and M. Rusinkiewicz. Specifying and enforcing intertask dependencies. In *The 19th International Conference on VLDB*, 1993.

[BDS+93] Y. Breitbart, A. Deacon, H.-J. Schek, A. Sheth, and G. Weikum. Merging application-centric and data-centric approaches to support transaction-oriented multi-system workflows. 22(3), September 1993.

[CR90a] P. Chrysanthis and K Ramamritham. Acta: A framework for specifying and reasoning about transactions structure and behavior. In *ACM SIGMOD International Conference on Management of Data*, 1990.

[CR90b] P. Chrysanthis and K. Ramamrithan. A framework for specifying and reasoning about transaction structure and behavior. In *ACM SIGMOD International Conference on Management of Data*, 1990.

[GH94] D. Georgakopoulos and M. F. Hornick. A framework for enforceable specification of extended transaction models and transactional workflows. *International Journal of Intelligent and Cooperative Information Systems*, sept. 1994.

[GR93] J. Gray and A. Reuter. *Transaction Processing: Concepts and Techniques.* 1993.

[Gru94] J. Grudin. Computer supported cooperative work: History and focus. *COMPUTER*, May 1994.

[Kle91] J. Klein. Advanced rule driven transaction management. In *IEEE COMPCON*, 1991.

[Loc94] R. Lockwood. Groupware and workflow: the european perspective. In T.E. White and L. Fischer, editors, *New tools for new times: The Workflow Paradigm*, chapter 12, pages 195–214. Future Strategies Inc., Book Division, Alameda, CA, 1994.

[PC94] K. Ramamritham P.K. Chrysantis. Synthesis of extended transaction models using acta. *ACM Transactions on Database system*, 19(3):450–491, sept. 1994.

[SR93] A. Sheth and M. Rusinkiewicz. On transactional workflows. 16(2), June 1993.

[Tra94] TransCoop. Transcoop deliverable 2.1, specification language requirements. Transcoop (ep8012) deliverable, University of Twente, Dec. 1994.

[VEH92] J. Veijalainen, F. Eliassen, and B. Holtkamp. The s-transaction model. In A.K. Elmagarmid, editor, *Database Transaction Models for Advanced Applications*, chapter 12, pages 467-513. 1992.

[Vei90] J. Veijalainen. *Transaction Concepts in Autonomous Database Environments.* R.Oldenbourg Verlag, 1990.

[Vei92] J. Veijalainen. Issues in open edi. In *Proc. of 2nd International Conference on Systems Integration*, pages 401–412. IEEE Computer Society, june 1992.

[Vei93] Jari Veijalainen. Heterogeneous multilevel transaction management with multiple subtransactions. In *Fourth Intl. Conference on Database and Expert Systems Applications, DEXA '93, LNCS Nr. 720*, pages 181–188, September 1993.

[Wäc91] W. Wächter. Contracts: A means for improving reliability in distributed computing. In *IEEE COMPCON*, 1991.

[Wor94] Workflow Management Coalition. *Glossary; A Workflow Management Coalition Specification*, nov. 1994.

[WR92] H. Wächter and A. Reuter. The contract model. In A.K. Elmagarmid, editor, *Database Transaction Models for Advanced Applications*, chapter 7. 1992.

[WS92] G. Weikum and H. Schek. Concepts and applications of multilevel transactions and open nested transactions. In A.K. Elmagarmid, editor, *Database Transaction Models for Advanced Applications*, chapter 13. 1992.

# APPENDIX 1 SUMMARY OF THE PRODUCT EVALUATION

**Technical details of the products**

| | Staffware | FlowMark | TeamFlow |
|---|---|---|---|
| Architecture | Client/Server | Client/Server | Client/Server, Mail-Based |
| Server platform | UNIX | OS/2, AIX | OS/2, Windows NT |
| Client platform | UNIX, Windows | OS/2, AIX, Windows | Windows |
| DBMS | Proprietary, Informix, Oracle | ObjectStore | Proprietary, (SQLServer or SQLBase for audit-trail log) |

**Workflow process definition functionality**

| | | | |
|---|---|---|---|
| **Graphical def.** | Yes | Yes | No |
| **Hierarchical def.** | No | Yes | No |
| **Reusability** | Poor reusability in definition | Every object can be reused | Existing definition as a template for a new one |
| **Language** | Script | FDL | No |
| **Process simulation** | No | No, only animation | No |
| **Testing before production use** | In separate test environment | By animation facility | No separate testing facilities |
| **Import/Export process definitions** | Yes | Yes, using FDL | Transferable internal representation |
| **Misc.** | Includes form tools | | |

**Workflow process definition features: activities**

| | | | |
|---|---|---|---|
| **Activity types** | Steps (with a form interface), automatic steps, external events, management reports | Program and process activity | Steps, co-operative and information steps |
| **Compensating or contingency activities** | No | No | No |

**Workflow process definition features: activity assignment**

| | | | |
|---|---|---|---|
| **Activity assignment** | Single user, group, role | Single user, role, organisational unit | Single user |
| **Dynamic assignment** | Yes | Yes | Yes (by user selection) |

**Workflow process definition features: control flow**

| | | | |
|---|---|---|---|
| **Dependencies between activities** | Release → Begin, Release → Release | Release → Begin | Release → Begin |
| **Routing** | Rules-based | Rules-based | Response-based |
| **Parallel routing** | Yes | Yes | Limited |
| **Synchronisation of converging control flows** | AND-join | AND-join, OR-join | No |
| **Iteration** | Yes | Yes | Yes |
| **Bundles** | No | Yes (by using ext. utility) | No |
| **Data flow definition** | No | Yes | No |

**Workflow process definition features: deadlines and other temporal dependencies**

| | | | |
|---|---|---|---|
| **Deadlines can be set to** | Activities, group of activities and whole process | Activities | Activities |
| **Deadline expression** | Duration, absolute, relative (to e.g. some variable) or calculated date and time expressions (years, months, weeks, days, hours, minutes). Deadlines can be conditional. | Duration (days, hours). | Duration (days, hours). |
| **Action if deadline exceeded** | Start user defined activities | Notify | Notify |
| **Other temporal dependencies** | No | No | No |

| | | | |
|---|---|---|---|
| **Workflow process management** | | | |
| **Activity delegation** | Yes | Yes (has also automatic delegation to the substitute user) | Yes |
| **Modify a process in execution (by an end-user)** | No | No | Yes |
| **Forward recovery** | Continue from the last saved state | Continue from the last saved state | Continue from the last saved state |
| **Backward recovery** | No | No | No |
| **Work balancing** | No | No | No |
| **Data definition features** | | | |
| **Basic data types supported** | Text, number, date, time, memo | String, long, float | String |
| **Structured data types** | No | Array, structure | List of strings |
| **Misc.** | User defined value lists and data tables | | |
| **Data management** | | | |
| **Management of the workflow process relevant data** | Global within a process instance. Parallel activities can have concurrent access (without any control). | Each activity has private data containers contents of which are exchanged between the activities as defined in data flow definition. | Data are stored in TeamMail mail items. In case of parallel activities, data items are replicated. |
| **Document management** | Pointers to physical files using attachment fields | No | Managed as TeamMail attachment files |
| **Concurrency control in the document management** | Yes (based on UNIX file handling) | No | Documents are shared as mail attachments |
| **Versioning of the data** | No | No | No |
| **User definition** | | | |
| **Single user definition** | Predefined set of attributes + user defined attributes | Predefined set of attributes | Predefined set of attributes |
| **Other user structures** | Group, Role | Role, organization | No |
| **Integration** | | | |
| **Integration mechanisms** | External program calls from Staffware forms. Forms can be replaced by another application. Very limited API support. Visual Basic Form helper utility. | External program (or DLL function) calls, APIs | external program calls, APIs |
| **APIs** | Proprietary SAL API, DDE | C/C++, REXX, Visual Basic, DDE, OLE, VIM, HLLAPI | C/C++, Visual Basic |
| **Administration and monitoring functionality** | | | |
| **Audit trail database** | Yes | Yes | Yes |
| **Built in audit-trail reporting** | Status of process instance, audit-trail report, customised reports | Graphical representation of the process instance status | Status of process instance, audit-trail report, predefined reports with user parameters |
| **Suspend/re-route/re-assign/terminate a process instance** | Yes/(Yes)/Yes/Yes | Yes/No/Yes/Yes | Yes/Yes/Yes/Yes |
| **Modify data of a process instance** | Yes | Yes | Yes |
| **Suitability for different workflow types** | | | |
| **Workflow type product suits best for** | Administrative and production | Production | Administrative and ad hoc |

3

# The Systems Integration Architecture: an Agile Information Infrastructure

*by John J. Mills, Ramez Elmasri, Kashif Khan, Srinivas Miriyala, and Kalpana Subramanian*
*The Agile Aerospace Manufacturing Research Center,*
*The Automation & Robotics Research Institute,*
*The University of Texas at Arlington,*
*7300 Jack Newell Blvd. S,*
*Fort Worth TX, 76118, U.S.A.*
*Principle Contact: Dr. John J. Mills, 010-817-794-5903; 010-817-794-5952 [fax]; e-mail: jmills@arri.uta.edu*

**Abstract**

The Systems Integration Architecture project is taking a fresh approach to integration with special emphasis on supporting Agile, Virtual enterprises and their unique need for reconfigurable, de-centralized information systems. SIA is based on a different conceptual model of integration - called the TAR model - one which allows higher level integration than the traditional common, neutral format, shared database. The basic concept is that all information processing consists of a series of transformations of data sets called "Aspects" into other "Aspects". The transformations are effected by what are called Functional Transformation Agents which provide a single function and have a well defined interface structure which allows them to be integrated in a variety of ways. The Systems Integration Architecture provides three high level services which allow FTA's to be defined, combined into diverse networks which provide transformations of aspects in a manner transparent to the user and executed under a variety of control algorithms in a heterogeneous, de-centralized environment. These are: an Executive--to provide business control services; a Librarian--to act as somewhat of a meta data dictionary, keeping track of FTA's and their input and output Aspects; and a Network--which is based on the Common Object Request Broker Architecture to facilitate communication between objects on a heterogeneous network. An extended entity relationship diagram is provided and each of the objects in the system is described. A simple example of its use is provided.

## INTRODUCTION AND BACKGROUND

Agile Manufacturing is a new paradigm in which manufacturers must be able to rapidly respond to unanticipated market demands, producing new products uwith resources outside of their immediate company in what has become known as "Virtual Corporations". In these, complementary core competencies from diverse companies including suppliers and customers, are combined temporarily into a new, decentralized company existing only to fulfill that market demand and dissolving when the demand is satisfied.

To support such rapid formation and reconfiguration of business processes, a unique information infrastructure will be required. The requirements of such an infrastructure are not clear at present, but some things are fairly clear. A business consists of a series of processes (order entry, generate purchase orders and invoices, design part or product, produce artifact, etc.). An individual business process consists of a series of functions or activities in IDEF0 formalism [1] which takes some input and "transforms" or converts it into an output. Both the processes and the lower level functions perform some action. The processes perform the action to achieve a business goal or objective, subject to a set of business rules.

Even if a company is not ready to become "Agile", to survive in today's competitive world, it must be continually seeking to improve itself. Such continuous improvement requires change; changes within individual processes and changes within the organization of those processes and activities.

There is a strong move in industry to treat these business processes like any other industrial process and to apply engineering principles to their design and implementation. This move is called Business Process Re-Engineering. If we are to be able to reconfigure the business functions or processes at any level, the information system supporting these must be modular in nature with clearly defined inputs and outputs. These modules must be supported by an information infrastructure into which the modules "plug" in such a manner that they provide integration at multiple levels. At this juncture, it is not necessary to define the granularity of the modules.

STEP is an international effort to standardize the exchange of data within an enterprise. While this effort will go a long way to addressing the issue of interfaces, we believe that it is based on a conceptual model which is no longer adequate for integration within an agile or continuously improving environment.

A conceptual or basis model is a simple model which is used to communicate the ideal which one is attempting to achieve when building some system. Another way of viewing it is that it is an abstraction of the purpose of the system.[2] Most implementations of integrated systems are based on a model consisting of a common, neutral format, logically unified, but physically distributed, shared database. This model has its problems as we have discussed elsewhere[3]. It requires mechanisms for "Unification" of the various views extracted from it [4]. It does not support time dependency of the data (being a static model), it is data centric, it ignores the processes which create the data in the first place and it does not provide an easy migration path to its eventual creation. The CIM-OSA project has defined at least three levels of integration as illustrated in Figure 1[5]. The common database model only supports one aspect of this concept.

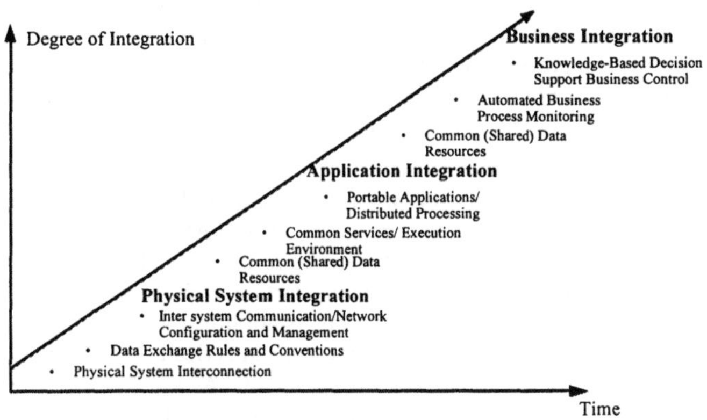


**Figure 1. CIM-OSA Levels of Integration**

The common shared database model is basically sound and should be incorporated in any model that replaces it. Elsewhere we are proposing a basis model derived from one emerging from the design theory world. We call it the Transformation of Aspects and Representations or TAR model and briefly describe it below. It supports all of the concepts in the CIM-OSA model.

*The Automation & Robotics Institute (ARRI)* is creating the *Systems Integration Architecture* that facilitates seamless integration of tools not necessarily designed to be used together. The *Systems Integration Architecture (SIA)*, based on the TAR model, was designed to integrate heterogeneous functional modules and systems with a minimum of effort, thus allowing the definition and execution of processes that use multiple application modules in an agile fashion. SIA also facilitates agility and flexibility in the integration of heterogeneous tools using an object oriented approach. The goal of SIA is to support the rapid reconfiguration of software modules into an information system supporting the enterprise as it is reconfigured. It can support integration, from the lowest level processes to the highest level processes in an enterprise, with any degree of business control desired.

Below we briefly describe the TAR model followed by an overview of SIA, with some further detail. We end with a short example of its use.

## TAR MODEL

The derivation of this model can be traced back at least two decades in the design theory arena [6,7,8,9,10]. In the latest instantiation, Fenves and Talukdar express it as the TAO model. We have expanded it out of the design theory world to encompass the whole product realization process from needs definition to product delivery and support -- and from order entry to shipping.

The model is quite simple in essence. The product realization process (PRP) is one or more transformations of information and material. The artist, or craftsman, takes a set of needs or requirements from inside themselves or from a customer and transforms these into the end product by a creative process with very few intermediate steps. In the engineering world, the realization of products is a process with many steps, each of which transforms a set of data or information into another data or information set, with the end result being a transformation of an information set and raw material into the finished product and supporting information.

For convenience we define two kinds of information sets which are transformed. The first, called "Representations" consist of all the information required at the completion of some phase or stage of the product realization process. The TAR model leaves the precise definition of these phases and their Representations up to the user. The PRP then consists of the transformations of the various Representations, starting with the needs and ending with the product. However, in reality, a "Representation" is not transformed in a single event, but in multiple parts and multiple steps, some of which are in series and some in parallel. We define a Representation, therefore, to consist of a set of "Aspects" which are subsets of Representations required by some function during the PRP and it is these "Aspects" which are transformed. Details of the model can be found in Reference 3

Transformations are effected by software applications which we call Functional Transformation Agents or FTA's. Fully manual transformation agents are humans performing some function for which an algorithm has not yet been defined. Computer aided transformations agents are applications which help a user either document the result of their creative activity or analyze, under human control, some data set or aspect. Fully automated transformation agents are applications which perform the transformations on their own. An example of a fully automated transformation agent is a rule based design system which transforms a set of specifications into a full design according to the rules embedded in it. A key feature of our model is the nature and structure of the interfaces between the transformation agents. Figure 2 illustrates the concept of the transformation agent and its interfaces.

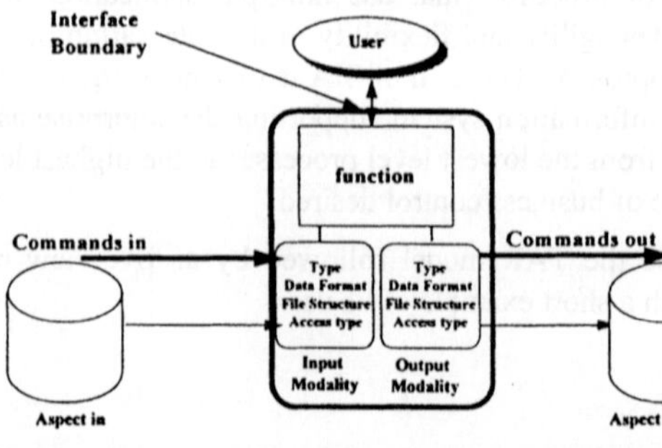


**Figure 2. The Concept of a Transformation Agent and Its Interfaces**

Systems engineering precepts imply a single function for each transformation agent. This has advantages, but most legacy software is not set up in that manner and they can provide many functions, each of which is an FTA. Transformations can also be combined into processes in any kind of network; each process carrying out a higher level function. Functional Transformation Agents transform an input Aspect into an output Aspect. To combine them, however, the interfaces between the agents becomes a critical part of the process design. If the output Aspect(s) of one transformation agent does not match the input Aspect(s) of the next agent, the process cannot be executed. However, just specifying the type of data (i.e. the Aspect) does not guarantee that the functions can be integrated. The Aspects can be in many different file structures and data formats. They can also be accessed in many different ways. Accordingly, we have defined each Aspect to have, what we have termed, a "Modality' with three attributes: the file structure, the data format and the access type. These are described in more detail later.

Commands are also part of the interface definition, since, for true integration, it may be necessary for one FTA to activate another.

The TAR model is suitable for an Agile Enterprise because each transformation agent forms a module which can be configured into a system with other modules as long as the appropriate Aspects and Modalities can be matched.

## THE SYSTEM INTEGRATION ARCHITECTURE

### *Overview*

SIA achieves the required integration as specified by the CIM-OSA model, by providing certain key services in data management, control and communications. In SIA three modules provide these three categories of services; the Executive, the Librarian, and the Communications Kernel. We discuss these concepts in more detail later in the paper.

The approach used in the development of SIA is different from what is used in some of the existing integration frameworks. *SIFRAME,* developed by SIEMENS/NIXDORF, for instance, is a domain-less framework that uses a work space concept to support teamwork.[11] However, concurrent development is hampered because the user keeps the rights to a particular data set or Aspect until they free it. In our view, an integration system needs to provide for a variety of data sharing modes, not just lockout. The framework also assumes a logically unified database which has inherent problems as discussed earlier.

*Khoros* and *PowerFrame* are two other applications that facilitate integration at workflow level, but these do not integrate the services that are required with the data. Product data management systems, such as SDRC's DCMS or the new Metaphase product data manager being created by a joint venture between SDRC and CDC, focuses on facilitating product data management. It facilitates the integration of the data and provides certain other services which activate the appropriate application associated with a set of data, but does not provide for work flow management.

The Systems Integration Architecture on the other hand allows true agile information processing by allowing integration at all three CIM-OSA levels: data, service, and business. In SIA, functions are integrated along with the data needed by the functions in a manner that is transparent to the user. The user can call up any function supporting the activity or process they need and the system provides the data set in correct file structure, format, and access type without the user having to worry about the location or format of the tool.

Like SIFRAME, PowerFrame and Khoros, SIA uses the concept of processes to allow the user to define a workflow by checking for the appropriate format for tool integration through a user interface called *Executive.* However, SIA also keeps track of the information interfaces through a data management system called *Librarian* via a *Communication* kernel which is based on the Common Object Request Broker Architecture. All these modules are described in the next section. Figure 3 illustrates the conceptual System Integration Architecture.

## *Executive Module*

The Executive module operates at the front end of SIA. It interacts only with the user and the Communications kernel module of SIA which in turn interacts with the Librarian module to provide the Executive with the required information. The primary objective of the Executive is to provide the user interface, which controls the user access to system data and resources, and to interpret user requests. The core idea of a minimal executive is, by invoking a specific control algorithm, it allows any degree of business control from a tight workflow management approach like SIFRAME, defining who does what and when, all the way to a fully autonomous system with autonomous agents reacting to a change in their environment. Hence, the executive acts as a client in SIA, with the Librarian and tools acting in the role of servers that provide specific services. The user interaction with SIA depends on the category of the user (i.e. project member or the project manager). It allows the team members to login and logout, browse through information about SIA objects, select a context, and launch enterprise processes. It helps the project manager to manage all the team member services along with storing and editing information about new or existing SIA objects, creating and editing enterprise process templates, and adding and deleting SIA objects. This feature is elaborated in the section below on Modes of Use.

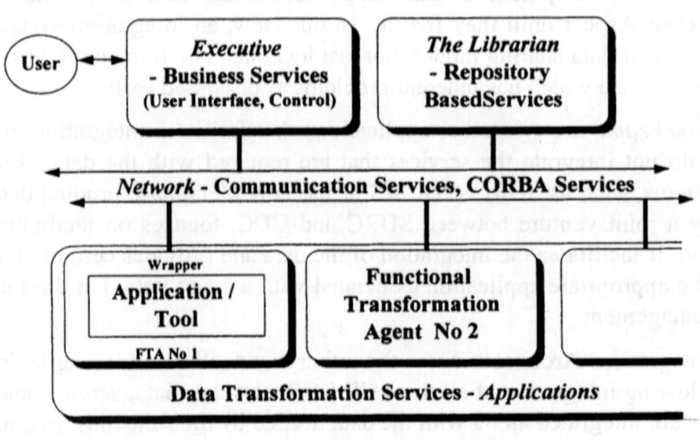


**Figure 3. The Conceptual Model of the Systems Integration Architecture**

The core Executive also allows the project manager to define transformation agents and their interfaces. Several other transformation modules are under development to provide other required services to the users, including a menu driven interface to facilitate setting a context for passing of these commands to specific transformation agents and a project management function to define the flow of transformations and information management.

The Executive can start, stop, and pause/resume processes as well as request status information. It may activate certain specific processes which provide more functionality to the user, such as a system configuration function to allow the project's leader to configure the system with the degree of control he desires. It may activate a process to provide very specific sequencing of functional transformations for all users, or may allow the users to select the functions they want in whatever order they prefer, subject to the availability of data.

The Executive also has naming algorithms which the Librarian uses to name the data files that are generated by the transformation agents. The names must be compatible with conventions used by tools for naming their files.

### *The Librarian*

The Librarian is the central object in SIA and its basic function is to manage the relationships among processes, tools, and data sets, and to maintain information about the existence and format of all data in the system. It acts as an information base in the architecture. The Librarian does not actually store items, it stores information about where and how the applications and data items are stored (i.e. meta data). It integrates both the data sets and the functionality.

The Librarian invokes modules for dealing with concurrency and sharing of data. It also responds to requests for access to data items as they are created. The Librarian maintains a list of all current objects (tools, transformation agents etc.) available in the system and enables the user to build new objects as needed. In addition, the Librarian maintains a history of all transformations performed on data items, as well as individual logs and versions for existing data files. The Librarian maintains knowledge about the capabilities and functions of tools, such as the transformations that the tools perform. It will allow the executive to return the user to the same place in his project on login. It also maintains records of all projects that are active, including the history of how, who, and when the data was created and where it is stored.

The Librarian also helps compute efficient transformation processes for data to be transformed from one format to another through the use of other modules. The Librarian stores these information paths for future reference. The Librarian manages all the configuration tables (that store information about the users, their access rights, and the status of each project) and addresses issues such as, how much information can one project access about any other project.

### *Communication Module*

The main function of this module is to provide communications services among distributed heterogeneous modules. It is, essentially, the lower six layers of the ISO/OSI communication protocol architecture plus a message passing protocol. While we initially created our own network kernel, we are currently re-implementing it using the Common Object Request Broker Architecture (CORBA)[12].

CORBA allows us to define SIA services provided by the tools, functional transformation agents, and Librarian. These services are implemented as SIA services. The SIA client, the Executive can now communicate with and invoke these services through CORBA anywhere on the network. This will allow us the advantages of an object-oriented framework with the obvious benefits of inheritance, encapsulation of services, etc., thereby allowing heterogeneous platforms to communicate.

## COMPONENT OBJECTS OF SIA

The Extended Entity Relationship[13] diagram, Figure 4, depicts all the component objects of SIA. A description of each follows.

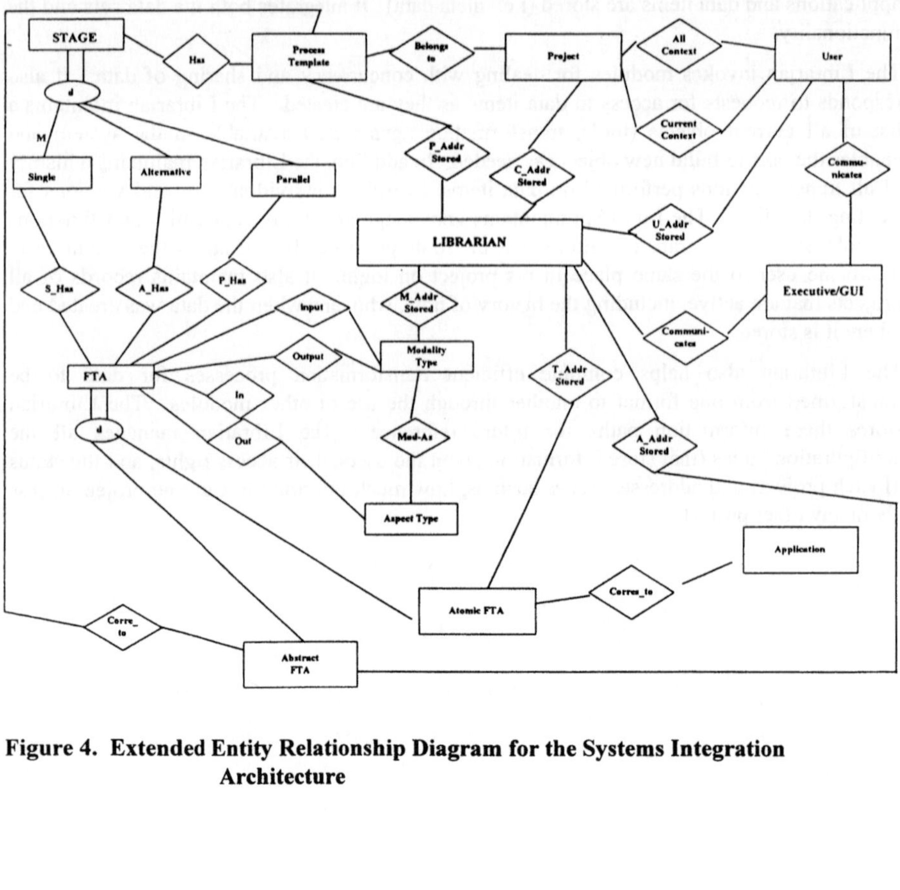


**Figure 4. Extended Entity Relationship Diagram for the Systems Integration Architecture**

### *Users, Contexts and Projects*

Users in the architecture represent the current users of the system. They are divided into two subgroups- ordinary users and project leaders. Project objects are the primary interfaces for users. Projects maintain a user list with information about users passwords and data access rights. One user in the list is designated as the Project Leader. Each Project maintains a list of Process objects and their possible interdependencies.

The User is capable of launching and shutting down processes. Also, each Project object maintains a project log, detailing users' connect times and the processes invoked during user sessions. Project objects, or their users, may have priority levels assigned to them, in which case the Project with the higher Priority would be granted access to the FTA. The notion of context is related to the project and the skills of the user.

### *Aspects, Modality, and Functional Transformation Agents*

Aspects in the Librarian module are represented as a combination of identifier and modality pair.

A ***data identifier*** is simply a unique name of an “Aspect” which is simply a specific set of information, such as a product part or a document. We term these “Aspects” since they can be considered as an "Aspect" or "View" of the product data. Each data identifier may have several modalities associated with it, representing different versions or formats of the information. In such a case, each modality represents either the same data in a different format, or another version of the information. The data item description contains a unique identifier associated with the data item and a time stamp used for version management. The combination of data items and description identifies a unique collection of data that can be stored as a file, or in a database, or in any other suitable data format.

***Modality*** is a triplet that is a specification of physical format of data (including storage and data format).

*Modality = { data_format, file_structure, access_type}*

where *data_format = {DXF, IGES, EXCEL, WORD, STEP, AUTOCAD native format }*

*file_structure = { ASCII, flat, binary, MacBinary, database}*

*access_type = { read/write, dbQuery, pipes, SDAI, RPC, API}*

The ***Functional Transformation Agent*** (FTA) is the function that provides mapping from an input Aspect/Modality combination to an output Aspect/Modality.

*FTA: input Aspect/Modality -------> output Aspect/Modality*

SIA has a graphical user interface that allows new FTA's to be defined as needed. The modalities of the FTA's can be used by the process object to determine the consistency of the input and output specifications on which the FTA's should operate. Once launched, an FTA object should be able to start, stop, and abort operation and report its status.

FTA is an abstract class which has two subclasses. ***Abstract_FTA*** is a process template, in its own right, with its Aspects and their Modalities. It represents a higher level abstract function that is defined as a process of lower level FTA's and allows a hierarchical design of a process template. An Abstract FTA can include other abstract FTA's, which are more detailed process templates, and provide a high level view of a complex manufacturing process included as a component of another process. This allows abstract FTA's to be recursively composed.

***The Atomic_FTA*** is the combination of Function and its interfaces. If the function is a computer based tool or application, then the ***Atomic_FTA*** also includes the enclosing wrapper of that function of the application. The wrapper in SIA encapsulates a function because each function requires a different aspect and, usually, a different modality. The ***Atomic_FTA*** is an FTA that can be directly executed using one or more available tools.

As each Atomic FTA is launched, the process will query the Librarian for the input and output modalities. These will be combined with the data identifiers listed in the transformation path and sent to a tool that performs the desired FTA function. If at some point a requested modality of an Aspect intended for input does not exist, the Process will request the Librarian to generate an extension to the transformation path. The Librarian will look up the existing modalities for the specified Aspect, and consult its list of FTA's, trying to locate one or more that can accomplish transforming one of the existing modalities into the requested one. If the Librarian succeeds in generating a sub-path that will produce the requested modality, the path is returned to the process, which incorporates it into its existing transformation path for future use.

***A Process*** is the most autonomous action that a user can request. It represents a production, design or business process transformation path with a sequence of stages to be invoked. Processes are thus composed of FTA objects arranged in a transformation path, which represents a series of FTA's and the data items that are input and output from them.

***A Process Template*** is a description of a process. It describes a process transformation path for the sequence of Functional Transformation Agents (FTA) to be invoked. Each process template can be used by several users to launch the corresponding process and each launched process is associated with only one process template. The process template consists of several stages, and each stage is either single, parallel, or alternative. A ***Single Stage*** consists of only one FTA. A ***Parallel Stage*** consists of several transformation agents, all of which must be invoked in parallel. An ***Alternative Stage*** consists of several FTAs, only one of which must be invoked. Figure 5 illustrates this concept.

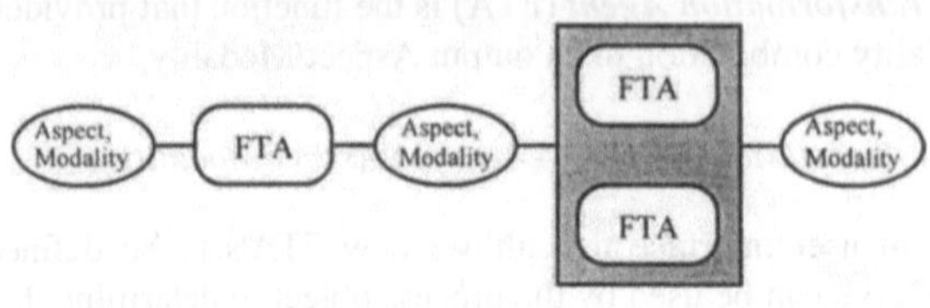


**Figure 5. Concept of Stages in a Process Graph**

# MODES OF USE OF THE SYSTEMS INTEGRATION ARCHITECTURE

## *Modes of Systems Integration Architecture*

To obtain its goals, the Architecture operates in three modes. *Application Integration mode* is used for defining a new tool or application and its location and launching mechanism. It assists in creating wrappers when necessary. It also allows the systems engineer to define the functionalities for a tool. *Process Definition Mode* allows SIA to check the compatibility of FTA's input/output while defining a new process. Transformation of FTA's can be used to make the input and output modalities compatible. *Process Launching Mode* helps keep track of current progress in a launched process, location of I/O files, etc.

## Application integration mode

Application Integration deals with the principles and mechanisms that help us make the functions provided by the software tools of the environment cooperate efficiently towards the smooth flow of the transformation of information. SIA supports the integration of in-house and commercial tools. When a tool/platform is incompatible with SIA, a wrapper is developed to provide the capability for connecting the tool to SIA. This allows SIA modules to communicate with the new tool in the SIA protocols. The wrappers will allow seamless data communications between tools or applications that are normally not compatible. The architecture allows many diverse computer based tools to be integrated and interact in such a manner that is transparent to the user. The architecture allows any software application to be pluggable, which means that any application can be removed from a system and a new application, providing the same functionality, can be inserted without having to do a major rewrite of the integration software.

## Process definition mode

Process in SIA can be compared to a workflow - a long duration, multi-step activity with some data and control flow between the constituent steps of the workflow. The basic reason for workflow is to automate routine work. It provides a structure to accomplish a series of tasks in an automated fashion,[14] the same objective being desired in SIA through the use of processes.

In process definition mode, SIA allows the project managers to design processes that require routine automation. This is achieved through the use of defining a process through different stages by the project manager based on FTA's needed to perform that particular task. If the output Aspect and its Modality of the first tool matches with the input Aspect/Modality of the other, the next stage can be defined; otherwise, SIA will search for a transformation tool that converts the output of the stage to the modality compatible with the input of the next stage.

A mark of a good workflow system is flexibility - both in design and operation.[15] SIA provides this flexibility by allowing the user to pick any tool out of the list of tools that can perform the same function. If the tool is not available, another tool, able perform the same function, can be specified.

### Process launching mode

The process launching mode deals with the execution of an already defined process.

Each FTA in the path is executed in order. In the case of multiple tools/applications that can perform the same function, the user may select which function they prefer. As each FTA is launched, the Process will query the FTA for its input and output modalities. These will be combined with the data identifiers listed in the transformation path and sent to the Librarian. The Librarian will then return file names for each data item.

The Process will start the FTA, passing it the filenames to be used for input and output. Each reference to data may be flagged as persistent or transient data. In the case of transient data no query to the Librarian is made. Instead, the two FTA's on either side of the data are launched with an interposed communication channel, established between them. This facilitates real-time function interaction in the system. Also each reference to an FTA object may or may not be flagged 'must run'. If the FTA is not flagged "must run", the output file is compared to the input file's data to determine if the output data is out of date. FTA is launched only if it is out of date.

Finally, if at some point a requested piece of data intended for input does not exist, the Process will request the Librarian to generate an extension to the transformation path. The Librarian will look up the existing modalities for the specified data, and consult its list of FTA's trying to locate one or more that can accomplish transforming one of the existing modalities into the requested one. If the Librarian succeeds in generating a sub path that will produce the requested modality, that path is returned to the Process, which incorporates it into its existing transformation path for use.

## IMPLEMENTATION EXAMPLE

Suppose a user wants to define a process for designing an assembly of a new product using a Create Geometry function; passing this design to an assembly planning function; converting the assembly plan to a robot assembly program; and finally executing the robot assembly program.

The user first logs into SIA through the Executive module. The user may browse through a list of FTA's providing Create Geometry services available through SIA and select the desired FTA for the first step. The FTA selected is placed as the first stage in a Process Graph, which represents the process template being created. There could be several FTA's based on different CAD tools placed in parallel to allow the eventual user a selection based on his expertise. Each commercial application providing this functionality is encapsulated in a Wrapper to allow the association of the Aspect/Modality Definition with the appropriate functionality. The user then selects the planning FTA required for the assembly planning step, and attempts to place it as the second stage in the Process Graph, Figure 6.

SIA checks whether the output Aspect and Modality of Stage 1 (Create Geometry FTA) is compatible with the input Aspect and Modality of Stage 2 (planning FTA); if they are not compatible, SIA may search for a FTA that converts the output of Stage 1 to an Aspect/Modality combination compatible with the input of Stage 2. If such a FTA is found , it is inserted as Stage 1a in the process - otherwise, Stage 1a may be designated as a manual stage in the process. User may then select a FTA to convert the output of the planning tool into a robot assembly program (Stage 3); alternatively, Stage 3 could be designated as a manual stage.

Stage 4 in the Process Template could be manual stage to check that the robot used for assembly is properly set up. Stage 5 is then specified as invoking the Assembly Robot FTA with the file that is output from Stage 3. No output is shown from Stage 5 since the major output is the assembled artifact. There could be a status report as an output if that was desired, however.

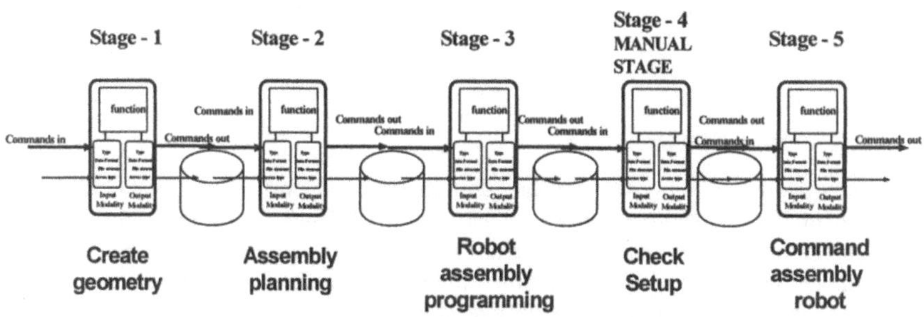


**Figure 6. A Specific Process Graph for Integrating CAD to Robot Assembly**

In the process definition scenario presented, we assume that the user wants to launch that process. A user logs in through the Executive module and selects the previously defined process template from the Librarian and launches the process. SIA identifies the first stage in the Process Template and starts the designated CAD tool, via its wrapper, to provide the required functionality of that tool. SIA keeps track of the stage of the user in the process. Once Stage 1 is completed, the output file from the CAD tool is registered with the Librarian.

SIA can now automatically invoke Stage 1a in the process (by starting the transformation tool with the appropriate input file). The output file, from the transformation FTA, is then provided as the input to Stage 2 in the process (invoking the assembly planning FTA).

The file created by Stage 2 is then input to Stage 3. If Stage 3 is a manual stage, SIA notifies the user that the function of Stage 3 must be performed manually and the process waits till the user provides the input file to Stage 4. SIA now informs the user to perform Stage 4 by checking that the robot is set up properly. After the user indicates that Stage 4 is completed, SIA can invoke the assembly robot (Stage 5 in the process) by providing the output file from Stage 3 (the robot assembly program).

## CONCLUSIONS

The Systems Integration Architecture is based on a different model of integration than the traditional model of a shared, common database. The new model, called the TAR model, views all data processing as one or more transformations of data sets called Aspects. SIA integrates these data sets and the Functional Transformation Agents, which perform these transformations, by keeping track of the input and output Aspects and their structure called Modalities. SIA is currently being implemented in C++ on a variety of machines, including a Silicon Graphics Indigo, a Sun Sparcstation and a DEC ALPHA, all running with a UNIX operating system on a local area net within the Institute. When completed, SIA will, not only support business process re-engineering by facilitating the reconfiguration of the information systems to support the newly engineered business processes, but the concept of virtual companies as well. Specifically, the heterogeneous design of SIA, the use of standards and the definition of the standard module interface structure allows companies to manage the integration of their information systems with those of other companies to form the information system supporting the virtual company.

## ACKNOWLEDGMENTS

The authors would like to acknowledge the financial support of the National Science Foundation under Cooperative Agreement No DDM-9320949, April 15, 1994, the Agile Aerospace Manufacturing Research Center. The assistance of Pulin Chhatbar and Anup Bhatt in implementing the Executive and the Librarian and Neil d'Cunha in implementing the preliminary network kernel is also gratefully recognized.

## AUTHOR'S BIOGRAPHIES

John J. Mills is the Director of The Agile Aerospace Manufacturing Research Center(AAMRC) and The Automation & Robotics Research Institute(ARRI). He also holds positions as a Professor, Mechanical Engineering at The University of Texas at Arlington and is the Fort Worth Chamber Foundation Chair in Automation and Robotics. He holds a Ph. D. in Applied Physics from The University of Durham, England and a B.Sc. Physics from The University of Glasgow, Scotland.

As the Director of the Automation & Robotics Research Institute, Dr. Mills manages a multi-million dollar institute dedicated to helping U.S. industry become globally competitive. In addition to his duties as director, Dr. Mills leads the Information Technologies Research Group, studying computer architectures and methods to support concurrent engineering approaches to the design, development and commissioning of complex manufacturing systems. He is also a Principle Investigator on the project to develop the Dynamically Reconfigurable Assembly System under Texas State funding. As Director of the Agile Aerospace Manufacturing Center, Dr. Mills heads one of three Agile Manufacturing Institutes in the nation. Funded by an ARPA/NSF Agility Initiative, the Center is helping to define agility in aerospace manufacturing in the United States.

Ramez Elmasri is an Associate Professor in the Department of Computer Science and Engineering at The University of Texas at Arlington. He has worked in database research for over 15 years and holds M.S. and Ph.D. degrees in computer science from Stanford University. Prior to joining The University of Texas at Arlington in 1990, he was an Associate Professor at the University of Houston and a Principal Research Scientist at Honeywell. Elmasri is co-author, with S. Navathe, of the textbook "Fundamentals of Database Systems", Benjamin/Cummings, 1989 (Second Edition, 1994).

His work on a Tool Integration Architecture (TIA) for manufacturing systems is at the Automation & Robotics Research Institute (ARRI) at UT-Arlington, and focuses on developing an underlying architecture that supports agile manufacturing by quickly integrating new tools and processes. His work on software maintenance environments focuses on developing software maintenance process models and utilizing advanced database technologies in a maintenance environment.

Kashif Khan has an M.S in Computer Science and Engineering (1995) and MBA (1992) from The University of Texas at Arlington, and a B.S. in Electrical and Communications Engineering from the University of Engineering and Technology, Pakistan. He is currently working as a Research Assistant at the Automation & Robotics Research Institute, Fort Worth, Texas.

Srinivas Miryala has an M.S. (1995) in Mechanical Engineering from The University of Texas at Arlington. He is currently working for Erricson in Dallas, Texas.

Kalpana Subramanian is currently student of graduate program in Computer Science and Engineering at The University of Texas at Arlington. She has a B.S. in Electrical Engineering and is currently working as a Graduate Research Assistant at the Automation & Robotics Research Institute Fort Worth, Texas.

## REFERENCES


[1] Mayer, R.J., "IDEF0 Function Modeling," Pub. by Knowledge Based Systems, College Station, TX, 1990.

[2] Mettala, E. Private Communication, September, 1994,

[3] Mills, J.J., "A Basis Model for Agile Computer Integrated Manufacturing," to be presented at ICCIM '95, Singapore, September, 1995.

[4] Fulton, J.A., PDES/STEP Model Unification: SUMM," Product Data International, May, pp. 6-7, 1992.

[5] Anon, "CIM-OSA Reference Architecture Specification,," ESPRIT Project Nr 688, pub. by CIM-OSA/AMICE, Brussels, Belgium, 1990.

[6] Balzer,, R., Goldman, N., and Wile, D "On the Transformational Implementation Approach to Programming," Proc. 2nd International Conference Software Engineering, pp. 337-343, 1976.

[7] Mostow, J., "Program Transformations for VLSI,' IJCAI-83, 1983.

[8] Ullrich, K., and Seering, W, Conceptual Design: Synthesis of Systems of Components," in Intelligent and Integrated Manufacturing Analysis and Synthesis, PED Vol. 25, ASME. NY, 1987, PP 57-66.

[9] Shah, J.J., and Wilson, P.R. "Analysis of Knowledge Abstraction, Representation and Interactions Requirements for Computer Aided Engineering," Computers in Engineering, Vol. 1, 1988, Pub. by ASME, New York, pp. 17-24.

[10] Talukdar, S.N., and Fenves, S.J., "Towards a Framework for Concurrent Design, in D. Sriram et. al, Computer-Aided Cooperative Product Development, MIT-JSME Workshop, November 1989, Lecture Notes in Computer Science No. 492, Springer-Verlag, 140-151.

[11] "SIFRAME V6.0 System Overview," Siemens Nixdorf, New York, 1992

[12] Betz, M., "Interoperable Objects," Dr Dobbs Journal, pp 18-39, October, 1994.

[13] R. Elmasri and S. Navathe, *Fundamentals of Database Systems*, Second Edition, Benjamin/Cummings, 1994

[14] Davis D.B. "Software that makes your workflow," Datamation, April 15, 1991.

[15] Dyson E. "Workflow," Forbes November 23, 1992.

4

# Message Flow Control

*A.T.M. Aerts*[1], *W. Hofman*[2], *L.J. Somers*[1]
[1]*Dept. Math. and Comp. Sci., Eindhoven Univ. of Technology,*
*P.O. Box 513, 5600 MB Eindhoven, The Netherlands,*
*+31 40 472733, 436685 (fax), {wsinatma,wsinlou}@win.tue.nl*
[2]*Bakkenist Management Consultants,*
*P.O. Box 23103, 1100 DP Amsterdam, The Netherlands*

**Abstract**

High level communication by means of the exchange of messages between different organizations or organizational units is studied. The concepts of business transaction and business transaction protocol are discussed. Message exchanges are controlled by a message handler that enforces a transaction protocol. The design and implementation of a generic message handler is described. The design is independent of a specific application. It offers a flexible implementation of protocols: dedicated subprocesses handle each message type. Changes in a protocol can easily be accommodated by adapting the subprocesses. A prototype has been written in the executable specification language ExSpect. The protocols can be validated by simulating the message exchange for a number of cases. As an application of the prototype, a party in a logistic chain using EDI is described.

**Keywords**

Business transactions, Transaction protocol, Simulation, EDI, Petri nets

## 1 INTRODUCTION

When organizations grow and become decentralized, the need for communication between the units increases. A similar situation arises when different organizations have a stable and intensive business relation. Communication between these organizations, which we will regard as parties or actors in a communication network, will have to satisfy high standards with regard to such aspects as timeliness and correctness.

Electronic interchange of normalized and standardized data (messages) between the (automated) information systems of different parties, EDI for short, has become an important technique for the implementation of information flows between such systems (Leyland, 1993). Information flows are used to exchange reference data, such as product information. They are also used to conduct business transactions between parties, such as the control of the flow of goods or services. In the latter case EDI is used to implement the information flows that control the primary flow of work or goods.

Information is exchanged in the form of messages. To conclude a business transaction, such as the ordering of transport, usually a number of messages have to be exchanged.

These messages are related to one another. Their order and significance with respect to the business transaction is expressed in a business transaction protocol (Hofman, 1994).

The key issue of this effort is to make sure that the parties involved have a consistent view of the information exchanged.

Business transactions have been conducted long before the concept was introduced in database systems for describing a unit of work against the database (Gray and Reuter, 1993). In database systems various applications may concurrently need to access the database. In order to guard the data from becoming inconsistent concurrent execution of transactions has to be controlled (Bernstein et al, 1987). Data modified by a transaction is not released until that transaction has successfully completed. Other transactions that need to access that data have to wait in some schemes of concurrency control or are allowed to go ahead at the risk of having to restart at a later stage in some other schemes.

When a database is distributed over a number of sites, concurrency control has to take this into account. A transaction may need to access data at various sites. Work for the transaction then is performed at various sites and the sites have to agree that work everywhere is done correctly and consistently. Distributed commit protocols are enacted to make sure of this.

Database transactions are controlled by transaction managers, that keep track of the progress of the work at various sites and initiates the various steps in the transaction protocol. Since database systems are meant to achieve a large throughput of work, the transaction manager is an automated part of the system.

Business transactions are becoming in some respects comparable to database transactions. When business relations are stable the larger part of a transaction may be routine and proceed without interruptions by human operators, possibly subject only to a final approval. In addition, because of the automatic support, information exchanges will no longer be suspended until some point in time when the transaction has gained some critical mass, but they will become smaller in volume and proceed at the earliest time possible in order to gain certainty about the feasibility of the transaction as soon as possible. The number of transactions and therefore also the number of messages will increase.

A further complication is that transactions may become nested: in order to proceed with a transaction the support of third parties (subcontractors) may be needed. This situation occurs quite frequently when the two parties involved are part of a logistic chain. One party, that has a freight to be transported may contact a transporter, who will accept the job. This transporter may choose to do part of the work himself and have other transporters do other parts for him. Of course, he can only commit himself after he has obtained the commitment of the other transporters. At this point it may become a problem to keep the exchanges as well as their mutual dependencies manageable.

A solution for this problem can be achieved by automation of the control of the message exchange. A software utility is needed that monitors and controls routine message flows. In this paper the software solution takes the form of a generic transaction protocol handler. The transaction protocol handler maintains the correctness of the transaction as specified in the protocol. A transaction can be regarded as a collection of messages that are mutually related. The exchange of these messages is subject to a number of rules regarding order and content of the messages.

The transaction protocol handler will coordinate the communication (exchange of messages) with the other parties (actors) in the communication network, who may have transaction handlers of their own. It will constitute the interface of a party with the external world. Internally, the transaction protocol handler interfaces with a business process providing the physical activities (transportation in our example).

For a prototype to work, this aspect of the system has to be accounted for. In our prototype we therefore include a component representing a business application process. The application process serves as a model for the relevant parts of the capacity planning of the system. It decides on providing activities to external parties when requested. It generates messages on the basis of incoming messages and local information. In other words, it acts as a terminator for the network. The combination of a transaction protocol handler and an application process, which we will call message handler for brevity, models the communication behavior of a party in a communication network.

In this paper we discuss the design and implementation of a prototype for a message handler. In particular we will focus on the generic part of the prototype: the transaction protocol handler. The business application has been instantiated for the case of a logistical chain. Such a chain can be regarded as a decentralized system of autonomous units. It may involve parties ordering transport, brokers arranging transport, and carriers executing transport. In addition, also warehouses and distribution centers may be involved for temporary storage and distribution of the goods to be transported. The prototype therefore simulates the information exchange between parties in a transport chain. Alternate instantiations, e.g., internal logistics in a hospital, using HL7-messages, follow the same pattern. In this example, patients have to be admitted to the hospital, transferred between wards, laboratory tests have to be ordered and surgery has to be planned and carried out.

The prototype has been implemented in ExSpect(van Hee et al, 1989), a tool for writing executable specifications, which provides extensive support for performing and analyzing simulations of systems. This paper is based on the work described in (Koop, 1993). In the remainder of this paper we will focus on the architecture of the transaction protocol handler.

## 2 GLOBAL SOLUTION

The solution for efficiently dealing with the increase in the number of messages is sought in the form of a general utility for controlling the message flows. This utility has to satisfy a number of requirements following from the fact that it has to be able to recognize the state of a particular transaction and from the fact that one transaction may spawn off a number of secondary transactions. This is discussed in the following section. In the section after that we will show how the requirements lead to a general architecture for the message handler. In the final section some features of the implementation will be discussed. The solution proposed here is quite general and does not depend on the example chosen for the purpose of illustration: the control of EDI-message exchanges in a transportation chain. In order to emphasize this the following discussion will refer to *actors* instead of *parties.*

## 2.1 Requirements

The usefulness of a generic transaction protocol handler derives from the fact that it is able to keep track of the progress that has been made with a given business transaction, and of the relations between various business transactions. In order to understand the architecture it is necessary to have some appreciation of the complications arising in a business transaction and the difficulties a transaction protocol has to deal with. It is not our aim to discuss the design of protocols here.

### *Business Transactions*

A business transaction, in the context of this paper, is regarded as the information exchange between two actors, needed to control a single physical activity, such as the transportation of a given number of goods from one location to another. The information is exchanged between two actors (parties): a *superior* who initiates the transaction by requesting the activity and a *subordinate*, who is asked to carry out the activity.

A business transaction has to satisfy a number of conditions, which resemble those for database transactions. An important difference here is that transactions control physical activities:

- An activity has to be carried out either completely or not at all. Partial completion of an activity is not allowed.

- The information about a given activity as stored by the superior has to be identical to that stored by the subordinate.

- To the superior it must appear as if the activity of a subordinate is executed independently of other activities executed by the same subordinate. This implies that the bound resources of these transactions, such as the means of transportation and the goods to be transported, have to be different.

- Once an activity has been completed no more messages may be exchanged concerning that particular activity. The result of an activity may only be changed by starting a new one, e.g., to compensate the effect of the activity.

These conditions appear to be the usual properties required for database transactions. With business transactions, however, some differences occur. First of all, parties are autonomous. Business transaction protocols there for are agreements that may be fixed between two business partners but may vary with different partners. Communication therefore is always between two parties. A transaction may involve more than one subordinate, but subordinates don't communicate with each other within the context of the transactions.

Local autonomy, that is the autonomy of each party implies, that in general no atomicity can be guaranteed (Mullen et al, 1991). There is no global transaction manager and only bilateral agreements can be used.

The information exchange is split up into an exchange of (standardized) messages. In order to preserve the properties mentioned above, a transaction is characterized by a special attribute: its state. In each state only certain messages can be meaningfully sent and received. What these states are and which messages may be exchanged is specified in a protocol and represented in a state transition diagram, such as shown in Fig. 1. The labels used in this figure will be explained below. Fig. 1 is just one of many possibilities.

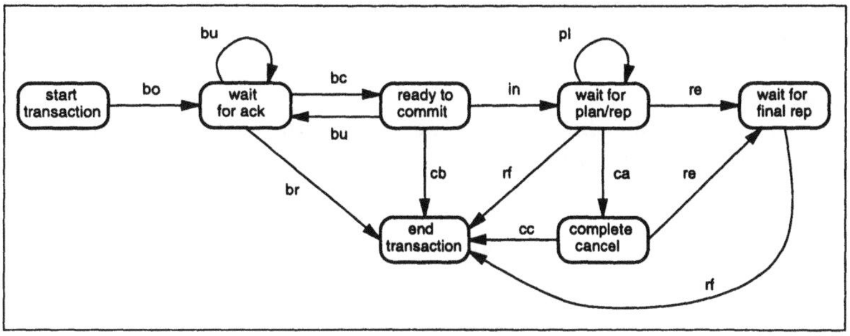


Figure 1: State transition diagram for a transaction.

The exchange of a message may change the state of the transaction as decisions with regard to certain aspects of the requested activity are communicated. In Fig. 1 an example of the various states of a transaction are given. Other possibilities are discussed in (Hofman, 1994). The arrows indicate the transition of one state to another (possibly the same) state, and are labeled by the type of message exchanged in making the transition. We will illustrate the diagram for the case of external logistics, but it is applicable to other situations (e.g., distribution) as well. Similarly, alternate state transition diagrams, involving more or different transitions and messages may be devised to reflect more properly the protocol needed.

The state transition diagram summarizes the protocol by specifying in which state which type of messages may be sent or received. The information exchange pass through three phases. In the obligatory **prepare** phase of the transaction the resources needed for a certain activity are reserved. The superior sends (from the initial state) a *booking* (bo-message). When the subordinate wants to carry out the activity and has sufficient resources to do so, he replies with a *booking confirmation* (bc-message). The resources needed will be reserved and become 'bound' resources. This compares to the locking mechanism used to implement database transactions. In the other case a *booking reject* is sent (br-message). By means of a *booking update* (bu-message) the superior may communicate modifications or additional information. The activity may not be changed, however. (When a different activity is required, the current transaction has to be canceled and a new one has to be started.) The superior may call off a transaction in this phase by sending a *cancel booking* (cb-message).

The **commit** phase begins as soon as the superior sends an *instruction* (in-message). The subordinate keeps the superior informed of the schedule of the required activity by sending a *planning* (pl-message). Information about the actual progress of the activity is transmitted by means of a *report* (re-message). When the activity is completed a *final report* (rf-message) is sent by the subordinate and the transaction ends.

When the superior decides in the commit phase to call off the activity, he sends a *cancel* (ca-message). The transaction now enters the **abort** phase. When the subordinate has already started the activity, he may reject the cancellation by sending a *report* (re-message). If not, he sends a *cancel confirmation* (cc-message) and the transaction ends. Note that the protocol has to exclude concurrency between various subordinates, in order to avoid conflicts between some subordinates having started the (physical) activity and others still waiting for the confirmation.

### *Relationships between transactions*

The role of superior or subordinate is only fixed within the context of a single transaction. The dual role of an actor with respect to transactions in general is illustrated in Fig. 2.

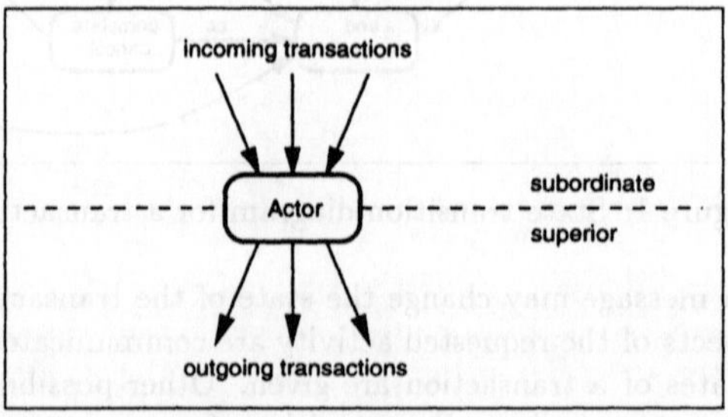


Figure 2: Incoming and outgoing transactions.

When we are dealing with a chain of activities an actor may act both as a superior and as a subordinate (for different transactions). For instance, an actor, say $\text{Carrier}_1$, who is asked by another actor - $\text{Shipper}_1$, acting as a superior - to provide transportation services, acts as a subordinate. In case $\text{Carrier}_1$ doesn't have the capacity needed, he may initiate an outgoing transaction to ask a third actor, say $\text{Carrier}_2$, to provide the missing capacity (as a subcontractor) and then acts as a superior to $\text{Carrier}_2$. Note that the incoming transaction is dependent of the result of the secondary, outgoing transaction: $\text{Carrier}_1$ can't confirm the booking of $\text{Shipper}_1$ before the missing capacity has been reserved elsewhere. Such an outgoing transaction is called an *inserted* transaction (see Fig. 3). It satisfies the following two conditions:

- A message of the outgoing transaction can only be sent after a message of the same type of the incoming transaction has been received.
- A message of the incoming transaction can only be sent after a message of the same type of the outgoing transaction has been received.

For instance, an *instruction* message of an inserted transaction can only be sent after an *instruction* message of the corresponding incoming transaction has been received. Every phase has to be initiated by $\text{Shipper}_1$, the superior of the initial transaction.

In case an incoming transaction causes an outgoing transaction but doesn't depend on the result of it, the outgoing transaction is called a *decoupled* transaction (see Fig. 4). E.g., a supplier may be able to fill an order for a certain quantity of goods (a booking message), but may be obliged to put out an order to a producer for the same type of goods, because the stock level has fallen below some limit. Clearly, the completion of the first transaction doesn't have to wait for the progress of the second one. The store of the supplier acts as a decoupling point.

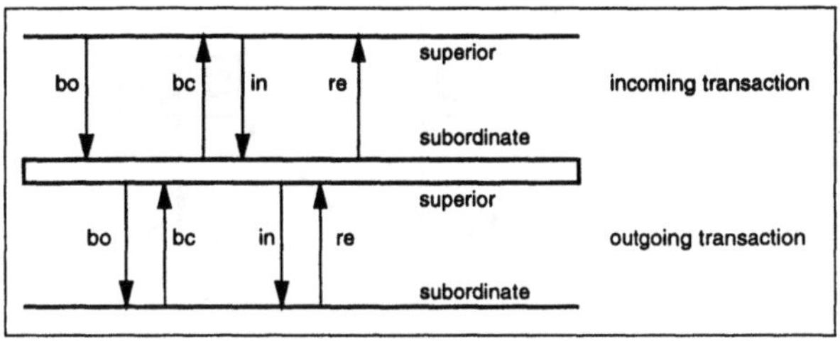


Figure 3: Inserted Transaction.

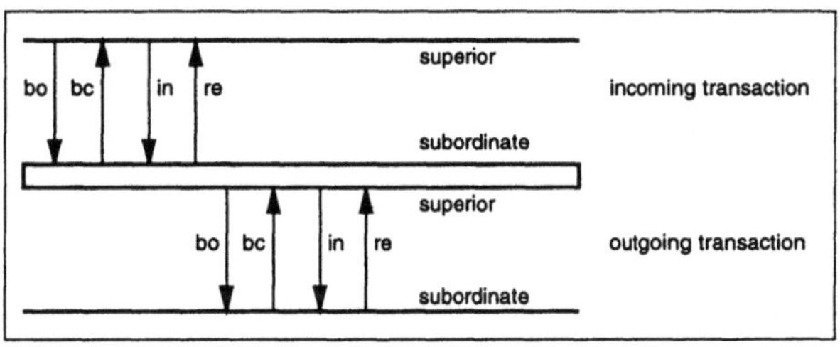


Figure 4: Decoupled Transaction.

## 2.2 Architecture

The requirements of the preceding section may be summarized as follows:

- We have to distinguish between incoming and outgoing messages. Depending on the role of an actor and the state of the transaction, a message of a certain type may be sent or received.
- We have to distinguish between incoming and outgoing transactions. An actor may act as a superior or as a subordinate. In the former case a transaction is called outgoing, in the latter incoming.
- We have to keep track of the relationship between transactions. An outgoing transaction may be inserted into an incoming transaction or it may decoupled from it. In the former case the incoming and outgoing transaction have to be synchronized.

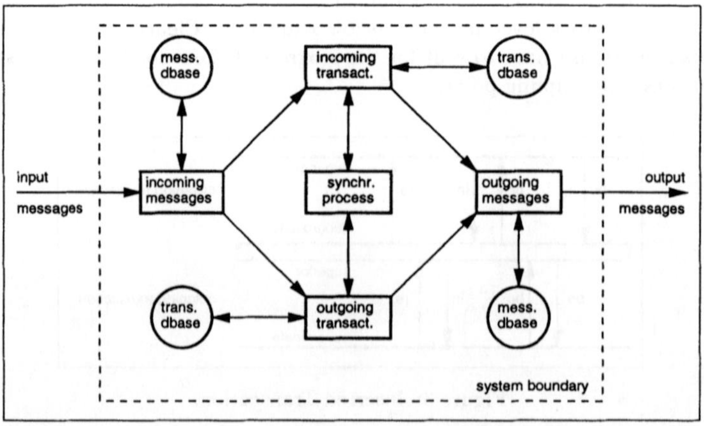


Figure 5: System architecture.

The requirements above lead to the architecture, shown in Fig. 5 (subsystems, i.e. processes, represented by squares, stores by circles, flows by arrows).

# 3 EXSPECT

ExSpect (Executable Specification tool) is a formalism to describe distributed systems (van Hee et al, 1989). It is based on timed hierarchical colored Petri Nets. (For colored Petri Nets, see e.g. (Jensen, 1992).)

Basically, the description of a system in the ExSpect formalism consists of two kinds of objects: channels (places) and processors (transitions). A channel is passive, it serves as a place holder of so called tokens: at any moment in time it contains a number of these tokens. A channel can serve as input or output channel for a processor, see for example Fig. 6.

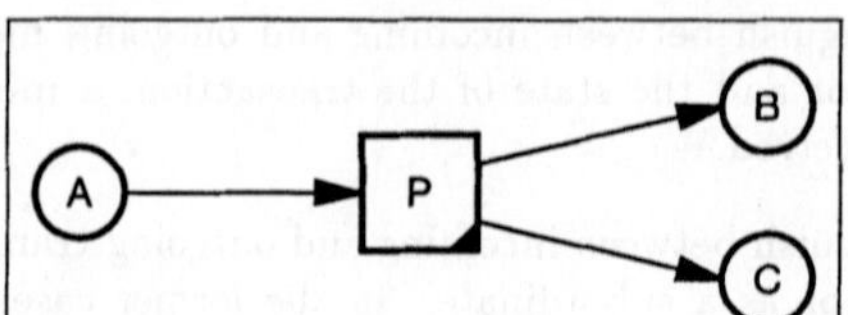


Figure 6: A processor (P) with input channel A and output channels B and C.

A processor is active: if all input channels of a processor contain at least one token, the processor may fire. If a processor fires, it removes (consumes) a token from each of its input channels and produces tokens for its output channels.

Each channel has a type that specifies which values (colors) are allowed for the tokens in that channel. The values of the tokens that are produced when a processor fires depend upon the values of the tokens that are consumed. Thus, a processor can be seen as a function from the types of its input channels to the types of its output channels.

A processor may have a precondition: only tokens with values that obey this precondition will be consumed.

Tokens also carry a time stamp. A token may not be consumed before the (simulated) time is greater than or equal to its time stamp. In the processor a delay is specified for each produced token. The time stamp is equal to the time of firing plus the delay.

```
proc P [in A: num, out B: num×str, C: str] :=
   if A > 0 then
      B ← ≪A+1,'ok'≫ delay 3.5
   else
      C ← 'invalid'
   fi
```

Figure 7: A possible definition of processor P.

The example in Fig. 7 represents a processor that consumes one numerical token from channel A at a time. If this token is positive then a token is produced for channel B. Its value is a pair consisting of the incremented value of the consumed token and the string 'ok'. The time stamp of this token will be equal to the time of firing plus 3.5. If the consumed token is not positive, a token is produced for channel C without delay.

The colors of the tokens may represent very complex data. The ExSpect type system has a few basic types and type constructors to build more complicated types. Among the basic types are the booleans (bool), rational numbers (num), floating point numbers (real) and strings (str). The type constructors allow for the construction of Cartesian products, sets, finite mappings (sets of pairs with unique first component) and tuples.

Models of large systems will become very soon too complex to understand if they consist of only channels and processors. The hierarchy concept solves this problem. Channels and processors may be grouped into subsystems ('processes'), such subsystems may be used in other subsystems and so on.

ExSpect has been implemented in a set of cooperating tools to design, simulate and analyze a specification. A graphical editor may be used to create the flow diagrams, a type checker checks the consistency and correctness of the specification and the simulator offers the possibility for interactive or batch simulation. During an interactive simulation the user may interact with the running simulation (inspecting places, adding tokens, reading from and writing to files or other applications) without stopping the simulation. Animation of token production and consumption is optional. Furthermore a static analysis tool to calculate some structural properties and timing properties is available.

The results of a simulation may be analyzed on-line or off-line by means of other software, like a spread sheet program. Alternatively, the simulation results may be used for conformance testing of a final application.

# 4 IMPLEMENTATION

When we analyze the architecture, proposed in Fig. 5, we can identify a number of system components. The resulting (ExSpect) process model is given in Fig. 8. In the diagram only the processors and the channels having to do with the processing of the messages have been shown. The database aspect has been suppressed, as well as a number of channels that can be attached for error handling and simulation purposes.

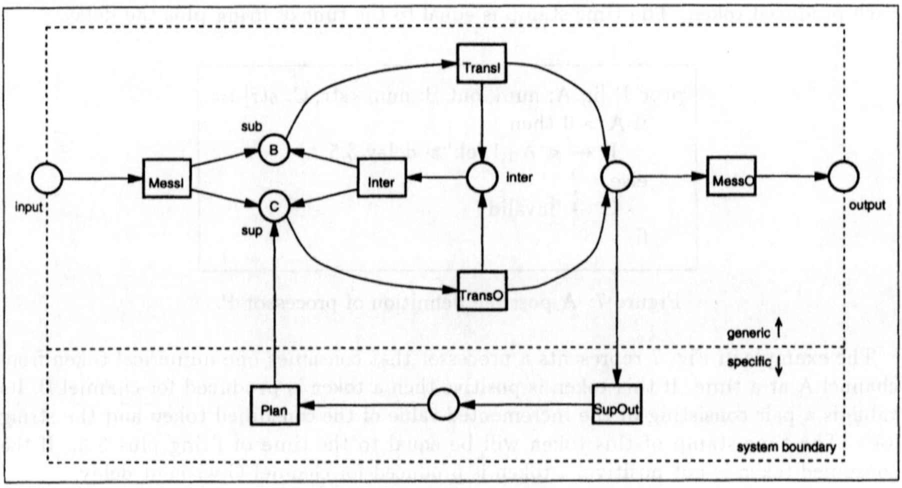


Figure 8: Process Model.

To arrive at the model of Fig. 8 starting from the architecture in Fig. 5 some observations need to be made. The heart of the transaction handler is formed by the processes 'TransI' and 'TransO'. 'TransI' and 'TransO' keep the state of incoming and outgoing transactions, respectively, up to date. Process 'Inter' keeps track of the relationships between incoming and outgoing transactions.

The generic transaction handler is formed by processes 'MessI/O', 'Inter' and 'TransI/O'. The application dependent part is limited to 'SupOut' and 'Plan'. So, if we want to use the message handler for a field other than external logistics, we only have to adapt these two processes.

When we treat requests for activities that are offered by the actor itself (i.e., for which it has sufficient resources in a given period) in the same manner as requests for which the cooperation of other parties is needed (i.e., the actor does not have sufficient resources itself or has none at all), the functionality of 'TransI' and 'TransO' becomes identical. This has as a consequence that for every bo-message entering the system from the outside an inserted outgoing transaction will be started.

Consider, e.g., what will happen when a bo-message is received. 'TransI' notes the start of a new transaction and passes the request on to 'Inter'. 'Inter' notes that an inserted transaction will be needed and generates the required bo-message for 'TransO'.

'TransO' notes then the start of an outgoing transaction. When the booking is destined for an external actor, it passes 'SupOut' and is processed by 'MessO' into an external message. When the bo-message is destined for internal processing, 'SupOut' filters it out and passes it to 'Plan', where a decision is taken: reject or confirm on the basis of the available capacity. A br- or bc-message is generated, respectively, and sent to 'TransO' which notes the change in state of the transaction. The message then is propagated further via 'Inter' and 'TransI' to 'MessO' from where it is sent to the superior.

We will now discuss each of the processes in more detail for the case of external logistics.

## *MessI*

The messages enter the system via a single (complex) process. It is implemented as a single processor as can be seen in Fig. 9. In this figure channel 'err' and store 'message' are shown that had been suppressed in the main diagram of Fig. 8. Channel 'out1' is connected to 'sub' and 'out2' to 'sup'.

As can be seen from the specification in Fig. 10, the processor that handles the incoming messages (labeled 'messInfilter') checks to see if the message hasn't been previously received (not(MessPresent(kk,Message@MESS))), determines whether it is part of an incoming (mm ∈ {'bo',...}) or outgoing transaction (mm ∈ {'br',...}), and whether it has its logical place (i.e., the correct sequence number) for the transaction concerned (MessSucc(kk,Message@MESS)). If so, the message is stored (Message ← ...) and converted to an internal representation, which is passed on (out1,2 ← ...). If not, an error message is generated. The precondition (pre r = me) guarantees that only messages for this node are selected.

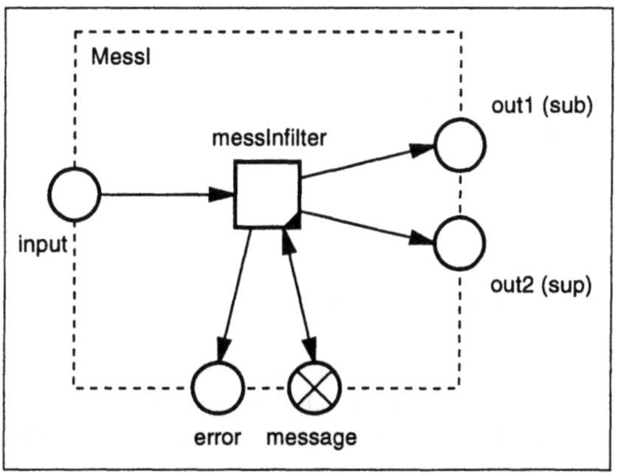


Figure 9: The handler of incoming messages (MessI).

## *TransI/TransO*

Incoming messages of incoming transactions, i.e., messages of type 'bo', 'bu', 'cb', 'in' or 'ca' (see Fig. 1), which come from a superior and are called superior messages, are passed on to the process 'TransI'. Those of type 'br', 'bc', 'cc', 'pl', 're' or 'rf', which come from a

```
proc messInfilter
 [  in      input: Mess,
    out     out1: Token,
            out2: Token,
            error: Error,
    store   Message: MESSAGE,
    val     me: Id |
    pre     r = me
 ]
:=
   if not(MessPresent(kk,Message@MESS)) and MessSucc(kk,Message@MESS) then
      if mm ∈ {'bo','bu','cb','in','ca'} then
         Message ← upd(Message, [MESS:InsMessIN(kk,d,Message@MESS)]),
         out1 ← upd([k:p],d)
      elif mm ∈ {'br','bc','pl','re','rf','cc'} then
         Message ← upd(Message, [MESS:InsMessIN(kk,d,Message@MESS)]),
         out2 ← upd([k:b],d)
      else
         error ← 'MessIn error'
      fi
   else
      error ← 'MessIn error'
   fi
where
     kk  := input@k: MessKey;
     mm  := input@m: MessType;
     r   := kk@receiver: Id;
     s   := kk@sender: Id;
     t   := kk@trans: Id;
     d   := [m:input@m, a:input@a, l:input@l]: MessData;
     b   := [sub:s, sup:r, trans:t]: TransKey;
     p   := [sub:r, sup:s, trans:t]: TransKey
end
```

Figure 10: The definition of processor 'messInfilter'. Mess is a tuple type containing a.o. a field of type Messkey with label k and a field of type MessType with label m: type Mess := [k:MessKey, m:MessType, ...].

subordinate and are called subordinate messages, belong to an outgoing transaction and are passed on to the process 'TransO'.

The processes 'TransI' and 'TransO' are instances of a common process, 'Transaction'. The difference between these two instances lies in the fact that the role of the two output channels has been interchanged. Both processes fulfill the task of keeping the transaction data up to date. In addition the correctness of the data about the activities which are being required, planned or performed, is checked and in case of violations an error message is generated.

When the process 'TransI' is activated, the system is acting as a subordinate. The process will generate superior messages for the synchronization process 'Inter', and subordinate messages for the process 'MessO'.

When the process 'TransO' is activated, the system will act as a superior. The process will generate superior messages for the process 'SupOut' and subordinate messages for the process 'Inter'.

The process 'Transition' consists of a number of elementary subprocesses, one for each type of message. Each subprocess picks out only those messages from the input channel that belong to its message type. The subprocess then checks to see whether the message can be received in the current state of the transaction. It also checks whether the data are consistent with previously received messages.

E.g., consider the subprocess 'TransBu', which handles booking updates and processes exclusively messages of type 'bu'. TransBu checks to see whether the current state of the transaction is "wait for ack" or "ready to commit", which, according to Fig. 1 are the only states in which a booking update message may be received. Then it checks to see whether the data have acceptable values (i.e., belong to the right type) and whether the required activity is the same as the one in the original booking for the same transaction. If all checks out to be correct, the booking is updated (e.g., a different date or time is set) and the state of the transaction is changed to 'wait for ack'. The message is sent to the process 'Inter'.

### *Inter*

The process 'Inter' takes care of the synchronization of the incoming and the outgoing transactions. It is at the core of the message handler. For this purpose it records status information about the relationships between transactions. 'Inter' initiates inserted transactions and generates the proper messages for 'TransI' and 'TransO' in response to messages (information) it receives from 'TransO' and 'TransI' respectively.

The process has one input channel, which receives messages of both incoming (via TransI) and outgoing (via TransO) transactions. It can send messages to either the superior or the subordinate system.

Again the process is split up into a number of subprocesses, one for each message type. In this case the subprocess handling the booking messages has a special structure: it has an extra input channel. There it can receive not only the bo-messages of a new incoming transaction but also the confirmation and rejection of an outgoing booking. This may cause the start of a new outgoing transaction, in the former case because certain (supporting) activities should only be requested once the main activity is confirmed. In the latter case, because a rejection may necessitate the request of an activity from an alternate supplier.

E.g., a booking update (bu) message from TransI will nullify the number of acknowledged outgoing transactions. For every outgoing transaction a new bu-message is composed and passed to the superior output channel.

### *SupOut*

An actor in the role of a subordinate has the choice between performing a requested activity itself and asking a third actor to carry out the activity, when its own capacity appears to be insufficient. When we introduce a special subordinate actor, representing the internal capacity, the process Inter can be specified at a completely general level, without the need to make a distinction between internal and external processing. It just starts up transactions to potential suppliers of activities, including itself. The messages requesting activities from external suppliers are passed to 'MessO'. The other messages requesting internal activities do not need to leave the system but are, instead, filtered out by 'SupOut' and sent to the 'Plan' process.

### *MessO*

This process translates internal messages to external ones. It checks to see if the superior identification of messages of type 'bo', 'bu', 'cb', 'in' and 'ca' and the subordinate identification of messages of the type 'br', 'bc', 'cc', 'pl', 're' and 'rf' is the identification of the actor itself. If so, the message is translated, stored in the message database and sent out. If not, an error is produced.

### *Plan(ning)*

This process models the interface between the transaction handler and the application. It simulates the capacity planning aspects of the problem. The process has three major subprocesses: 'Reserve', 'Release' and 'Monitor'.

When a booking message is received, it is passed to 'Reserve'. There the available capacity is checked and a decision is taken. In case of sufficient capacity, i.e., sufficient resources that haven't been bound yet in the period at hand, the requested resources are bound for the period and a confirmation (bc-message) is sent to the superior component. If not, a br-message is generated.

Messages of type 'bu', 'cb' and 'ca' are passed to 'Release' and cause bound resources to be released. The 'bu' message then is passed on to 'Reserve' to see if the new requirements can be met. In response to a 'ca' message a confirmation is generated (cc-message). In case of a 'cb' message no action is needed (in this simulation).

The 'Monitor' checks for activities that should start. When the transaction is still in the preparatory phase, a 'br'-message is sent. In the commit-stage a 're'-message is sent. Finally when an activity is about to end an 'rf'-message is generated, in case the transaction is in the commit-phase.

The response to an 'in'-message is to generate a forecast (pl-message) of the expected activities.

# 5 CONCLUSIONS

In this paper an ExSpect prototype of an actor in a logistic chain has been described. The prototype contains generic software for supporting Electronic Data Interchange. The prototype implements a utility for processing data and controlling various primary business processes.

The utility has been illustrated for the case of external logistics but we could have equally well taken our case from the storage and distribution areas. The instantiation of the solution to another application area will not have any consequences for the systems architecture. The architecture is based on the processing of data by means of transactions, and is independent of the content of the messages used.

The system offers a flexible implementation of protocols. We have demonstrated that not only simple protocols, but also the weaving of protocols can be handled in a flexible way. This flexibility stems from the architecture of the system: dedicated subprocesses for each message type and clear modules for handling the control of single transactions and the interplay between transactions respectively.

The use of an executable specification language for designing the system offers the advantage of being able to simulate the message exchange between a number of parties, each of which is an instantiation of the message handler system with its own set of resources and activities offered. By simulating the message exchange for a number of cases, the protocols can be validated. It then becomes possible to design tailor made protocols which are optimally suited for the control of message exchanges between specific parties. Having a flexible system then pays off: the impact of adding a message or transition is quite local and its consequences are easy to grasp and validate.

The prototype supports the modeling and analysis of various designs for a decentralized organization. Various assignments of tasks to locations (system configurations) can be proposed and subsequently analyzed in terms of the complexity of the communication needed to control the flow of work or goods between these locations. This should yield useful insight in the viability of the various designs.

# 6 REFERENCES

Bernstein, P.A., Hadzilacos, V., Goodman, N. (1987) *Concurrency Control and Recovery in Database Systems.* Addison-Wesley Publishing Co.

Gray, J. and Reuter, A. (1993) *Transaction Processing: Concepts and Techniques.* Morgan Kaufmann Publishers Inc.

van Hee, K.M., Somers L.J., Voorhoeve, M. (1989) Executable specifications for distributed information systems, in *Information system concepts: an in-depth analysis,* (eds. E.D. Falkenberg, P. Lindgreen), North-Holland.

Hofman, W.J. (1994) *A conceptual model of a Business Transaction Management System.* Tutein Nolthenius, Amsterdam.

Jensen, K. (1992) *Coloured Petri nets. Basic concepts, analysis methods and practical use.* Vol. 1: Basic concepts. EATCS monographs on Theoretical Comp. Sci., Springer-Verlag.

Koop, C. (1993) *ExSpect prototype of a party in External Logistics.* Masters thesis, Eindhoven University of Technology. (In Dutch.)

Leyland, V. (1993) *Electronic Data Interchange.* Prentice Hall International.

Mullen, J.G., Elmagarmid, A.K., Kim, W., Sharif-Askary, J. (1991) On the impossibility of Atomic Commitment in Multidatabase Systems, in *Proc. First Int'l Workshop on Interoperability in Multidatabase Systems*, pp. 625-634.

## 7 BIOGRAPHY

Ad Aerts received his Ph.D. from the University of Nijmegen in 1979. He has held several postdoc positions in the U.S. and Europe prior to his current position as lecturer at the Eindhoven University of Technology. He has published a large amount of papers on various subjects at conferences and scientific journals. His research interests currently include database models, integration of database systems and transaction management.

Wout Hofman is senior consultant in the area of telematics with Bakkenist Management Consultants. He holds a masters degree in electrical engineering and information processing. The subject of his Ph.D. thesis (1994, Eindhoven University of Technology) is the conceptual model of a Business Transaction Management System based on EDI communication. He has published a number of papers on the subject of EDI and is the author of the Dutch EDI handbook. He is also a member of the advisory board of the ministry of transport and travel with respect to telematics.

Lou Somers received his Ph.D. in theoretical physics from the University of Nijmegen in 1984. For several years he worked as a systems engineer at Philips Data Systems, a.o. on the design and development of a system for distributed databases and a user interface management system. Currently he is associate professor in the area of software engineering at the Eindhoven University of technology. He has designed the software package ExSpect. Furthermore, he has been involved in several national Dutch projects, the ESPRIT project PROOFS, and the TEDIS project EDISCAN.

5

# A Light Weight Name Service and its use within a collaborative editor *

*J.-C. Lugeon* *F. Pacull*
*Département d'Informatique.*
*Ecole Polytechnique Fédérale de Lausanne*
*CH-1015 Lausanne (Switzerland)*
*E-mail: {lugeon,pacull}@lse.epfl.ch*

**Abstract**

This paper presents the LWNS, a light weight name service specifically designed for groupware applications, and an example of its use. The chosen application, called DUPLEX, is a collaborative editing environment for users connected through the Internet. It proposes a model based on splitting the document into independent parts, maintained individually and replicated within a distributed kernel. Naming is an important aspect of such application since objects (document parts) are replicated and distributed over the large heterogeneous network. However, this set is small (typically a few dozen elements) and composed of objects whose names are contextual to the document. The replicas are maintained in heterogeneous file systems with no global naming scheme consistent with the name space of the collaboration. Therefore it requires a dedicated name service specifically designed to solve this problem in large scale distributed applications.

**Keywords**

Naming, large scale distributed systems, CSCW

## 1 INTRODUCTION

Distributed applications such as a collaborative editing environment use the network not only to exchange information, but also to share objects containing data. Sharing objects, in general implies that the users involved should have some knowledge about the objects: its name, generally given in a user friendly manner, but also the method used to access it. This second

*Research supported by the FNS and OFES under contract number 21-32210.91, as part of European ESPRIT Basic Research Project Number 6360 (BROADCAST).

component is generally related to a more computer-oriented pattern. The complexity of this pattern in linked to the complexity of the considered object and the underlying distributed system.

For instance, consider that objects are files. When all users work in the same integrated file system domain (e.g. NFS (Sandberg et al., 1985) or AFS (Howard et al., 1988)), the object reference is the path name, i.e. any composite path, the user is authorized to follow leading from the root of the shared file name space to the file. When the users and the resources reside in heterogeneous systems, access to the objects requires a more complicated protocol (e.g. file transfer service as FTP (Postel and Reynolds, 1985)). In addition to the the file name relative to this server, the server's address and the protocol (here FTP) are required.

When the object is replicated and spread over a large heterogeneous network, the object's pattern becomes more and more complex. It could include the list of the replicas, the protocol used for ensuring consistency or the address of a replicated service. Thus, the applications has to rely on a dedicated service that ensures the translation between the object name and the means to access it. This service has to ensure the following requirements:

- To name objects of any type, e.g. files and services.
- To provide name transparency, i.e. a name must not contain any information specific to the underlying system, and a name must refer to an object independently of the site where the user issue the requests.
- To be flexible, i.e. the name service should adapt itself to the requirements of the application and not the contrary.

A Light Weight Name Service (noted LWNS) has been developed in our laboratory to fulfill these requirements for applications considering a large scale distributed system like the Internet. This paper describes an experience of using the LWNS in a collaborative editing environment called DUPLEX (Pacull et al., 1994; Pacull, 1995) also developed in our laboratory.

The paper is structured as follows: Section 2 presents briefly the motivation that has conducted to the conception of the LWNS. The LWNS model is described in Section 3. Section 4 gives an overview of the DUPLEX collaborative editing environment and emphasizes the problems related to naming. Section 5 describes how the LWNS has been used to this end. Section 6 presents why existing name services cannot be used in the particular frame of collaborative application over a large scale distributed system. Finally, Section 7 concludes the paper.

## 2 MOTIVATION

The distributed system we consider is composed of a set of sites in a wide area network. We consider only the sites involved within a collaboration. Sites for different collaborations can be disjoint or overlap, but are managed as independent distributed systems so large scale does not necessarily imply a large number of sites. Large scale distributed system for the particular frame considered here means large distances between sites, since they might be scattered over continents and connected through the Internet (Comer, 1988).

For instance, if we consider collaborative editing, a site could be the workstation of an author, a data repository for parts of the document, or both. The set of sites evolves dynamically as users join or leave the collaboration, and parts of a document are added or removed.

Considering such a distributed system, the constraints of the large scale and the specificity of the collaborative application,should be taken into account.

The first point implies that failures (links or sites) have to be considered. In particular, two sites might be unable to communicate, though both can communicate with a common destination.

The second point has an influence on the naming aspect since the information useful to the collaboration is distributed over the large underlying heterogeneous system. The closure of the name spaces of all these heterogeneous systems is very wide, and considering naming within this context is costly even if the set of objects (information about the collaboration) is relatively small. Moreover, the names of the objects are contextual to the collaboration and do not correspond to the naming scheme of the underlying heterogeneous systems.

Our approach is to provide a dedicated name service (1) that is not dependent on the architecture of the underlying system, and (2) that ensures the availability of the service despite failures or network partitions.

# 3 THE LIGHT WEIGHT NAME SERVICE

This Section presents a context-relative name service, called LWNS for Light Weight Name Service, specifically designed for large scale distributed applications.

## 3.1 LWNS basic model

The LWNS manages the mapping of *contextual names*, meaningful for the users in the frame of a collaborative application, to information. By "information", we mean all that the users want to be associated with the contextual name.

The LWNS is a context-relative name service distributed over several name servers, where each name server is responsible for an independent part of the global name space. Therefore, the unavailability of one of the name servers (failure or network partition) does not have any harmful effects on the other name servers, i.e. users will only notice the failure if they need to access contextual names managed by the unavailable name server. Moreover, instead of other context-relative name services such as in ANSA (Linden, 1993), the naming is global to the collaboration and not context-relative to each name server.

The LWNS furnishes only basic operations (thus the term *light weight*) such as: to register a name and some information, unregister this information and look up a name to retrieve the associated information. Despite of this very simple interface and functionality, we claim that it furnishes the minimal required for many collaborative applications. The advantage of this simplicity is that the name service can be realized at a low cost. More complex features, if they are required, can be added on top of it (e.g. at the application level).

Each name server manages two contexts, a *shared* context and a *private* context. The shared context is exported to the collaboration, whereas the private context is only accessible by requesting directly the name server and permits to cache some information (Sollins and Clark, 1988). As will be described in the following, the cached information is used (1) for accelerating name resolution, and (2) in case of failures of parts of the name service.

### *Object references*

In general terms, accessing an object requires the following knowledge:

- the address of a service providing the access to the object, e.g. for remote access to a file, a service of the resident file system which can be invoked through the network.
- an access protocol, e.g. NFS, FTP, HTTP, ...
- the object's local name, i.e. the name of the object for the considered couple (address of service, protocol).

This information defines what we call the *object reference*. An *object reference* is associated to the *contextual name* manipulated by the users and the LWNS is in charge of the mapping between the *contextual name* and the *object reference*.

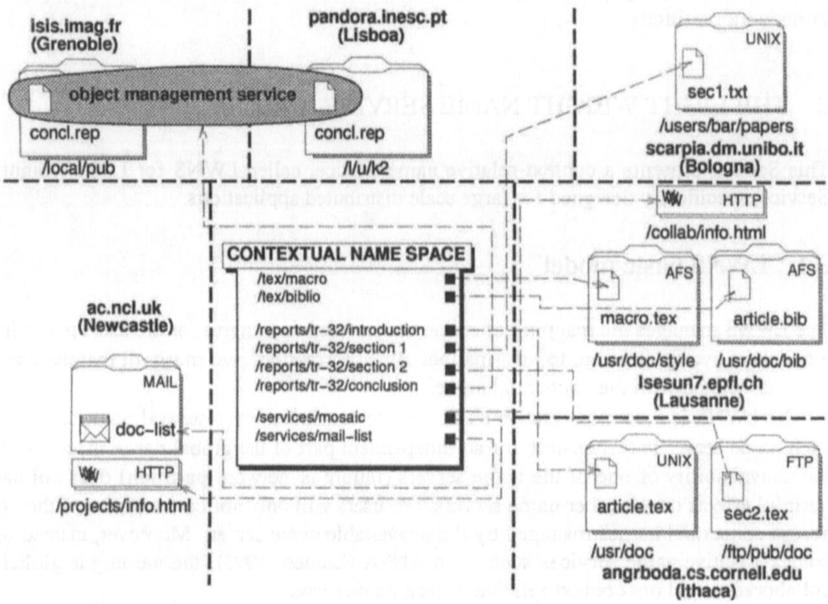


**Figure 1** Contextual name space with the object references mapping.

Figure 1 shows the mapping between a set of contextual names defined within the frame of a collaboration and the corresponding *object references*. An *object reference* is represented by a black square pointing to the object location.

An object can be a traditional file, maintained by a file system and accessible via the `FTP` protocol (e.g. the contextual name `/reports/tr-32/section2` corresponds to the file `/ftp/pub/doc/sec2.tex` on site `angrboda.cs.cornell.edu`). Other services of higher or lower complexity can also be considered. The service can be a mailing list maintained by one site, e.g. `ac.ncl.uk`, or two identical services, e.g. `HTTP` which can be offered either by `ac.ncl.uk` or `lsesun7.epfl.ch`. In this last case, the service is replicated but each server is independent. Finally, it is possible to consider a service maintaining a replicated object, `/reports/tr-32/conclusion`, which is maintained by a replicated service on two sites (`pandora.inesc.pt` and `isis.imag.fr`). The service in this case can be represented by the list of the involved sites or by a group name if a more complex paradigm is used for managing the replication. Note that the contextual name is completely independent from the way that the object is actually implemented.

## 3.2 Architecture of the LWNS

The name service is *distributed* over several independent name servers. We note $LWNS_{s_i}$ the server located on site $s_i$. Each $LWNS_{s_i}$ is independent of the others and only manages a subset of the references of the objects available in the system (i.e. a context). Depending on the properties that we require for the name service (e.g. availability, locality, etc.), the context managed by a $LWNS_{s_i}$ can be one of the following:

1. the contextual names corresponding to the objects located on $s_i$. This allows to enforce **availability** by ensuring that if a site $s_i$ is up then the object can actually be accessed, since the $LWNS_{s_i}$ and the service managing the object on site $s_i$ are reachable. If the two services were on different sites, the failure of one of the two sites would be sufficient to make the object inaccessible.
2. the contextual names corresponding to the objects which have been created by the site $s_i$. This does not mean that they are located on $s_i$ but only that the site $s_i$ had asked for the creation. This solution enforces **locality** for the object creation. This point will be discussed in Section 5 as it is the option used by DUPLEX.
3. any subset of the contextual name space providing that the whole contextual name space is distributed over the different $LWNS_{s_j}$.

This constitutes a flexibility, which is particularly interesting as it allows to adapt the LWNS to the requirements of the application.

Since each $LWNS_{s_i}$ is responsible for the management of a part of the global context, they should be grouped together in order to form a federation. This is realized thanks to a master server (noted $LWNS_m$) that has two roles: (1) it is used for federating the different $LWNS_{s_i}$ involved within a collaboration and can therefore be compared with a *Trader* (Deschrevel, 1993), and (2) it is used for accelerating the name resolution by maintaining a prefix table as in Sprite (Welch and Ousterhout, 1986) (name resolution is discussed in the next Section).

The location of the $LWNS_m$ is decided during the initial phase of the collaboration by the community that wants to collaborate; it is statically known. Upon its creation, a $LWNS_{s_i}$ registers itself at the level of the $LWNS_m$, and obtains the list of the previously registered $LWNS_{s_j}$ as a result. Moreover, the $LWNS_m$ forwards a notification of the existence of the new $LWNS_{s_i}$ to all the registered $LWNS_{s_j}$*.

As a result, each $LWNS_{s_i}$ knows all the other $LWNS_{s_j}$ registered; this information is used, as described in the next Section, for the name resolution.

*This communication as every communication within LWNS is not costly, because it uses a reliable datagram protocol ensuring good performance and reliability.

## 3.3 Name resolution

We will now describe the means by which the name resolution is performed. Consider, that the policy is to manage the contextual names on the same site as the objects. This is illustrated in Figure 2, where the contextual name space of Figure 1 is split into six parts, corresponding to the six sites storing objects. For example, the LWNS$_{lsesun7.epfl.ch}$ (noted LWNS$_{lsesun7}$ in the following) only manages a name space containing the contextual names `/tex/biblio`, `/tex/macro`, and `/services/mosaic`, which correspond to the files `/usr/doc/bib/article.bib` and `/usr/doc/style/macro.tex`, accessible through `FTP` and the service `HTTP`. The LWNS$_m$ is on `angrboda.cs.cornell.edu`.

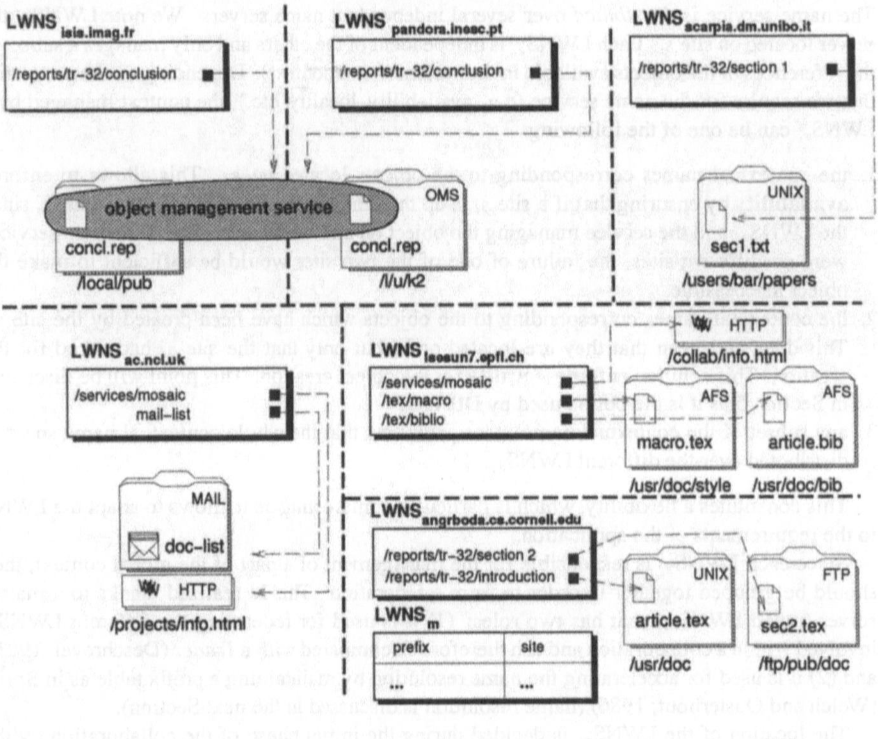


**Figure 2** Name distribution based on the location of the objects.

### *Local resolution*

The name resolution requested by the site $s_i$ is performed in the following way. First, the local LWNS$_{s_i}$ is enquired for the *o-ref* (object reference) corresponding to a given *o-ctxt* (contextual name). If *o-ctxt* is known by the LWNS$_{s_i}$ then the response is immediate. For instance, if *o-ctxt* is `/tex/biblio` and $s_i$ is `lsesun7.epfl.ch` then the corresponding *o-ref* `(lsesun7.epfl.ch,FTP,/usr/doc/bib/article.bib)` is returned by LWNS$_{lsesun7}$.

### *Remote resolution*

In case of a negative response, a remote interrogation will be necessary. For instance, if the *o-ctxt* is the same but the requester $s_i$ is now $isis.imag.fr$. Since LWNS$_{isis}$ does not manage the contextual name `/tex/biblio` it has no information on the location of the corresponding object.

There are two methods for locating the LWNS$_{s_k}$ that manages a contextual name *o-ctxt*: (1) an efficient optimized method, and (2) a costly brute force method. The optimized method is always applied first; if it fails (due to some site crash or link failure), the costly method is then applied (see §Failures of Section 3.3).

The optimized method uses a *prefix table*, a technique introduced by the Sprite File System (Welch and Ousterhout, 1986), which is located at the LWNS$_m$ level. The prefix table is a set of entries *(prefix, site)* where *prefix* is a prefix of a contextual name: e.g. `/tex` is a prefix* for the contextual name `/tex/biblio`. The prefix table ensures the following property:

> Consider *o-ctxt* a contextual name. If *(prefix, $s_i$)* is the entry of the prefix table that has the longest prefix of *o-ctxt*, then the contextual name *o-ctxt* can be resolved by the server LWNS$_{s_i}$ located on the site $s_i$.

An example of a prefix table is given in Figure 3. For instance, if the *o-ctxt* is `/tex/biblio`, the longest corresponding prefix is `/tex`. The entry `(/tex, lsesun7.epfl.ch)` tells that all contextual names beginning by `/tex` (and in particular `/tex/biblio` can be resolved by the LWNS$_{lsesun7}$.

| Prefix | Site |
|---|---|
| /service/mosaic | lsesun7.epfl.ch |
| /tex | lsesun7.epfl.ch |
| /reports/tr-32/section 1 | scarpia.dm.unibo.it |
| /reports/tr-32/introduction | angrboda.cs.cornell.edu |
| /reports/tr-32/section 2 | angrboda.cs.cornell.edu |
| /reports/tr-32/conclusion | pandora.inesc.pt |
| /reports/tr-32/conclusion | isis.imag.fr |
| /services/mail-list | ac.ncl.uk |
| /services/mosaic | ac.ncl.uk |

**Figure 3** Prefix table.

Thus, when LWNS$_{isis}$ is asked for a name resolution that it cannot resolve locally (e.g. *o-ctxt* is `/tex/biblio`) the LWNS$_m$ is first interrogated. The result of this first request is the LWNS$_{s_j}$ that manages this contextual name (LWNS$_{lsesun7}$ in our example). In a second step, LWNS$_{lsesun7}$ is requested for the corresponding *o-ref* as is shown in Figure 4.

*However, the prefix of a contextual name *o-ctxt* might be the full contextual name *o-ctxt* itself.

By consulting such a prefix table, the name resolution is very efficient since it requires accessing only two servers: (1) the server managing the prefix table (LWNS$_m$), and (2) a single remote LWNS$_{s_j}$ that manages the requested information.

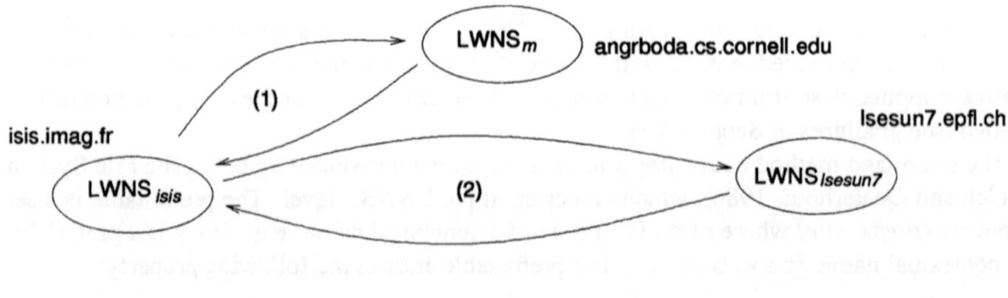


**Figure 4** Remote resolution protocol.

### *Optimization*

Each LWNS$_{s_i}$ can cache information in order to make the remote name resolution more efficient. This information constitutes what we have called *private context* in the beginning of Section 2. The information that is cached is (1) the result of the prefix table consultation and (2) the result of the remote LWNS$_{s_j}$ interrogation. For instance, in our example, the information returned by the LWNS$_m$ can be cached in order to short-cut the LWNS$_m$ interrogation for contextual names that have the same prefix as `/tex/biblio` (e.g. `/tex/macro`). In the same manner, information returned by the LWNS$_{lsesun7}$ about `/tex/biblio` can be locally stored in order to permit a local resolution by the LWNS$_{isis}$ at another time.

Concerning the caches, the flexibility of the LWNS permits the application designer to be free to choose the way he/she manages the information stored at the LWNS level. Thus, it is possible to register, in a LWNS$_{s_j}$, "shared" information (prefix table updated) or "private" information (prefix table not updated). The cached information will be accessed by a local request to LWNS$_{s_j}$ or by a brute force method interrogation.

By using cached information, once the resolution of a contextual name has been performed one time, the next resolution will be performed locally. Consistency can be maintained by detecting and discarding stale cache entries on use (Cheriton and Mann, 1989). Caching information is of particular interest for collaborative application, since generally the contents of a shared object can change but the reference to this object stays the same (in particular this is the case for DUPLEX).

### *Failures*

Unfortunately, this method for the remote name resolution cannot be used when either (1) the LWNS$_m$ or (2) the LWNS$_{s_j}$ maintaining the *o-ctxt* are not accessible. In the first case because it will not be possible to find which remote LWNS$_{s_j}$ should be interrogated and in the second because the remote LWNS$_{s_j}$ itself cannot be interrogated.

In both cases, the costly brute force method is applied. In this method, the local LWNS$_{s_i}$ that wants to make a remote name resolution multicasts directly the request to every LWNS$_{s_j}$ it knows. In case (1), such a brute force method permits to reach the information since a LWNS$_{s_i}$

knows all the other $LWNS_{s_j}$ registered. In case (2), as $LWNS_{s_j}$ may cache information about their previous requests, the brute force method gives a chance to find another $LWNS_{s_k}$ that has the information in its cache. In fact, if this object has already been accessed, the information is somewhere in a $LWNS_{s_k}$.

We see that caching of information is not only used for accelerating requests but also in order to ensure fault tolerance by replicating information for the brute force method. This is obtained for free since the caching of information will be performed, in any case, for the acceleration goal.

As a result, the name resolution of *o-ctxt* by the site $s_i$ can be performed in three ways : (1) by the local $LWNS_{s_i}$ if the object is managed by $LWNS_{s_i}$ or if the result of a previous request has been cached, (2) by the $LWNS_m$ managing the prefix table and the $LWNS_{s_j}$ managing the name *o-ctxt* if the $LWNS_m$ is available, or (3) by all the $LWNS_{s_k}$ if the $LWNS_m$ managing the prefix table or if the $LWNS_{s_j}$ responsible for *o-ctxt* is inaccessible (e.g. due to a crash). This architecture provides fault tolerance without relying on name server replication, which is important since a replicated scheme would imply to multiply the number of $LWNS_{s_i}$ by three or four. If the prefix table is inaccessible the multicast method can always be used to resolve a contextual name. If the $LWNS_{s_j}$ responsible for the *o-ctxt* is inaccessible then the probability to find the required information depends on the use of the object: the more often an object is used, the bigger the chance to find the requested information. Most of the time, the resolution will be fast and cheap; costly treatment is only due to failures.

## 4 OVERVIEW OF THE DUPLEX ENVIRONMENT

This Section presents an overview of the DUPLEX collaborative editing environment and points out the naming problem raised by this large scale distributed application. More details about the DUPLEX environment can be found in (Pacull et al., 1994; Pacull, 1995).

Within DUPLEX, the jointly edited document is partitioned into several parts. This partition is dynamic and driven by the authors themselves. Each author works more specifically on one or several parts, but, in order to enhance cooperation, all authors should have direct access to all parts.

Document parts are replicated, to ensure better availability and fault tolerance, and maintained by a *distributed kernel*. The distributed kernel is shared by all members of the collaboration and provides persistence and availability of the most recent document state. Thus, we call *kernel object* the set of replicas corresponding to a replicated document part maintained by the kernel.

The co-authors may be scattered over very large distances such as in an international research effort, and interact through the kernel in an asynchronous manner. Basically, as is shown in Figure 5, a user reads an object from the kernel and stores it within a *local object*. This local object can be modified (edited or decomposed) locally without any connection to the kernel. Finally, the user requests a flush of this local object to the kernel in order to make the new version of the object available to the others co-authors. The concurrency control is provided at the kernel level and several policies (optimistic, pessimistic or hybrid) are offered (Pacull, 1995). The result of the write to the kernel depends on the chosen concurrency control policy.

Thus, a user works locally, disconnected from the kernel, until either (1) a copy of a kernel object is required to continue work, and the user copies it from the kernel, or (2) the user

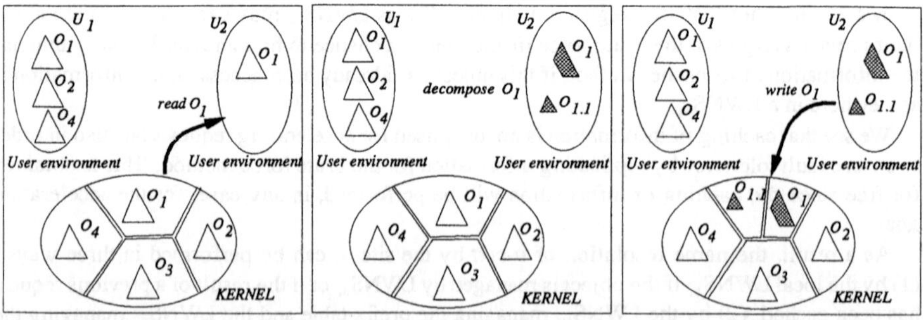


**Figure 5** DUPLEX architecture.

considers that a local object version should be shared, and updates the corresponding kernel object. This operating mode allows each user to work locally most of the time and limits the use of communication, that are known to be very costly in large scale.

## 4.1 Naming requirement

The solution we have adopted consists of a kernel distributed over a dozen of sites selected from the *domain* (local area network) of each collaborating team. Logical objects are partially replicated on these sites, which are chosen for their good communication performance.

Due to the heterogeneous system aspects, several ways to manage replicated objects at the kernel level have to be considered at the same time, implying different patterns for the *object reference*.

To a document correspond two views: (1) the user's view in which a contextual name corresponds to a *local object* that belongs to its local file system, and (2) a kernel view, in which each contextual name corresponds to a replicated service that manages the *shared object*. If the first correspondence *(contextual name, local object reference)* can be performed statically at the user file system, the second one *(contextual name, shared object reference)* needs the help of an external name service shared by the community. The set of shared objects is small (usually a few dozen elements) and composed of objects whose names are contextual to the document. Replicas are, however, maintained in heterogeneous file systems with no global naming scheme consistent with the name space of the collaboration. Thus, an important point is related to the way of naming shared objects and of retrieving the data associated to these names. Broadly speaking, the problem is how to embed the small document context into a large distributed system. This problem is delicate and a dedicated name service is required to manage the set of kernel objects distributed over the large heterogeneous network.

# 5 USE OF THE LWNS WITHIN DUPLEX

The concepts considered for the DUPLEX architecture have some influence on how the LWNS is used. We show in this Section how the LWNS can fulfill the particular requirement of DUPLEX.

## 5.1 Architecture of DUPLEX name service

The LWNS lets the application designer the free choice to decide upon the location of each $LWNS_{s_i}$ and of the $LWNS_m$, as well as how the name space is decomposed. The choice made by DUPLEX is to put the $LWNS_{s_i}$ close to the users' sites. In other words, if the collaboration involves four research teams whose respective domains are `epfl.ch`, `cornell.edu`, `unibo.it` and `inesc.pt`, a LWNS is present on one site of each of these domains (e.g. `lsesun7.epfl.ch`, `angrboda.cs.cornell.edu`, `scarpia.dm.unibo.it` and `pandora.inesc.pt`). The $LWNS_m$ is located on one single domain, e.g. `angrboda.cornell.edu`. The format of contextual name that we use ensures that each $LWNS_{s_i}$ manages objects created by the users working on the same local area network as $s_i$. The pattern of the contextual name in DUPLEX is the following: `/doc-name/domain-id/object-name.unique-id`. The two fields `doc-name` and `domain-id` ensure a correct management of the contextual name at the prefix table level: `doc-name` operates a segregation on the document name, and `domain-id`, a logical name defining the domain of a team*, permits to group all the objects created at the same domain, to be managed by the same $LWNS_{s_i}$. Finally, `object-name.unique-id` permits to define a meaningful name for the user that ensures at the same time the unicity of the contextual name in the frame of the collaboration. The user is not disturbed by such complicated contextual names since the graphical interface displays the structure of the document, and each independent object is labeled with the `object-name` chosen by the object creator. From the user point of view, this is sufficient for naming an object, without any risk of confusion.

Concerning the *object references* manipulated by DUPLEX, the flexibility of the LWNS permits to consider current implementations of objects, and future extension should not raise any problems. The three primitives of the LWNS, which permit to store, retrieve and delete such information are sufficient, since the validity of the object references is the responsibility of DUPLEX and not the LWNS.

Figure 6 represents several shared objects, corresponding to the document `TR-94-10`, maintained within the kernel. The boxes on the left hand represent the different local $LWNS_{s_i}$ in the domains `cornell.edu`, `epfl.ch` and `unibo.it`. The box on the right hand is the $LWNS_m$ that manages the prefix table. In the present example, the $LWNS_m$ is in charge of two documents (`TR-94-10` and `IFIP-paper`). All contextual names that have as prefix `/TR-94-10/lausanne` are managed by the $LWNS_{lsesun7}$ running on the host `lsesun7.epfl.ch`. That is not to say that each object created within the domain `epfl.ch` has to be managed by $LWNS_{lsesun7}$. For instance, $LWNS_{disun10}$ manages contextual names corresponding to `IFIP-paper`.

The flexibility of the LWNS lets the users choose if the $LWNS_{s_j}$ and the $LWNS_m$ manage information related to one or several documents. This choice is taken when the collaboration begins (for the $LWNS_m$), and when a new user enters within the collaboration (the local $LWNS_{s_j}$). In both cases it is possible to create a new one or use an already existing one.

*In the present example, we have chosen the name of the corresponding town.

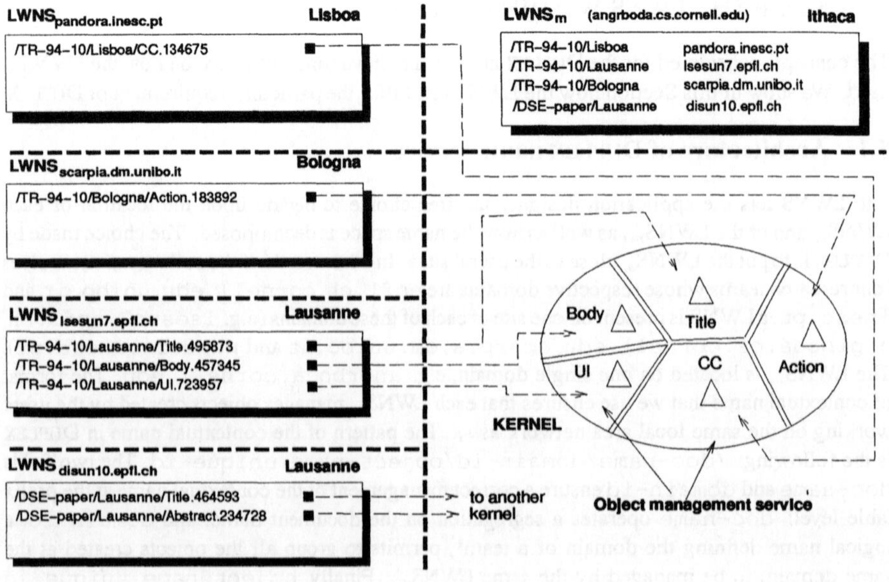


**Figure 6** Use of LWNS within DUPLEX.

## 5.2 Properties of this architecture

### *Efficient object creation*

When considering large scale, the response time is important. Thus, the creation of a new object has to be efficient. This implies that one cannot be delayed by a costly protocol checking if the new contextual name is valid for the registration.

To address this point, we use the fact that with the LWNS, the checking for conflicting names can be disabled. Thus, since (1) the contextual name pattern of DUPLEX permits to generate a unique name, and (2) all the contextual names of objects created at a given site $s_i$ are managed by the same LWNS$_{s_i}$, the registration can be performed locally. Practically, the creation of the first object by a site requests the LWNS$_m$ to modify the prefix table of the LWNS$_m$, and all the other creations need not contact neither the LWNS$_m$ nor any other LWNS$_{s_j}$. The contextual name is only registered at the LWNS$_{s_i}$ until a user from another domain asks for a remote name resolution. In this case, one of the mechanisms described in Section 3 is used.

### *Efficient name resolution*

The choice of putting the LWNS$_{s_i}$ at the level of the users' site, improves the availability of local resolution, which is one of the goals of the DUPLEX environment.

On one hand, this guarantees that an object created by an user is reachable provided that his/her site is up, and there is no partition isolating the user from the kernel. In this case, both the kernel and the local LWNS are accessible. On the other hand, this is also true for an object already used by a user, due to the cache mechanism.

*Fault-tolerance*

The fault-tolerance for name resolution and new object creation is ensured by the use of the brute force mechanism described in Section 2.

Considering fault-tolerance during the name resolution, we have to distinguish two kinds of failures: (1) the failure of the $LWNS_m$ and (2) the failure of the remote $LWNS_{s_j}$ that is in charge of the required information*. Due to the brute force mechanism, the first case can be hidden to the user since the required information will eventually be accessible with a longer delay. However, this is not the same for the second case of failure. The probability to resolve a contextual name in such conditions is proportional to the users working with the corresponding object. In fact, the fault-tolerance of the name service is provided by the propagation (in the caches) of information during its use. This guarantees, in particular, that the name resolution, corresponding to important objects, accessed by a large number of people, is always possible. The only problem arises when a contextual name is known only by one $LWNS_{s_i}$ and this latter has crashed. In this case, the object is not reachable during the time of the failure.

Even if the user is partitioned from the kernel, he/she is able to create new objects locally and to register them at the local $LWNS_{s_i}$. The new objects will be flushed to the kernel when the partition failure is repaired. This enforces the locality of the work for the users.

*Low cost name service*

Concerning the cost of the name service, we have to consider two parameters: (1) the cost of a name resolution request, and (2) the amount of information stored at the level of each $LWNS_{s_j}$. For the first point, we have already shown that only the first request is not performed locally, and this first request under normal conditions only requires the consultation of the $LWNS_m$ and of one remote $LWNS_{s_j}$. For the second point, the information stored by each $LWNS_{s_j}$ is minimal since only the contextual names of used objects are maintained either as a shared information or as private information (cache). Moreover, concerning the cost of propagating an information, it is distributed to the requesters and not only paid by the creator. This makes the registration efficient and scalable since it does not depend on the number of $LWNS_{s_j}$ belonging to the cooperation.

## 5.3 Discussion

The implementation of the name service of DUPLEX is not fully fault-tolerant. However, the unique case, (see §Faut-tolerance of Section 5.2), where fault-tolerance is not ensured is not frequent. Moreover, this "partial" fault-tolerance does not rely on any explicit replication. An explicit replication would require much more resources and a more heavy-weight administrative management when a team joins the collaboration. With the solution we have adopted, the new team just needs to launch a $LWNS_{s_i}$ and the name service is operational.

The second point to emphasize is that the fault-tolerance provided for the name resolution of a given contextual name is link to the importance of the corresponding object. Thus, the impossibility of resolving a contextual name does not block several teams at the same time since if several teams use an object this latter is known by several $LWNS_{s_j}$.

*A partition from the kernel has no influence on the name resolution even if, once the name resolution performed, the object is not accessible.

Finally, the low cost of the name service in absence of failures (which is the most frequent case), both for the name resolution and the registration, must be underlined. This is emphasized by the fact that the cache mechanism accelerates the name resolution corresponding to an already accessed object.

## 6 RELATED WORK

Although they are useful in some classes of applications, existing name services present restrictions that are not suitable for use in the specific domain of large scale distributed applications.

First of all, systems that integrate within the same system, a name service that is responsible for the mapping of an object name with the corresponding data, and the protocol required to access these data, could not be used since such systems are not adequate to manipulate general purpose objects (e.g. Ficus (Guy, 1991), Echo (Birrell et al., 1993) manipulate replicated files, and NFS (Sandberg et al., 1985), AFS (Howard et al., 1988), V-system (Cheriton and Mann, 1989), Sprite (Ousterhout et al., 1988) and Amoeba (Tanenbaum et al., 1990) manipulate non replicated files).

Thus, it is necessary to decouple the name service from the access service that manages the access and the storage of the objects. Hence, the name service is responsible for the mapping between a *contextual name* (the name of the object is the frame of the application) and an *object reference*. However, the naming service has to be flexible enough to leave the choice of the *object reference* format to the application builder. For instance, in the case of collaborative application such as DUPLEX, the same object can have two states (activated or desactivated). This requires that the object should be accessible through these two states and the *object reference* is more complex than a classical service address, since it has to contain the addresses of both the object management service and the activation service. Name services that impose the format of the information associated to a contextual name present a weakness in this matter (e.g. DNS (Terry et al., 1984)).

Moreover, large scale for collaborative applications generally means large distances, rather than a larger number of objects: when people cooperate they share information, so it is not because we have to consider several people that the number of objects will necessarily increase in an exponential manner. However, the probability that the objects and the people are spread over a large network is great, since it depends on the localization of the involved users. Thus, an important point is to provide an efficient name resolution in such a condition. As the number of objects useful for the collaborative application is small compared to the number of objects potentially manipulated by the underlying world wide distributed system, it is inefficient to rely on a global name service such as DCE (Lockhart, 1994). Indeed, the architecture of the underlying network makes the name services of DCE cumbersome to use since it is decomposed into two entities: a cell directory service and a global name service. The first manages the name within its corresponding cell and the second manages the cell name. With a large scale distributed application, the probability that each user is in a different cluster cell is great. Therefore, each resolution will use a costly mechanism even if only few objects are actually of interest for the application.

Another point to raise is that some knowledge about the application can be considered in order to increase the efficiency of the name service. For instance, the collaborative application

DUPLEX generates a unique contextual name, thus it is not necessary to perform a detection of conflicting names. This ensures a better locality and scalability for the registration since it is not necessary to verify all the entries maintained by the name service at each registration. Most name services (e.g. DCE's (Lockhart, 1994), X500 (CCITT, 1988)) suffer from the impossibility to disable this detection.

The way that the contextual name is used by existing name services is also characterized by a lack of flexibility. Systems like Propero (Neumann, 1992), DCE (Lockhart, 1994), X500 (CCITT, 1988), DNS (Terry et al., 1984) are hierarchical name servers that use the format of the contextual name for deciding which server will manage the name. Here, the server responsible for the management of an object is imposed by the system. In case of a failure of a given server, no other server can provide the same service, and some names might be impossible to register or retrieve during the server failure.

As a result, there is a lack of usable name services in this particular context since none of the existing system could be used for our purpose. The LWNS approach is not to implement a general purpose name service, but to provide a flexible efficient name service that can be adapted for large scale distributed application by providing what is really needed, at a low cost.

## 7 CONCLUSION

This paper has presented a Light Weight Name Service, which is particularly well suited for large scale distributed collaborative applications. We have designed such a name service because no existing system provides the features we need. The LWNS has been used in the design of DUPLEX, a collaborative editing environment, and its use has shown two things.

First, despite of very basic features, the LWNS is well suited for such a large scale application. Verifications are provided at the application level since it is the best way to benefit from the knowledge about the application. No useless work is performed, the application designer pays the price for the guarantees he/she really needs. Moreover, the application designer can adapt the LWNS to his/her requirements. It is not the application that should adapt itself to the name service. More efficient solutions can then be adopted. Second, by the result of its application, it has been proved that the performances were good (Lugeon and Sandoz, 1994) for a name resolution involving sites spread all over the world.

As a conclusion, the LWNS should be considered as a toolkit which permits to create a name service that exactly fits the requirement of a given application. It is not a general purpose name service but it offers a quick name resolution package that is easy to use and customize.

## 8 REFERENCES

Birrell, A., Hisgen, A., Jerian, C., Mann, T., and Swart, G. (1993). The Echo distributed file system. Technical Report 111, Digital Systems Research Center.

CCITT (1988). Recommendation X.500: The directory. *CCITT Blue Book*, VIII(8).

Cheriton, D. and Mann, T. (1989). Decentralizing a global naming service for improved performance and fault tolerance. *ACM Transactions on Computer Systems*, 7(2):147–183.

Comer, D. (1988). *Internetworking With TCP/IP: Principles, Protocols, Architecture.* Prentice Hall, Stevenage.

Deschrevel, J. P. (1993). The ANSA model for trading and federation. Technical report, APM Cambridge UK.

Guy, R. G. (1991). Ficus: A very large scale reliable distributed file system. Technical Report CSD-910018, University of California, Los Angeles. Ph.D. dissertation.

Howard, J., Kazar, M., Menees, S., Nichols, D., Satyanarayanan, M., Sidebotham, R., and West, M. (1988). Scale and performance in a distributed file system. *ACM Transactions on Computer Systems*, 6(1):51–81.

Linden, R. V. (1993). ANSA architecture report: The ANSA naming model. Technical report, APM Cambridge UK.

Lockhart, H. (1994). *OSF DCE Guide to Developing Distributed Applications.* Mc Graw-Hill.

Lugeon, J.-C. and Sandoz, A. (1994). A light weight name service for large scale distributed applications and groupware. Technical Report 94-63, Federal Institute of Technology of Lausanne, Computer Science Departement.

Neumann, B. (1992). The Prospero file system: A global file system based on the virtual system model. In *Proceedings of the USENIX File Systems Workshop*, pages 13–27.

Ousterhout, J., Cherenson, A., Douglis, F., Nelson, M., and Welch, B. (1988). The Sprite network operating system. *IEEE Computer*, 21(2):23–36.

Pacull, F. (1995). *Concepts et mécanismes pour la mise en oeuvre d'un environnement d'édition coopérative sur un réseau à grande échelle.* PhD thesis, École Polytechnique Fédérale de Lausanne (Federal Institute of Technology of Lausanne).

Pacull, F., Sandoz, A., and Schiper, A. (1994). Duplex: A distributed collaborative editing environment in large scale. In *Proceedings of the ACM Conference on Computer-Supported Cooperative Work (CSCW '94)*, pages 165–173.

Postel, J. and Reynolds, J. (1985). File Transfer Protocol. *Network Working Group, RFC 959.*

Sandberg, R., Goldberg, D., Kleiman, S., Walsh, D., and Lyon, B. (1985). Design and implementation of the Sun Network File system. In *Proceedings of the USENIX Summer Conference*, pages 119–130.

Sollins, K. and Clark, D. D. (1988). Distributed name management. In Speth, R., editor, *Message Handling Systems*, pages 97–115. Elsevier Science Publishers B.V. (North-Holland).

Tanenbaum, A., van Renesse, R., van Staveren, H., Sharp, G., Mullender, S., Jansen, J., and van Rossum, G. (1990). Experience with the Amoeba distributed operating system. *Communications of the ACM*, 33(12):46–63.

Terry, D., Painter, M., Riggle, D., and Zhou, S. (1984). The Berkeley Internet Name Domain server. In *Proceedings of the USENIX Summer Conference*, pages 23–31.

Welch, B. and Ousterhout, J. (1986). Prefix tables: A simple mechanism for locating files in a distributed system. In *Proceedings of the 6th International Conference on Distributed Computer Systems*, pages 184–189.

## 9 BIOGRAPHY

**Jean-Claude Lugeon** was born in Geneva in 1964. He obtained a technical degree in Electronic and Computer Science from Engineer School of Geneva, Switzerland, in 1984, and a Master in Computer Science from the Federal Institute of Technology of Lausanne (EPFL) in 1989. He worked in the Operating System Laboratory at the EPFL until end 1994. His research interests are in the area of distributed file service and large scale name service. He is currently system engineer in the Corporate Advanced System Engineering at Landis&Gyr.

**François Pacull** received a BSc in Mathematics from the University of Marseille, France, in 1986, and a BSc in Computer Science from the University of Grenoble, France, in 1988. He graduated in Computer Science from the National Polytechnic Institute of Grenoble in 1989. In 1992 he joined the Operating System Laboratory of the Federal Institute of Technology in Lausanne (EPFL), Switzerland, as a research assistant. He received his Ph.D. in Computer Science from the EPFL in 1995. His dissertation was concerned with the impact of large scale distributed systems within the frame of collaborative editing. His research interests are in the area of fault-tolerance and computer supported collaborative work, in particular in the context of large scale distributed systems.

# 6

# Organizational management system in an heterogeneous environment - A WWW case study

*A. Silva, J. Borbinha, J. Delgado*
Telematics Systems and Services Group
INESC - Instituto Engenharia de Sistemas e Computadores
Rua Alves Redol, 9, 1000 Lisboa, Portugal
*Alberto.Silva@inesc.pt, Jose.Borbinha@inesc.pt, Jose.Delgado@inesc.pt*

**Abstract**

W3 (World Wide Web) technology is being used over the world by a growth number of users. However that technology is mainly used to navigate or to retrieve hypertext information over the Internet. This paper describes some experiences currently tried at INESC, a Portuguese research institute. W3 and data bases technologies were used to develop, in a novel way, traditional information systems, that could be executed and accessed in a client-server model from a great variety of platforms and from any computer connected to the Internet.

**Keywords**

WWW, client-server computation, information systems, CGI gateways, databases, Internet

## 1 INTRODUCTION

Nowadays the spectacular Internet growth over the world is intrinsically due to the characteristics of the W3 model and its technology. the easy of use of its hypermedia navigation model, associated with its language (HyperText Markup Language) and protocol (HyperText Transfer Protocol), the availability of high quality W3 clients, like Mosaic or Netscape Navigator, hosted in a broad range platforms and environments, were decisive to the proliferation and the success of W3 and therefore to the Internet growth.

At INESC, a research institute in the areas of information technology, the Telematics Systems and Services Group has started in 1994 a few projects in the W3 area. One of those projects is the InInWeb (INESC In The Web), an administrative and general information system presented in this paper.

It is not the objective of this paper to explain what is the W3 [Berners-Lee 94], what are relational data bases [Codd 70], SQL [CODASYL 78], or even analysis and design methodologies [Rumbaugh 91]. These technologies were used direct or indirectly in this project but are conveniently described in other documentation.

The document is organized in the following way:

- Section 2 shows the computational model subjacent to the W3 architecture;
- Section 3 presents the organization INESC, the services developed and some particular characteristics of the system;
- Section 4 presents the GENESIS library, a C++ library developed to help the developement of W3 services in an object oriented manner (and which is the base of the InInWeb sistem);
- Section 5 depictes the service developed and the perspective of integration with other similar administrative services;
- Section 6 points briefly related or similar projects that are being developed around the world;
- Finally, section 7 concludes the work done and makes some considerations to the future.

# 2 THE W3 COMPUTATIONAL MODEL

W3 follows basically the client-server model that uses a simple stateless protocol (HTTP) over the current TCP/IP stack. This protocol is very adequate for the retrieval of hypermedia information but presents some drawbacks when used to simulate interactive connections, or when the clients need to handle some event notification occurred at the server side.

In general, the W3 clients (also called "browsers") have GUI capabilities, are multi-platform (X-Windows, MS-Windows, Macintosh, etc.), are multi-protocol (HTTP, FTP, GOPHER, NEWS, file, etc.), and parse and show conveniently HTML information. Recent clients have additional capabilities, for instance: built-in visualisation of different image formats (e.g. GIF, BMP), capability to invoke external multimedia players, availability of a CCI (Common Client Interface), or even secure transactions. Mosaic, from NCSA, was a great contribution to the W3 wave and nowadays the majority of the relevant clients are Mosaic-like.

From the other extreme there are the W3 servers (also called "HTTPd" or "HTTP daemons"). HTTP servers are in general multi-thread (it means they accept concurrently multiple requests), have configuration, logging and protection/authorization files, and support the CGI (Common Gateway Interface) protocol.

Servers answer client requests by returning HTML pages retrieved from the file system or by forwarding the data received from the CGI.

The CGI provides a mechanism to extend the basic functionality of an HTTP server by connecting it to other specific processes, called "gateways", invoked at run time. It is important to note that those gateways are completely independent processes that are launched by the HTTP server process. The way the data is communicated between the server and the gateway is conditioned by the CGI specification.

Figure 1 illustrates the general computation model above described.

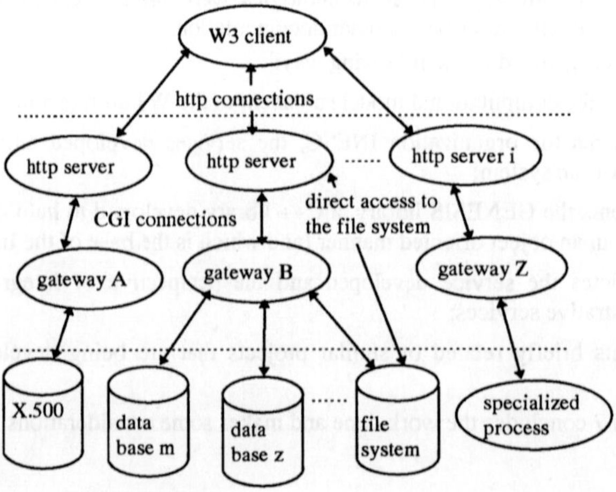


**Figure 1** The W3 computational model.

Gateways are specific applications that can interact with several data repositories (e.g. relational data bases systems, file systems, X.500 distributed directories, etc.) or even with other specialised processes. However all the CGI gateways are "short life" processes, this means that they are not interactive processes. Any CGI gateway presents the following basic functionality:

1. It is created by the HTTP server;
2. It receives data via the CGI channel, by its standard input and by environment variables;
3. It parses the received data and checks its validity;
4. It executes some queries or calculations;
5. It produces some results (usually information in the HTML format) that will be read by the HTTP server which will redirect it to the client;
6. It ends itself.

# 3 THE INESC CASE STUDY

## 3.1 The INESC organization

INESC is a relatively complex and particular organization of the Portuguese academic and entrepreneurial society with some similar aspects to a services' organization. However, INESC is a not-for-profit R&D institute, having public universities and telecommunication operators as associates. It is present in such geographical areas as Lisbon, Porto, Aveiro, Coimbra and Braga.

The organizational units at INESC are groups, centers and departments. Groups and centers are the operational units, while the departments are the supporting ones. Groups develop, as their main goal, R&D projects, while the main function of centers is to execute technology transfer. Groups and centers are distributed according strategy vectors. INESC has also developed, indirectly through its participated organizations, other complementary activities, such as professional training and company incubation.

The information system of INESC is very complex. It has very heterogeneous environments, either at the software or hardware level. It has machines from different manufacturers with different operating systems. Happily, the majority of its machines are connected to Internet (TCP/IP) and, consequently, they can share information and other resources using the W3 technology.

For a deep analysis of the INESC organization the reader can consult the specific documentation provided by its Communication Department [INESC 94].

## 3.2 The "INESC In the Web" service

The "INESC In the Web" ("InInWeb") service is an information and administrative support service to be used by people from and outside the organization. The InInWeb service has currently the following functionalities:

- A generic information service about INESC, that gives access to a well structured set of public information about INESC in an easy way (from or outside the organization), its collaborators, its functional units (groups, centers and departments) or its activities. This service was based in the concept of "Organizational Folder" (OF) that was firstly implemented in a paper support, where all the relevant entities had textual or image information, such as historical view, curriculum, objectives and activities.
- An administrative service called "Timecards", which is a service to manage and control the labour distribution, by each person, for activities and for work units. Because it handles information about people, work units and groups/centers, it makes sense to integrate it with the previous one.
- An administrative service called "Project Management", which intends to give support to the management and control of the projects developed by different groups. This service handles basic information, such as European programs and projects, consortiua, partners, etc., but also handles other resources such as labour, timecards, and financial (budgets and cost statements) information. One special emphasis was given to the management of European projects (such as Esprit or Race projects) because they are an important area of research and labour at INESC. Because this service also handles information about people, work units and groups/centers, it also makes sense to integrate it with the previous two mentioned.

The home page of the InInWeb is ilustrated in the figure 2.

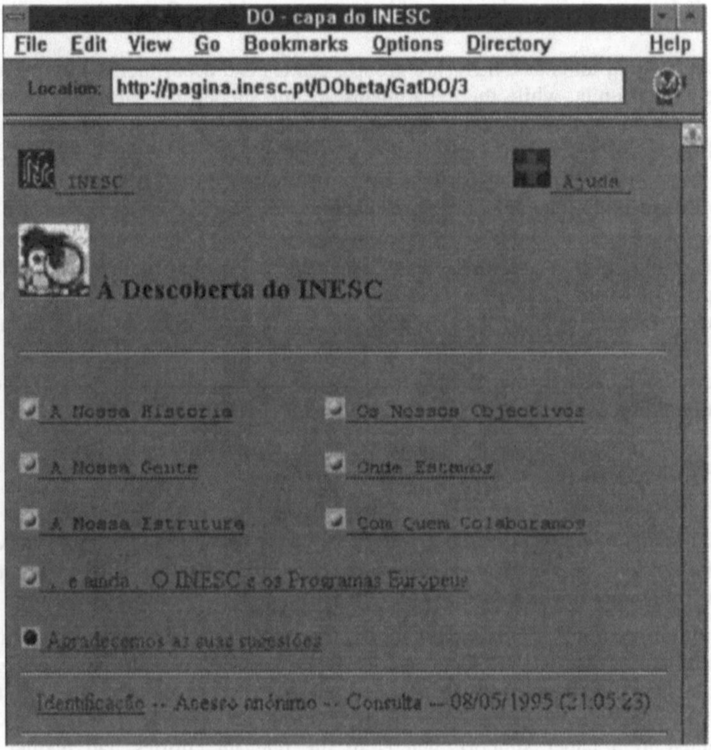


**Figure 2** The InInWeb service home page.

The information handled by the InInWeb service is stored in a file system and in a relational data base system (SQL Server from Sybase [Sybase 94]). The information saved in the file system is mainly text and image information, e.g. histories, objectives, photos or other pictures from people. All the other information is organized in a relational way.

# 4 THE GENESIS LIBRARY

## 4.1 Introduction

GENESIS is a C++ library developed to help the authoring of W3 services. It brings the details of the construction of W3 gateways and HTML pages to a higher level (C++ classes), so that the programmer doesn't have to be a "W3 expert".

Distributed services (gateways on different machines) using heterogeneous repositories of information (such as Relational Data Bases and HTML or even non-HTML files) are supported.

Using GENESIS, a significant number of details in the construction of W3 gateways and HTML pages are hidden from the author, who can concentrate in the authoring work.

The actual version of the GENESIS library intends to be used directly by programmers, but future versions will be targeted to be integrated in authoring environments.

## 4.2 The Basic GENESIS Components

The current version of GENESIS library consists of a group of C++ classes that can be inherited to construct W3 services. Each class supports a concept, offering a group of basic functions related to it.

A service that intends to use GENESIS must be conceived from two perspectives:

- Actions: a service is structured as a web of actions (or sub-services);
- State: the state of the service is represented by the state of its resources.

A request to the service is an action to change and/or access resources.

Actions are performed by a special kind of objects, named agents. The main function of a gateway receives a request, parses the CGI parameters, discovers the classe of the requested agent and creates it. The agent gets the remaining parameters from the CGI and performs the request accessing to the resources, which are encapsulated in a special kind of classes named entities. In the end it is generated an HTML page as answer.

In a more detailed way GENESIS offers the following basic concepts, described below.

### 4.2.1 Gateways

A service is a web accessible through one or more gateways. A gateway gives access to a group of actions, which are performed by agents.

Gateways can be located in different machines, but this only has to be specified once by the programmer, in a configuration phase. Apart from that, the author can program all the service as if were in the same homogeneous environment, using logical references (the generation of the real gateway addresses will be automatic and transparent to the programmer).

The passing of parameters from one access to the next one (such as the user identification, for example), is completely managed by the gateways, so the programmer only has to deal with objects (e.g., the parameters passed from one action to the next one are, at the programming level, objects).

### 4.2.2 Agents

An agent is a specialized class, responsible for a specific part of the service (a specific group of actions). An agent can be accessible from one or more gateways, which can be in different machines. This is possible because agents represent parts of the service (functions), and are not directly related with the state of the service. An agent has two basic kinds of methods:

- methods to help other agents in the processing of their requests.
- methods to answer user's requests;

The first kind of methods represent the contribution of the agent for the service (the requests it knows how to answer), while the second ones are the answers to those functions.

To answer an user's request, an agent performs three steps:

- interprets and validates the request, checking the level of the user and what kind of answer he/she will have access;
- processes the request (changing the data repositories, if it is the case);
- builds the HTML answers page.

In the third step it can be requested the help of other agents, in order to get information to build anchors to give access to them.

### 4.2.3 Pages

The answer to an user's request is always a HTML page. Each agent has a group of pages to answer to all of the requests it can perform. Pages have a structure with three parts: a header, a body and a footer. Each of these three parts consists of a list of elements.

Classes of pages can share the same header and/or footer in order to uniform all the service or only some parts of it (for example, all the pages of the service or of a specific agent can have the same header and footer).

### 4.2.4 Elements

Pages are composed of lists of elements. There are two basic kinds of elements, HTML elements and high level elements.

HTML elements are classes that represent all the HTML types. If the programmer uses these classes he/she doesn't have to worry about the HTML details.

On the top of the basic HTML elements were also built a group of more complex elements. These elements were found to be very common in the applications where GENESIS has been used, and they include examples such as tables and composed forms (forms mixing radio buttons and boxes). Elements are very useful because they permit to manipulate HTML and complex HTML structures at a C++ level.

### 4.2.5 Entities

Entities are abstractions on the top of the data repositories, offering an object oriented layer of them. Agents can change the state of the entities, which means they can change the state of the service. Pages can read the state of the entities in order to present that information to the user.

Each entity class has two kinds of methods: methods independent of the repositories and methods dependent of them. Methods dependent on the repositories have to be all written by the programmer, but an entity class can use more than one repository (a data base and a file system, for example).

### 4.2.6 Users and Security

An user is a special kind of entity. Users are identified by a name and a password. Users can have capabilities, which can be checked by agents, for requests processing, or by pages, for answers to requests.

The Genesis library offers a prototype of an user's class as also an authentication agent, which offers a group of pages to support the process of user authentication. Once an user is identified, an encrypted timestamp key is passed from page to page, simulating a connection oriented session.

The CGI mechanism recognizes the user entity, giving a special support to this feature (the author only has to program the repository dependencies for the user element).

## 5 THE ININWEB SERVICE ARCHITECTURE

### 5.1 The InInWeb computational model

Currently the InInWeb service corresponds to just one CGI gateway that handles all the requests about the three integrated functionalities described in section 3. The figure below depictes its computational model.

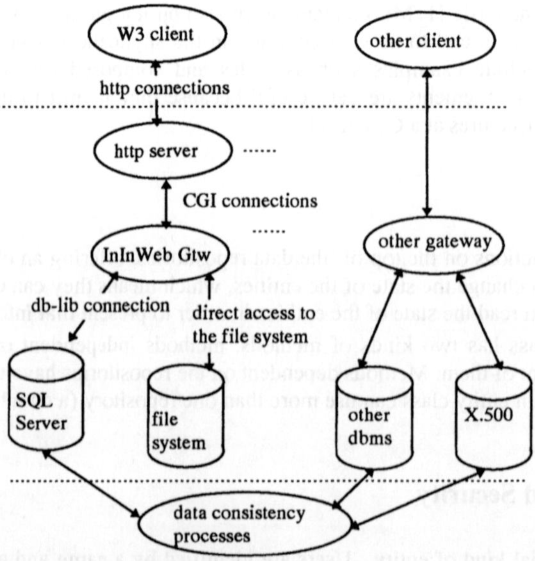


**Figure 2** The InInWeb service computational model.

All the information of the service is stored in a data base of the SQL Server, from Sybase, and in a hierarchical structure of the file system. The data and control communication between the gateway and the SQL Server is supported over a DB-Library connection. That kind of connection was chosen because both processes are running in the same computer and it was the easiest and fastest connection found. However, future experiences will take into account the ODBC connection standard.

The previous model raises some questions that were taken during the analysis phase. One of them was how to maintain the consistency of the information managed in the InInWeb data base with equivalent information (such as the telephone or room number) kept by other services in different computers and different data repositories (such as X.500 or other DBMS). The first idea was to integrate a transactional capability into the InInWeb gateway. However this solution became impractical with the increasing number of potential interdependencies between services, and the need for efficient and simple CGI gateways. So, it was decided that the data consistency problem would not be solved at the gateway level, and that it will be handled by another independent and specialized processes.

Other important question was about the concept of a cooperative gateways pool. If the InInWeb gateway presents three integrated functionalities would it be divided in three cooperative gateways? One specialized on the Organizational Folder service, other in the Timecards and the third on the Project Management service? This solution apparently has the advantage to be lighter (i.e. each separated process seems to be lighter and more efficient than the sum of all of them), but presents the drawback of the mutual interface knowledge between all the cooperative gateways. This question needs to be better analysed and detailed in future work.

## 5.2 Some architectural aspects

This sub-section presents some important or interesting aspects that were realized during the InInWeb service realization.

### 5.2.1 HTTP - A stateless protocol

As it is mentioned at section 2, the HTTP is a stateless protocol very adequate to the retrieval of hypermedia information. However the class of applications proposed initially is mainly interactive. So, the initial problem was: how to establish and to maintain an interactive session over a stateless protocol? This question can be asked from another, more technical, point of view: how can the gateway know what will be the HTML document to be generated?

The solution is the use of state variables, this means variables that are created and passed in the URL (Uniform Resource Locator), in the form name/value pair, whose values indicate the actual state. So, the gateway behaves itself as a state transition machine. Depending on the current state (passed on the current URL), the gateway analyse the other parameters and its standard input and based on that it will generate a HTML page whose links will correspond to URLs with future state values.

This mechanism of passing parameters in URLsis used in several situations, whenever necessary, such is the case of the authentication information. However all the parameters are conveniently coded with a way that nobody, even who sees the URL, can understand its meaning. The next figure illustrates an URL with encoded parameters.

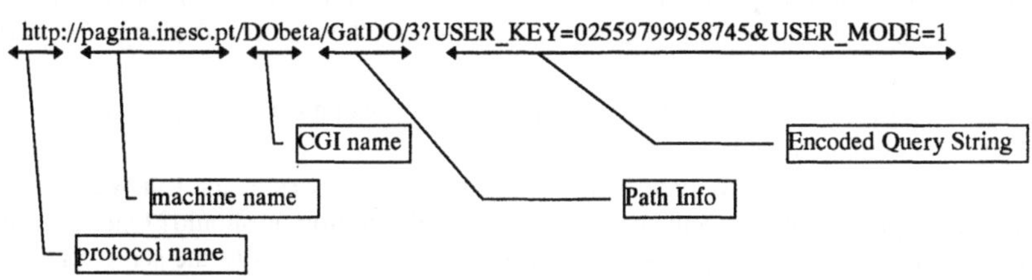


**Figure 4** Example of an URL with some encoded parameters.

### 5.2.1 Security considerations

Due to the InInWeb service characteristics, some information is public (mainly the institutional INESC's information) but other (the administrative information such as some generic reports, or private information about people, units, or work units) must be protected and have access conditioned. Consequently it was conceived a generic mechanism able to handle the user level in a protected way.

With the INESC reality in attention it was defined the following users levels:

- *SuperUser*, corresponds to the service manager, the user level that owns all the potential capabilities.
- *Director*, corresponds to a member of the board of directors.
- *Administrative*, corresponds to the collaborator responsible for doing the administrative tasks.
- *Unit Leader*, group, center or department leader.
- *Unit Secretary*, group, center or department secretary.
- *Work Unit Leader*, corresponds to the work units leader.
- *Collaborator*, corresponds to a regular collaborator.
- *Anonymous User*, corresponds to a non identified user.

These levels are not hierarchically organized in any capability order. Instead they would be better understood as several levels to control access, in either consulting or change mode, to different information classes depending on the person and on its own user level.

Any access to the InInWeb service will start, by default, in the *Anonymous User* level. Therefore the user will be able to only consult the institutional, or public, information. To change to an authenticated level and so to have access to different service capabilities, the user must select the Identification link that is present at all services pages' footer. The next figure shows the generic identification page.

After the identification link selection, the user must introduce his name, his password, and the desired operation mode (consulting or change). In this page he also could change his password to a newer one.

All the information concerning the authentication mechanisms: user, user levels and passwords are stored in the SQL Server.

In the meantime, how can we ensure that in successive accesses to the InInWeb service the user remains properly identified and accesses only the information he should? One solution is to request the user to systematically supply the password in each access to the server. This would be a very cumbersome solution. Another solution is to pass the password, eventually encrypted, in the URL as a name/value pair. This is a more attractive on the point of view of the user but is not as safe, since any user that somehow got access to the URL of these documents could subsequently access them directly.

Our proposal is based on the latter solution, but introduces a new variable in the model: time. When the URL to access a given restricted document is created, a password (pw') is generated as a result of an encrypting function (cript), whose parameters are the user's original password (pass) and a timestamp (ts). Therefore, pw' = crip(pw, ts).

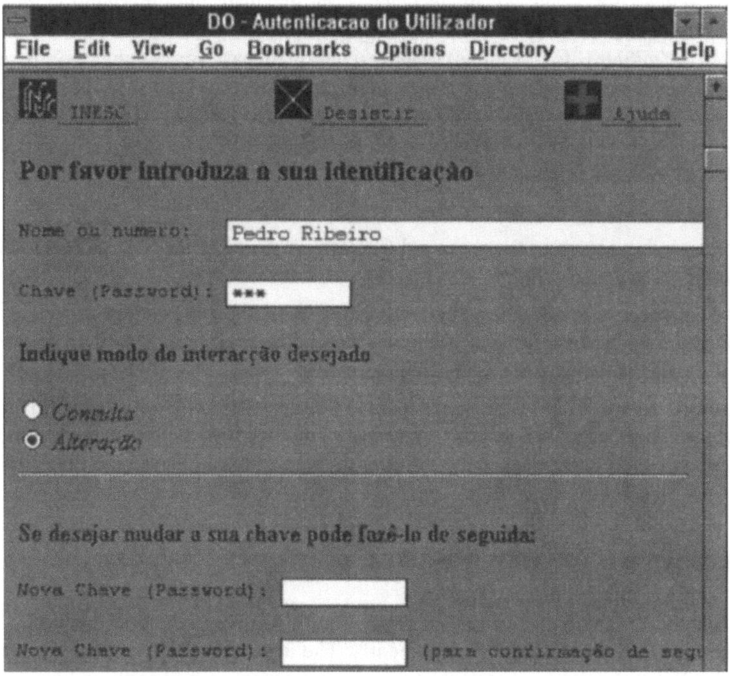


**Figure 5** The generic identification HTML page.

Whenever a request for a new document reaches the gateway, the timestamp stored in that file is checked to ascertain whether the time during which the password would be valid has already expired (5 minutes, for example). The re-encrypted password is then compared with another one generated locally from the password and the timestamp stored in the password file and, if valid, a new timestamp is obtained and a new password is coded. This password is then used to travel across the network. This process is repeated indefinitely.

The effectiveness of this scheme is guaranteed by:

- The user's password is not known;
- Even if someone has access to the password file (that is stored at the SQL Server), will only find encrypted passwords (with UNIX's crypt());
- If someone has access to the encrypting algorithm with the timestamp, won't be able to reproduce the URLs because he doesn't know which is the timestamp stored in the password file, even if he knows which is the encrypted password;
- If someone has access to a re-encrypted password, this one will only be valid until the authorized user makes another access, or at most until a given period (say, 5 minutes) is passed. This is due to the update of the timestamp in each access and to the time limit of its validity.

### 5.2.3 Integration services considerations

In the INESC context it will be developed other administratives services, such as "Human Resources Management" or "Library Management". The implementation of these services will be based on the W3 technology. Therefore one relevant aspect to be handle is how to design and how to build a good integration of the services.

The integration of the various services (gateways) is based on their mutual knowledge, that is, on the knowledge of the URL's each one knows how to deal with. It should be noted that each service must know the address and interfaces that the other services export. But then what happens if one of the gateway is moved to another computer? Or if the interface exported by a service is changed? These aspects are relatively important in the development of distributed applications.

There are several technological solutions (DCE [DCE 92], CORBA [CORBA 91], COM [Udell 94]), each with its own specificities. The solution we used, W3, presents some of the problems referred above and which other technologies try to solve, namely the problem of name identification in distributed environments. Ideally, documents should be accessible independently of their physical location. This requirement implies a name server, which is still a research issue in the W3 context.

## 6 RELATED WORK

The W3 services construction, i.e. the development of CGI gateways that could dynamically generate HTML pages based on heterogeneous data repositories, is currently one important research and industrial area of interest. There are around the world others projects more or less similar to our, which are relevant to be referred:

- OMNIWeb [Matheus 95], from the National Space Science Data Center (NSSDC), USA. OMNIWeb provides access to a wide variety of data from NASA missions, allowing users to produce plots and retrieve data.
- Hyper-G [Andrews 95], from the Institute for Information Processing and Computer Supported New Media (IICM), USA. Hyper-G is a large-scale, multi-protocol, distributed, hypermedia information system that uses an object oriented database layer to provide information structuring and link maintenance facilities.
- OMNIS-WWW server [Clausnitzer 95], from the Technical University of Munich, Germany. OMNIS is a multimedia information retrieval system for the administration of documents in libraries and offices, and OMNIS-WWW server is a gateway between the OMNIS server and any W3 client.
- O2Web [O2Web 95], from the O2 Technology - SA, France. O2Web is said to integrate all the benefits of database technology with a complete set of tools to develop and deploy a W3 server based on the proprietary O2 system.

## 7 CONCLUSIONS AND FUTURE WORK

This paper has tackled the problem of management of institutional and administrative information in medium to large organizations, in which the information is distributed in various formats and data repositories. An adequate solution, which uses different technologies of informatics and telecommunications, such as W3 and relational databases, has been presented. The feasibility of the integration of different services and applications, namely the "Organization Folder", the "Timecards" and the "Project Management" executed in heterogeneous and distributed environments, supported by the technologies referred to above, has been demonstrated.

The most relevant advantages of the services developed and the technology used are:

- Computation based on the client-server model over an heterogeneous and distributed environment.
- Information locality transparent to the final user. Some information is kept in data bases in one, or more, machines. Other part of the information (mainly text or image information) could be kept locally at the chosen machine of each entity.
- Attractive user access and interface. Possibility of using graphical interfaces (GUI) with all of their inherent characteristics.

- Multi-platform clients, which means that the services developed could be accessed and executed from multiple environments, namely MS-Windows, Macintosh, X-Windows or VT-terminals.
- Possibility to mix traditional information with multimedia such as text, images, graphics, sound and video.
- Possibility to access different and heterogeneous data repositories.
- Guarantee of privacy and security in the information access and its management.

Although some limitations of the current W3 technology became apparent. There are important restrictions in the development of services whose aim is to be more than simple hypertext search and retrieval systems. The main limitations for our purposes have been the following:

- The W3 tools (clients, servers, editors, application development) are still in an initial stage of development (and not a mature technology)
- The hypertext paradigm underlying the W3 is not always the most adequate, specially in the tasks to manage database information (creation, modification, deletion)
- Definition of forms with several management, control and visualization limitations
- The HTTP protocol does not support secure (privacy and authenticated) transactions, namely:
  - the confidentiality of the information in the transaction is not guaranteed;
  - there is no guarantee of the identification of the entities involved in the transaction.

  The evolution of the protocol to support security is now under discussion [S-HTTP94].
- HTTP is a stateless protocol not very adequate to the traditional informatic services.

The work described in this paper, although interesting to the operation of the organization where it was developed, was mainly a case study to try out the emerging W3 technology. Future developments include:

- New administrative services.
- Continue with the design and implementation of new GENESIS library functionalities.
- Authentication and security mechanisms to be analyzed and thought out at the level of the definition of user profiles and concession of associated privileges, in a coherent and normalized way for an increasing number of services.
- Start the design of an authoring environment to help the W3 services development.
- Follow W3 and telematics technology tendencies, namely the Http-New Generation protocol and its specifications in the field of security, distribution and client-server interaction.

## 8 REFERENCES

Andrews, K. et al. (1995) Serving information to the Web with Hyper-G. *Computer Network and ISDN Systems*, vol.27 nº6, 819-26, April 1995.

Berners-Lee, T.; Cailliau, R.; Luotonen, A.; Nielsen, H.F. and Secret, A.. (1994) The World-Wide Web. Communications of the ACM., 76-82, August 1994.

Clausnitzer, A. et al.(1995) A WWW interface to the OMNIS/Myriad literature retrieval engine. *Computer Network and ISDN Systems*, vol.27 nº6, 1017-26, April 1995.

CODASYL (1978) Data Description Language Committee Report. Information Systems. vol. 3 nº4, 247-320.

Codd, E.F. (1970) A Relational Model for Large Shared Data Banks. *Communications of the ACM*, vol.13 nº6, 377-87, June 1970.

CORBA (1991) OMG. The Common Object Request Broker: Architecture and Specification.

DCE (1992) OSF. Introduction to DCE. Prentice-Hall.

INESC (1994) INESC's Institutional Information.

Matheus, G. J. and Towherd, S. (1995) NSSDC OMNIWeb: The first space physics WWW-based data browsing and retrieval system. *Computer Network and ISDN Systems*, vol.27 nº6, 801-8, April 1995.

O2Web (1995) O2 Technology. O2Web - Using object technology to build an Enterprise WWW Server. Commercial information. See also: HTTP://www.o2tech.fr.

Rumbaugh, J. et al. (1991) *Object-Oriented Modelling and Design*. Prentice Hall, New Jersey.

Sybase (1994) Sybase, Inc. Open Client DB-Library/C Reference Manual Release 10.0..

S-HTTP (1994) Draft of the Secure HTTP (S-HTTP) Protocol.
ftp://ftp.commerce.net/information/standards/drafts/sHTTP.txt

Udell, J. (1994) Componentware. *Byte*, May 1994.

## 9 BIOGRAPHY

Silva, A. is a researcher at INESC and an assistant lecturer at the IST/UTL (Technical University of Lisbon). His main interests are distributed computation, authoring tools, data bases and telematic applications development.

Borbinha, J. is a researcher at INESC and an assistant lecturer at the IST/UTL (Technical University of Lisbon). His main interests are in the telematic systems, in the organizational engineer and interfaces.

Delgado, J. is a researcher at INESC and a teacher at the IST/UTL (Technical University of Lisbon). His main interests are in the areas of domotic systems and telematic systems for the end users.

# 7

# A Federated Information System for Quality Management Processes*

*P. Peters, P. Szczurko, M. Jarke*
*Informatik V, RWTH Aachen,*
*Ahornstr. 55, 52056 Aachen, Germany*
*email: {peters,szczurko,jarke}@informatik.rwth-aachen.de*
*Phone/Fax: +49 241 8021521/ +49 241 8888321*

*M. Jeusfeld*
*University of Science and Technology, ISMT, Kowloon, Hong Kong*
*email: jeusfeld@usthk.ust.hk*

**Abstract**

As the structure of modern organisations changes to networks of decentralised, autonomous units, the demands on information systems alter from simple sources of data to links that connect those units along the workflows and support groups of knowledge workers with timely and task appropriate information. Fulfilling this task depends heavily on the ability to change the information system according to the business process evolution. As our approach to deal with those problems, we present a task oriented, federated information system architecture. We show the impact of this approach in an example where quality management tasks and systems in the industrial product life cycle has been integrated. Starting from the integration of task and information modelling based on a repository architecture, we show how conceptual models support communication and information access in the heterogenous environment by directly relating tasks to the information they need or provide. Furthermore, we propose an information system change process that exploits the described relations between task and information modeling.

**Keywords**

Federated Information System Architecture, Quality Management Processes, Repositories, Information Access Mechanisms

---

* This work was supported by the German Ministry of Research and Technology under grant 02QF3004/1, by the DFG Graduate College 'Computer Science and Technology' at RWTH Aachen and by the European Community under Information Systems Interoperability Project No ECAUS003 and Basic Research Working Group No.8319 (ModelAge)

# 1 TASK ORIENTED INFORMATION SYSTEMS

In order to improve business processes, the organisation of industrial work is in the midst of transformation. Functionally divided, vertically integrated and hierarchically organised firms give way to process networks of islands integrated by flows of material and information ((Brynjolfsson and Mendelson, 1993), (Davenport *et al.*, Fall 1992), (Hammer and Champy, 1993), (Warnecke, 1992)). The interplay of ideas from Organisational Theory and the technological development in information science established the ideal of the 'flexible corporation' that meets customers' needs, makes effective use of assets and is able to adapt itself to new ways of working or changing business demands ((Hammer and Champy, 1993), (Markus and Robey, 1988), (Scott-Morton, 1994)).

Organsational consequences of this idea mainly deal with matters of distribution: How should information be distributed along the business processes? What responsibilities should be given to the agents performing the process steps? How much distribution is needed at all? What are the main aspects of integration is this distributed environment? ((Hammer, 1992), (Pels and Wortmann, 1992), (Veryard and Macdonald, 1994)) Based on these questions several proposals for both federated management concepts ((Huber and McDaniel, 1986), (Warnecke, 1992)) and information systems ((Davenport *et al.*, Fall 1992), (Sheth and Larson, 1990) , (Sol, 1992)) argued that responsibilities for tasks as well as information resources should be distributed along the defined processes. From the information systems viewpoint, computer networks and access mechanisms to distributed information sources stored in databases are the technologically available backbone for the implementation of federated information systems ((Abramovici and Bickelmann, 1993), (Sol, 1992), (Arens *et al.*, 1993), (Brodie and Ceri, 1992)). Nevertheless, there are a multitude of organisational, conceptual, and information management problems to be solved in designing and implementing **process oriented information storage, access, or manipulation** of data.

Hierachically structured departments have to be reorganised and integrated with respect to the business processes that should be supported. In addition to the spatial distance between working groups along the process chain there always exists a **conceptual distance**. For historical, technical or educational reasons, people use different language to describe their work and the information they need to perform it. Ideas proposed for the conceptual integration of distributed information sources range from information descriptions using standards or company-wide data dictionaries ((Scheer, 1994), (Shaw, 1991)) to fully federated systems where all sources provide interfaces to outside users (Menzel *et al.*, 1992). In recent years, the repository approach is becoming popular for the conceptual integration of systems in the business process reengineering context, because it allows modeling the relations between information and the environment in which it is used at various levels of abstraction (see, e.g., (Carlson and Ram, 1992), (Chen *et al.*, 1992), (Jarke *et al.*, 1993), (Woo and Lochovsky, 1992)).

Another problem is the **task-oriented access to and availability of information**. Information is just a means to support effective and efficient action of the responsible teams and persons ((Huber and McDaniel, 1986),(Gerrits, 1993)), and the access to information should fulfill the needs of the task performing agent. But it also has to be restricted to information necessary to perform the task in order to avoid information overload phenomena. Concepts for task adequate information management have been developed (e.g. (Daft and Lengel, 1986) and (Hammer, 1992)). Though they have influenced data modeling , they are rarely implemented with respect to business process oriented information distribution and access today.

A third major problem is the **management of change** once a information system is installed. Implemented technical solutions tend to freeze the state of the organisation because they support given work structures. That's why process changes often are costly and lengthy ((Sol, 1992), (Warnecke, 1992)). But in an environment of steady changes the ability of fast adaptation to new requirements is a major competitive advantage. With business processes in the center of interest, the consequences of changing processes or products should lead directly to the identification and implementation of change with respect to the information system. This is possible only if process and information models are intertwined and is manageable with acceptable costs only if all parts of the system are clearly separable not only technologically but also conceptually.

The contribution of this paper is an information system design that is a trade off between high conceptual and system integration which facilitates fast business process execution, and clear system separation allowing better management of change. We will start with a description of the repository-based federated information system architecture developed during the WibQuS project. This project deals with the integration of quality management methods along the product life cycle in manufacturing. After reviewing the impact of conceptual modeling on the method integration task, we will show how communication and information access tasks are managed in the given architecture. Based on the experiences in the project, information access mechanisms at various levels of automation are presented. Finally, we will describe, how change processes and database evolution are facilitated by the knowledge stored in the repository and the developed communication mechanisms.

## 2 THE WIBQUS PROJECT

The goal of the Germany-wide WibQuS project is the integration of quality management methods based on information flows. In order to achieve high quality goals, those methods are embedded in all stages of the product life cycle from design tasks supported by Quality Function Deployment (QFD) to methods and tools for service engineers ((Jarke *et al.*, 1993), (Peters and Jeusfeld, 1994)). Quality management processes are of special interest in task oriented information management because information flows occur in various types (data, knowledge, strategy) between differing method executing agents (automated systems, engineers, teams). Additionally, the transfer of product and process information not only follows the product life cycle, but is crucial also along multiple control loops from the manufacturing floors back to work preparation and product planning. The implementation of those control flows is essential in order to achieve and maintain high level product and process quality (Pfeifer, 1993).

Information system development in the WibQuS project is based on a repository approach (ISO/IEC 10027, 1990). It started with a conceptual modeling phase, where all engineering teams, located at seven research institutes in four cities, had to develop a model of their

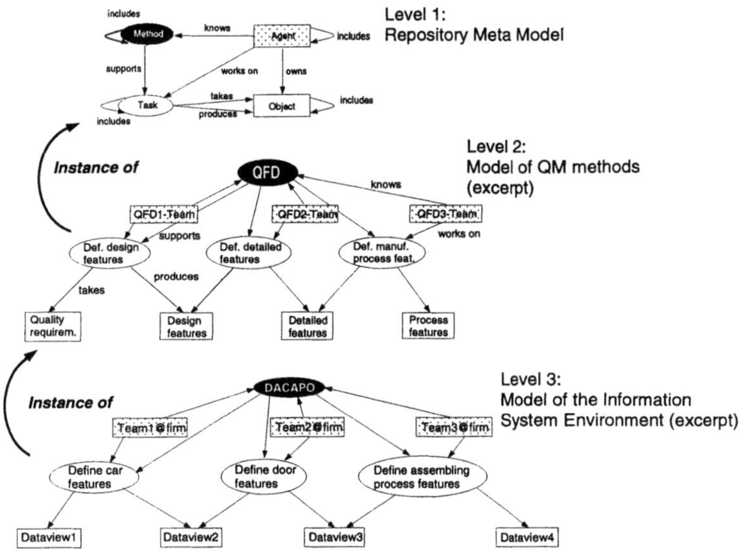


**Figure** 1 The levels of the WibQuS repository

method by instantiating the meta model depicted at Figure 1. This process, facilitated by the client-server architecture of the object base management system ConceptBase (Jarke *et al.*, 1995), was performed mainly for two reasons*:

1. To facilitate interoperation between the performing agents by establishing a common language (the conceptual model). In the model that forms this language, the methods have been related semantically by detecting information needs and sources that connect the various methods (represented by **objects** that connect **tasks** performed by different **methods** in Figure 1). These connections served as a starting point for information modeling on the data level.
2. To explicitly relate informations to the tasks that consume or produce them and to the agents that perform the tasks (see also (Mylopoulos *et al.*, 1993)). This way the needs, skills and responsibilities of agents in a specific decision process can be taken into consideration which is a first step to 'task and decision process oriented' information management.

The result of the modeling process was the integration of all models in one model of quality management methods containing 500 objects at level 2 of the repository. This model is a central element of the WibQuS information system architecture, because it describes conceptually the possible information flows with respect to the tasks to be solved (see Figure 1). Based on that model, the engineers in the next phase formulated the data models of their databases and the technical means for information exchange between the tasks at level 3 of the repository.

* A more detailed description of the distributed modeling process is given in (Peters and Szczurko, 1994).

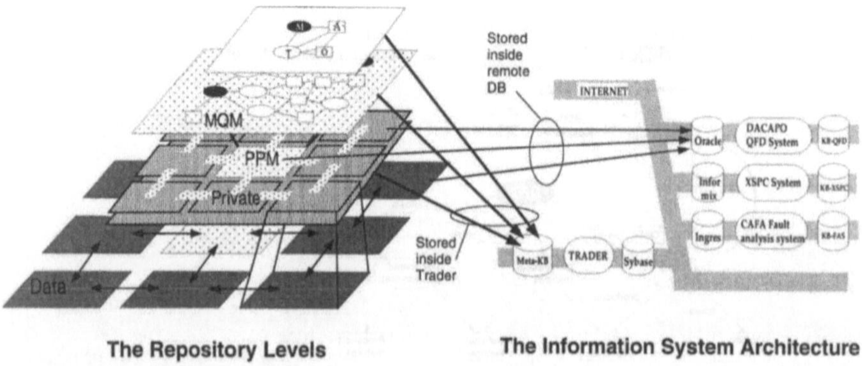


**Figure** 2 The WibQuS project

This was done by instantiation of the modeled **objects** at the method model level with relational schemas on the data level describing the contents of the **object**. The information needed for a specific **Task** form a view on these relational schemas (see Figure 5 for an example). **Agents** and **Tasks** are instantiated by an example organisational setting used in the WibQuS project and the **Methods** are instantiated by objects describing the tool configuration developed by the engineers for this specific method.

Technologically, standards like Internet as network communication protocol and SQL-databases as interfaces of the knowledge-based systems form a good framework for the federated architecture. This setting describes the typical industrial situation quite well. In order to keep the methods as autonomous as possible we needed a central communication manager that performs and controls information exchange. The *Quality Trader** stores and provides knowledge about the data and services of the whole information system (see Figure 2): It consists of an SQL-gateway that handles the technical connection to the federated databases, a number of communication processing mechanisms described in the following sections, and the repository stored in ConceptBase. In addition to the already described models at the higher levels, it contains all schema information of the SQL-databases that form level 3 of the repository with respect to the concept **Object**. This schema information consists of two parts :

1. The *Product and Process Model* (PPM) which is a globally available schema describing information that requires overall agreement because it is used in (almost) every method, e.g., product structure trees, or manufacturing process information.
2. *Private exchange schemas*, describing information of interest only for few agents like specific method results, e.g., matrix structures of QFD.

The distinction between those schema types prevents the company data schema from getting unmanageable, because changes in a special method might lead to changes in the relational schema of that method, but it does not influence other system schemas as long as the PPM is

---

* This approach is similar to the trader concept of Open Distributed Processing ((Raymond, 1995), (Bearman, 1995)) but restricted to database functionality.

not changed. Additionally, it emphasizes the autonomy of the participating groups: As long as information provided by a group is of interest only for one or two methods in the system, the group remains responsible for the schema, its evolution, or bilateral negotiations about information needed by other methods (c.f. sections 4,5). Only information of global interest should be represented in a globally identifiable and accessible way.

Nevertheless, all schemas, private or global, in WibQuS have to be represented in the Quality Trader, because it is responsible for the execution of all communication based on relational queries, especially if it refers to data distributed over several systems. The mechanisms underlying the communication in the given setting are described in the following section.

## 3 COMMUNICATION IN THE TRADER ARCHITECTURE

Queries, the basic communication technique of the Trader Architecture, are facilitated technically in two ways: First, all system configurations and their Internet addresses are represented at level 3 of the repository, instantiating the described **Methods**. So, in addition to the relational schemas, all routing informations are part of the Trader's knowledge base and the user need not care about where information is stored. Second, the SYBASE OmniSQL* server is able to connect to and communicate with all databases included in the system architecture if the routing informations are given. This simplifies the query formulation and data transfer between the four used database brands, because the user (or the knowledge-based system) must know only his own SQL-'dialect'.

Although these technical preconditions are helpful in implementing communication mechanisms, using SQL as a language is too restrictive to support efficient communication for several reasons:

1. It restricts system interfaces to relational databases.
2. The user has to learn the complex language to use the system. Even if he knows the language he still has to look up the schema information, find the information sources, and formulate the probably lengthy queries when he needs fast information access.
3. It restricts communication to the pure database access.

Because we wanted to embed other communication mechanisms like message broadcasting or assignment negotiation in the system, especially the last point caused the definition of a more abstract request language. It is based on relational concepts and predefined queries but is easily transferable to other environments. This communication exchange relation schema (see Figure 4). allows to take a relatively simple predictable view on information requests using predefined queries or by naming a **predicate**, filling in the **argument list** and putting the **order** into the systems order request list.

The whole process is exemplified by the search for features of a specific Product Structure Element (PSE) in Figure 3. The requesting agent puts a tuple with the predicate and its arguments into his order relation. The Quality Trader recognizes the requests, looks up the

* SYBASE OmniSQL is a trademark of Sybase Inc.

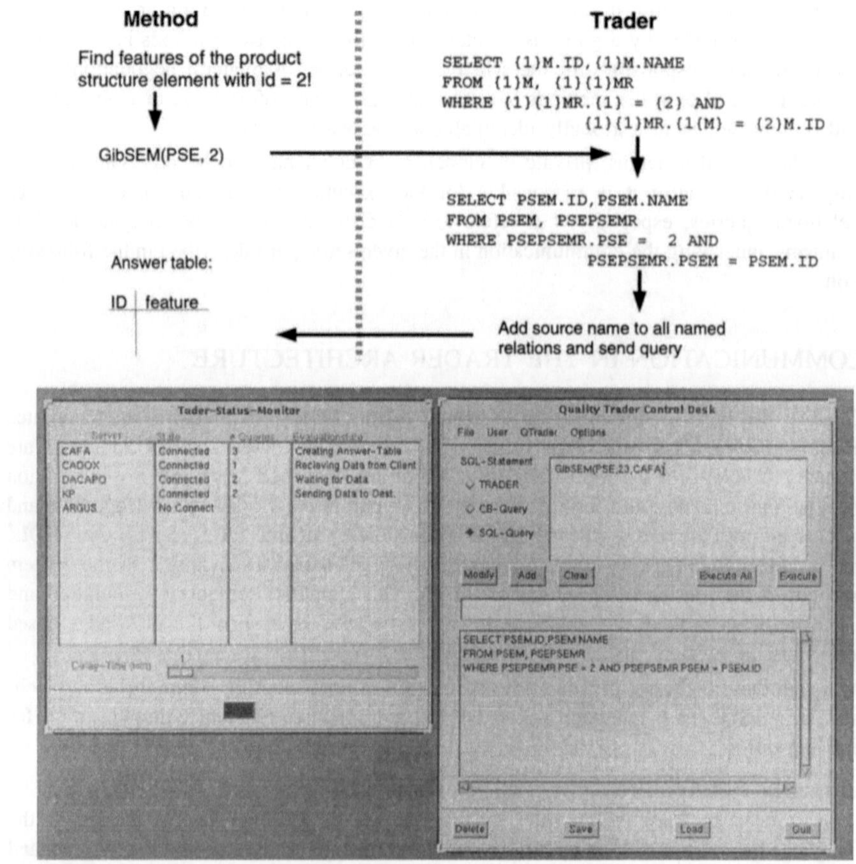


**Figure** 3 Requesting product element features using the **order** concept

query template related to the predicate, fills in the argument, and performs the query. He collects the answer tables and sends them back to the requesting system.

The Quality Trader windows depicted in Figure 3 are an application built for system engineering and control in the federated environment. The control desk allows manipulations on the repository using the ConceptBase Query Language and on all SQL-databases connected by using the facilities provided by OmniSQL. The status monitor gives an overview of the systems connected at the moment and the state of the queries currently under evaluation.

In detail, the process of order evaluation is the following (see also Figure 4): Placing the **predicate** and the **argument list** in the **order** relation and setting the value of the **comstate** relation to 1 initiates the order evaluation process by the Quality Trader based on triggers defined on the **comstate** relation:

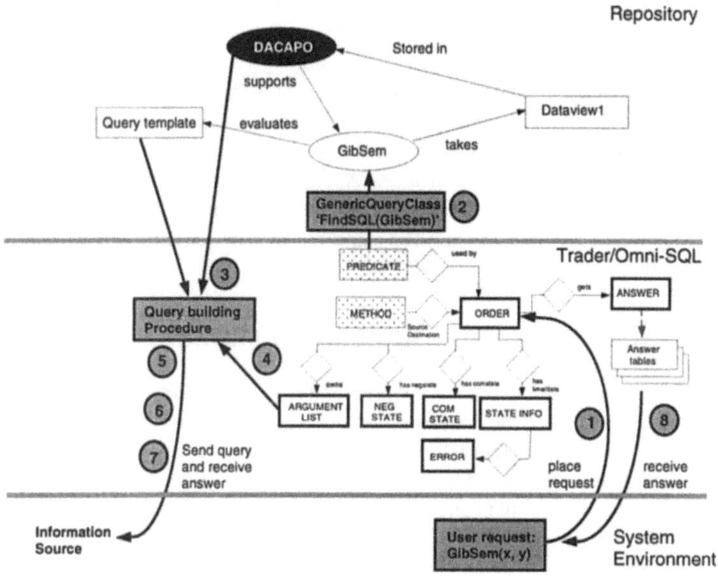


**Figure** 4 The order evaluation process.

1. **comstate** = 1: The Quality Trader checks the **comstate** relation of every system frequently and starts the query evaluation procedure.
2. The Quality Trader looks up the query represented by the **predicate** (Figure 4). This is done by evaluating the GenericQueryClass 'findSQL(**predicate**)' on the repository. Each predicate is represented as an instance of **Task** at repository level 3.
3. The relations which are involved into the query are related to the systems in which they are stored. The Quality Trader finds those information source(s) using the **stored in** attribute added to the structure of the repository.
4. The query variables in the predefined **query template** are instantiated with the **argument list** and the locations found in step 3.
5. SYBASE OmniSQL transfers the query into the database dialect(s) of the source(s). **Comstate** = 2
6. Execution of the (distributed) query.
7. The Quality Trader collects the answer(s) and transforms it into the dialect of the requesting system. **Comstate** = 3
8. The answer table is sent to the requesting system. **Comstate** = 4
9. The Quality Trader documents the querying process for statistical purposes.

Depending on the type of predicate referred to in the request, the **order** can be a query as in the example of Figure 3, a message to be broadcasted or a real assignment. This would lead to the initiation of a negotiation process between the involved methods supported by a mechanism based on the **negstate** relation that is currently under development.

Therefore, the implementation of the **order** concept solves the problems mentioned in the beginning of the section: It is at least more user-friendly than SQL, it allows other communication than pure data queries, and the language need not to be changed from the user's point of view if information sources other than SQL databases are added to the system. Because of the predefined queries the developed mechanism is restricted to a limited number of communication processes: *Highly standardised negotiation processes or information requests that can be detected and defined in advance.* According to the engineers using the system, there exist a lot of requests that are predictable or even automatable (embedded into the knowledge-based systems), but at least the same number of requests are *ad hoc* and needs different support.

# 4 GRAPHICAL INFORMATION ACCESS TO FEDERATED DATABASES

As a lot of the information needs are not predictable during quality management processes, the need for user-friendly ad hoc information access becomes obvious. But the classical problems of query languages (hard to learn, difficult to use, not adapted to the specific domain) are even more complicated in federated information systems. First, there are several query languages used in the system and second, there is no central database schema known by all system members but a number of loosely coupled schemas where structure and contents of the database are not easily understandable at once for someone looking for information. The advantages of graphical database browsing and access mechanisms for central databases have been pinpointed in various publications ((d'Atri, 1989), (Wong and Kuo, 1982), (Zhou, 1994)) and they are at least as striking for federated systems as we will show in this section.

The conceptual models of method interaction and product-/process structures were the starting point for a browsing and querying tool currently under development. Starting from the browsing facilities of ConceptBase and recent approaches in graphical query languages ((Consens *et al.*, 1992), (Zhou, 1994)), we are currently creating a *task and view-oriented information system browser* that allows direct access to information provided by the systems in the WibQuS environment.

As mentioned before, the model of quality management methods and all schema information are stored in the Quality Trader. This adds up to about thousand objects and searching the whole repository would be inefficient. Therefore, we started structuring it by first separating the method model from the database schema information and second dividing the schema information into PPM (general interest) and private schemas. This led to the browsing window layout shown in Figure 5. To adjust the search space to the tasks to be supported we have developed a view concept that restricts the information provided at the windows (Peters *et al.*, 1995a). The given instances of views were the result of various discussions with the quality management engineers:

1. **The Method View:**
   This view puts the method and its tasks into the center of focus. All information flows (**objects**) **taken** by a specific **Task** and its subtasks are displayed at the MQM window. All schema information to a selected **Object** in the MQM window is displayed in the database schema window (These are the relations named 'dataview' in Figure 1 and 4).

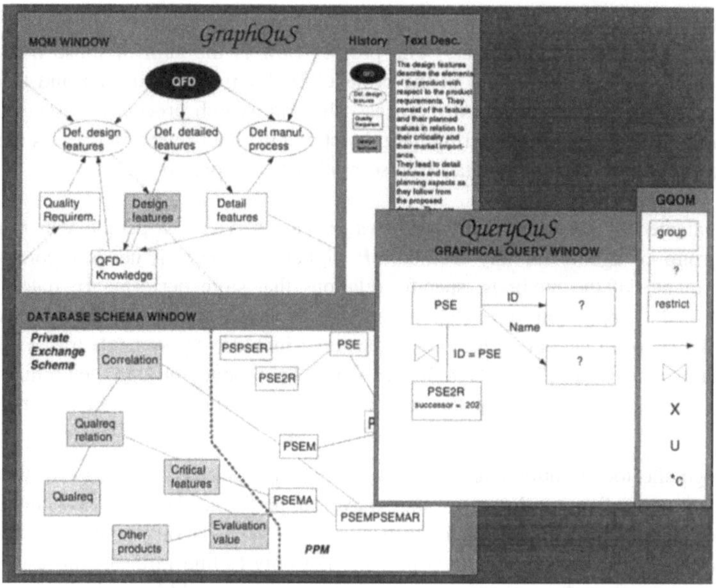


**Figure** 5 The information search and access tools

E.g., if an engineer working on a QFD uses the method view, all tasks related to QFD come up together with the connecting information flows (Figure 5). If he selects the 'Design features' object, the schema window displays relations representing the designed product structure (PSE, PSE2R) together with the product features and their values (other displayed PPM objects). Additionally, private relations are displayed describing relations between the features and the quality requirements to be fulfilled. Now the engineer can compose the query he wants to ask using the graphical query window.

2. **The Information View:**
   While the first view groups around the method, the second focuses on the information related to a specific product. If information about a specific product structure is needed, selecting the PSE relation leads to the display of the method from which the PSE relation originates. This is he method that first fills the relation during the product life cycle or the one responsible for the administration of the relation (In WibQuS for PSE this would be QFD.). The schema window display relations with distance one, meaning that the primary key of PSE is foreign key for the distant relation or the other way round. Further information could be provided by selection of any relation, causing that its connected relations will be displayed.
3. **The Project View:**
   As engineers fill several roles in method performing teams* an overview about a project's specific information context inside the environment is often helpful, because it facilitates

* E.g., there is always a manufacturing plant engineer in a QFD team, who is also responsible for work preparation tasks and the manufacturing process.

the transfer of experiences from one task to another by displaying the specific interrelations among the project informations. The project view is the sum of those method views that show methods performed in the project. If, for instance, design and test data are needed to start the manufacturing process, the data search process is restricted to those methods already performed during the project and the data selection process is facilitated by restricting the available data to those related to the project.

4. **The Service View:**
   As indicated by the name, service views provide services to people which are not in the group of **agents** for any method. If higher management needs reports about the performance of the methods, specific relations that store performance data (like tasks performed, information accesses,...) will be displayed at the schema window. If the contract between the enterprise and its customer include requirements traceability efforts or quality reports fulfilling ISO 900x, the way of the product through the product life cycle could be traced by following the information objects through the quality management tasks.

Although the tool is built mainly to satisfy information needs of users in the WibQuS environment according to the tasks they have to perform, the last view indicates that accelerated search for information in distributed databases is only one advantage of this view concept. Using this concept, it is possible not only to find information fast but also to present it in an task and user appropriate way. Every view could be embedded in a specific presentation tool that might generate quality reports from the SQL-databases or could display charts of the performance results. That way, the interpretation of data would be facilitated causing better and faster decisions (Daft and Lengel, 1986).

After finding the relations from which data should be retrieved, a graphical query can be formulated by shifting relations to the graphical query window and grouping them with operators from the graphical query operations menu (Figure 5). Two operations are performed together with the shift: The database where the relation is stored is attached to the relation (as described in the previous section) and after all needed relations have been shifted, the connections between the relations in the are computed and displayed in order to find possible join paths defined by foreign key dependencies.

The menu provides all operations that are necessary to ensure relational completeness plus a group operator and an operator for recursive queries which is useful especially in engineering environments because a lot of data are described in tree structures (products, machines, processes). The recursion is limited to simple one involving a maximum of two relations.

The formal query definition (Figure 6) follows an approach similar to (Angelaccio *et al.*, 1990). In a first step an SQL-independent representation of the queries is derived when the user formulates his graphical query. The representation consists of a triple *(N, A, X)* for every relation in the window where *N* denotes the relation name, *A* are the selected attributes, and *X* is a relational clause naming the operator and its arguments. Every unary operator causes a change in the related triplet (see projection and selection in figure 3) and every binary operator causes the definition of a new triplet that refers to its argument triplets (see join in figure 3). Because these triplets can be embedded recursively, relational completeness is ensured.

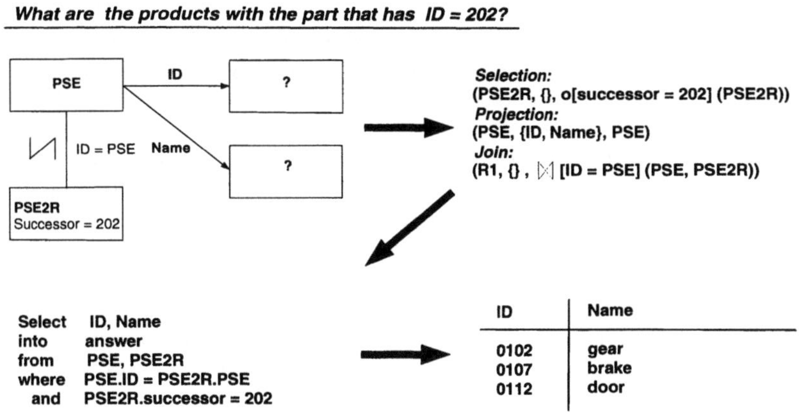


**Figure** 6 Definition and evaluation of a graphical query

In the next step, the generated triplets are translated into the specific SQL-dialect. This can be done by building a query tree (Elmasri and Navathe, 1989) where the whole 'triplet tree' is evaluated from the leaves upward by formulating a query for every triplet and using the results for the evaluation of the father query. This approach causes high network load because a lot of queries have to be sent. We used another approach by defining an interface for the translation of the whole query into OmniSQL, what might lead to higher costs for large join operations but keeps the network load relatively low. As recursive queries cannot be formulated in SQL, we implemented a 'stored procedure' that controls the recursive loop of the querying process performed by OmniSQL. Both the interface and the stored procedure can be transformed easily without changing the formal representation if another SQL-dialect is required.

As mentioned in section 3, the technical part of the querying process is performed by the Sybase OmniSQL gateway. The query answer appears in an separate window as table visualization. As we learned from the engineers, often a sequence of queries is performed, either because the information was not as complete as needed or additional information needs where triggered by the results. To support these step by step processes, we are currently working on query chaining mechanisms for a faster formulation of query sequences.

# 5 MANAGING CHANGE IN THE WIBQUS ENVIRONMENT

The models and information system structure implemented at the moment reflect the state of quality management processes and their support systems as perceived in the WibQuS environment. In this paper we will not reflect on technological changes of the latter, but on the agreement on the processes which are subject to continuous change: the composition of the expert groups may change, new methods are selected depending on management decisions, and the relevance of information is re-evaluated because of growing experience or changing market demands.

In a task oriented approach, changes of the federated information system reflect changes of the supported business processes. Therefore, based on the WibQuS experiences, we propose conceptual modeling of the changes as mediation between the agents perception of change and its representation in the database schemas (see also (Alonso and Barbara, 1989), (Jeusfeld and Szczurko, )). The renewed process model facilitates implementing changes of information access, information needs or content of databases using the Quality Trader functionality.

As the described mechanisms support both communication and information access in a federated information system, they can assist change processes from the introduction of a new method to the schema change of an information object. The first step is the announcement of the possibility of, or the need for, a change in the whole system. In addition to frequent system engineering team meetings this can be done by sending messages using the Trader facilities. To support this change initialisation, we defined two special order types called request announcement and availability announcement. This messages will be send to every method in the system and their arguments describe the subject of change. A comment gives further specifications about the needed/provided information.

The implementation of the two steps of change, conceptual modeling and database adjustment are currently possible only using the quality trader control desk described in section 3. Together with the browsing facilities of ConceptBase it forms a system engineering environment for the repository but changes cannot be propagated to the remote databases and working with this interface turned out quite complicated for the engineering groups. The development of the browsing and access tool described in the previous section provides a more easy-to-use front-end to the repository and even more, together with the OmniSQL-Gateway, to the whole system. We are currently working on an enhancement of the graphical query window to allow its usage as a system design window that supports tell/untell operations on the ConceptBase repository as well as create/update/delete operations on the relational databases.

This allows an engineering process according to the proposal above (Peters *et al.*, 1995b). In a first step the repository is changed using the access mechanisms to the repository. This step consists of changes of the model of quality management methods that induce changes of the relations of the private exchange schema or the PPM. These changes have to be translated into SQL commands using the graphical design mechanisms provided. Finally, order templates can be formulated using the graphical query language.

The information system change process is facilitated by the described tools mainly with respect to **system representation, operation formulation** and **enactment** in all steps. The processing of process changes into relational data model changes into database changes has to be performed by the system engineer together with the user groups. How adjustment in the latter steps depends on changes of the method model is subject of current research (Jeusfeld and Szczurko, ).

# 6 CONCLUSIONS

The method integration approach presented here follows the tradition of heterogeneous database integration (e.g., CORBA (Murphy and Grimson, 1994), MRDSM (Litwin *et al.*, 1990), or CIM/Z (Norrie *et al.*, 1994)) and Distributed Object Management ((Manola *et al.*,

1992), (Saake *et al.*, 1993)). Most of the approaches presented in the field concentrate on information modelling and leave the supported tasks implicit. Influenced by the ideas of business process re-engineering, the explicit connection of the concepts of **task**, the **needed information**, and the **performing agent** has been considered recently as a necessary feature of task adequate information and database management (e.g., (Mylopoulos *et al.*, 1993)).

The evolution process during the WibQuS project showed that business process change management goes hand in hand with engineering information systems on the technical as well as on the conceptual level. Project results and various interviews with the participating engineers validated the feasibility of the implemented information system approach that is based on the idea of integrated task and information modeling. The modeling of quality management methods and their interactions proved to be a right-sized starting point for process integration, information system engineering in the given environment, and task oriented information and change management along the described quality management processes.

The repository based integration of conceptual models of the processes and the information flowing between them forms the cornerstone of the Quality Trader architecture. It is the starting point for the technological solution related to the presented management approach and fits typical business settings in both intra- and interorganisation cooperation, because it is based mainly on standard technology like SQL databases or Internet. Built on those standards, conceptual models and Trader architecture constitute the technical and conceptual environment for several tools currently under development, supporting information management at various levels of automation and enabling fast adaptation to changing information needs.

The advantage of the proposed approach — relying on standard technology — is its disadvantage at the same time: Support is restricted by the technological means integrated into the architecture. Though we are implementing several communication and cooperation mechanisms on top of this technology, one thing we've learned during WibQuS is that communication should be performed using various channels to optimise task performance and workflow. This includes a certain level of redundancy which is often needed as well as task oriented suitability of media (see also, e.g. (Daft and Lengel, 1986)). Certainly, database technology will become more powerful with respect to multimedia, but the integration of multiple communication channels is a main challenge for task oriented information system management.

## REFERENCES

M. Abramovici and S. Bickelmann. Engineering Data Management Systems – Requirements, State of the Art, and Potentials (in German. *CIM*, (5):20–28, 1993.

R. Alonso and D. Barbara. Negotiating Data Access in Federated Database Systems. In *5th Intl. Conf. on Data Engineering*, pages 56–65, 1989.

M. Angelaccio, T. Catarci, and G. Santucci. QBD*: A Graphical Query Language with Recursion. *IEEE Transactions on Software Engineering*, 16(10), 1990.

Y. Arens, C.Y. Chee, C.-N. Hsu, and C.A. Knoblock. Retrieving and Integrating Data from Multiple Information Sources. *Int. Jour. of Intelligent and Cooperative Information Systems*, 2(2):127–158, 1993.

M. Bearman. Trading in Open Distributed Environments (Tutorial). In *International Conference on Open Distributed Processing*, 1995.

M.L. Brodie and S. Ceri. On Intelligent and Cooperative Information Systems: A workshop summary. *Int. Jour. on Intelligent and Cooperative Information Systems*, 1(2):249–290, 1992.

E. Brynjolfsson and H. Mendelson. Information Systems and the Organization of Modern Enterprise. *Journal of Organizational Computing*, 3(3):245 – 256, 1993.

D.A. Carlson and S. Ram. A Knowledge Representation for Modeling Organizational Productivity. *Journal of Organizational Computing*, 2(2):155 – 180, 1992.

M. Chen, Y.I. Liou, and E.S. Weber. Developing Intelligent Organizations: A Context-Based Approach to Individual and Organizational Effectiveness. *Journal of Organizational Computing*, 2(2):181 – 202, 1992.

M.P. Consens, I.F. Cruz, and A.O. Mendelzom. Visualizing Queries and Querying Visualizations. *ACM SIGMOD*, 16(3), 1992.

R.L. Daft and R.H. Lengel. Organizational Information Requirements, Media Richness and Structural Design. *Management Science*, 32(5):554 – 571, 1986.

A. d'Atri. From Browsing to Querying. *IEEE Database Engineering*, 8:110 –117, 1989.

T.H. Davenport, R.G. Eccles, and L. Prusak. Information Politics. *Sloan Management Review*, pages 53 – 65, Fall 1992.

R. Elmasri and S.B. Navathe. *Fundamentals of Database Systems*. B. Cummings Publishing Company, Inc., 1989.

H. Gerrits. Business Process Redesign and Information Systems Design: A happy couple? In N. Prakash, C. Rolland, and B. Pernici, editors, *IFIP Transactions: Information Systems Development Process*. Elsevier Science Publishers B.V., 1993.

M. Hammer and J. Champy. *Reengineering the Company*. Harper Business, New York, 1993.

D. K. Hammer. Lean Information Management: The Integrating Power of Information. In H. J. Pels and J. C. Wortmann, editors, *IFIP Transactions: Integration in Production Management Systems*, pages 147–163. Elsevier Science Publishers B.V., 1992.

G.P. Huber and R.R. McDaniel. The Decision-Making Paradigm of Organizational Design. *Management Science*, 32(5):572 – 589, 1986.

ISO/IEC 10027. Information Technology – Information Resource Dictionary System (IRDS) - Standard. Technical report, 1990.

M. Jarke, M. Jeusfeld, and P. Szczurko. Three Aspects of Intelligent Cooperation in the Quality Life Cycle. *Int. Jour. of Intelligent and Cooperative Information Systems*, 2(4):355–374, 1993.

M. Jarke, R. Gallersdoerfer, M.A. Jeusfeld, M. Staudt, and S. Eherer. ConceptBase – A Deductive Object Base for Meta Data Management. *Journal of Intelligent Information Systems*, 4(2), 1995.

M.A. Jeusfeld and P. Szczurko. Evolution of Federated Database Schemas by Trading Information Resources (*submitted for publication).*

W. Litwin, L. Mark, and N. Roussopoulos. Interoperability of Multiple Autonomous Databases. *ACM Computing Surveys*, 22(3):267–293, 1990.

F. Manola, S. Heiler, D. Georgakopoulos, M. Hornick, and M. Brodie. Distributed Object Management. *Int. Jour. of Intelligent and Cooperative Information Systems*, 1(1):5–42, 1992.

M.L. Markus and D. Robey. Information Technology and Organizational Change: Causal Structure in Theory and Research. *Management Science*, 34(5):583 – 598, 1988.

C. Menzel, R.J. Mayer, and L. K. Sanders. Representation, Information Flow, and Model Integration. In C. Petrie, editor, *Enterprise Integration Modeling*, pages 131 – 141, 1992.

J.P. Murphy and J.B. Grimson. A CORBA based Architecture for Multidatabase Systems. In *Int. Conf. on Data and Knowledge Systems for Manufacturing and Engineering*, pages 630–635, Hong Kong, 1994.

J. Mylopoulos, T. Rose, and C. Woo. Task-Oriented Development of Intelligent Information Systems. In M. Papazolou, editor, *Int. Conf. on Intelligent and Cooperative Information Systems*, pages 206 – 219, Rotterdam, The Netherlands, 1993.

M.C. Norrie, W. Schaad, H.-J. Schek, and M. Wunderli. CIM through Database Coordination. In *Int. Conf. on Data and Knowledge Systems for Manufacturing and Engineering*, pages 258 – 263, Hong Kong, 1994.

H. J. Pels and J. C. Wortmann. Integration in Production Management Systems: An Integrating Perspektive. In H. J. Pels and J. C. Wortmann, editors, *Integration in Production Management Systems*, pages 1–13. Elsevier Science Publishers B.V., 1992.

P. Peters and M.A. Jeusfeld. Structuring Information Flow in Quality Management. In *Int. Conf. on Data and Knowledge Systems for Manufacturing and Engineering*, pages 258 – 263, Hong Kong, 1994.

P. Peters and P. Szczurko. Integrating Models of Quality Management by an Object-oriented Repository. In *2nd Biennal European Joint Conf. on Engineering Systems Design and Analysis*, London, England, 1994.

P. Peters, U. Loeb, and A. Rodriguez Pardo. A Task-Oriented Graphical Interface to Federated Databases. In *Proc. of 3rd Int. Conf. of the Int. Soc. for Decision Support Systems*, Hong Kong, 1995.

P. Peters, P. Szczurko, M. Jarke, and M. Jeusfeld. Business Process Oriented Information Management: Conceptual Models at Work. In *Proc. of Int. Conf. on Organizational Computing Systems*, San Jose, Calif., 1995.

T. Pfeifer. *Quality Management (in German).* Carl Hanser Verlag, Muenchen, 1993.

K. Raymond. Reference Model of Open Distributed Processing (RM-ODP): Introduction (Tutorial). In *International Conference on Open Distributed Processing*, 1995.

G. Saake, R. Jungclaus, and T. Hartmann. Application Modelling in Heterogeneous Environments Using an Object Specification Language. In M. Papazolou, editor, *Int. Conf. on Intelligent and Cooperative Information Systems*, pages 309–318, Rotterdam, The Netherlands, 1993.

A.-W. Scheer. *Wirtschaftsinformatik (Reference Models for Industrial Business Processes, in German)*. Spriner Verlag, Berlin, Heidelberg,..., 1994.

M.S. Scott-Morton. The 1990s research program: Implications for Management and the Emerging Organization. *Decision Support Systems*, 12(2):251–256, 1994.

N. Shaw. STEP Part 1 – overview and fundamental principles. Technical report, 1991.

A.P. Sheth and J.A. Larson. Federated Database Systems for Managing Distributed, Heterogeneous, and Autonomous Databases. *ACM Computing Surveys*, 22(3):183–237, 1990.

E.-J. Sol. CIM – Communication and Information in Manufacturing. In H. J. Pels and J. C. Wortmann, editors, *IFIP Transactions: Integration in Production Management Systems*, pages 13–21. Elsevier Science Publishers B.V., 1992.

R.A. Veryard and I.G. Macdonald. EMM/ODP: A Methodology for Federated and Distributed Systems. In A.A. Verrijn-Stuart and T.W. Olle, editors, *IFIP Transactions: Methods and Tools for the Information System Life Cycle* . Elsevier Science Publishers B.V., 1994.

H.-J. Warnecke. *The Fractal Factory (in German)*. Springer-Verlag, 1992.

H.K.T. Wong and I. Kuo. GUIDE: Graphical User Interface for Database Exploration. In *Proc. of the 8th Very Large Databases Conference*, 1982.

C.C. Woo and F.H. Lochovsky. Knowledge Communication in Intelligent Information Systems. *Int. Journal of Intelligent and Cooperative Information Systems*, 1(1):203–228, 1992.

J. Zhou. GUI to Databases – Survey and Practice. *GI Datenbank Rundbrief*, 13:49–51, 1994.

# 7 BIOGRAPHIES

Peter Peters studied computer science and medical informatics at the University of Dortmund, Germany. He is currently a doctoral student at the 'Graduate College for Computer Science and Engineering' and a member of the Information Systems group at the Technical University of Aachen. In his research he investigates the modeling, enactment, and analysis of information flow and communication in distributed organisations. During this work he has been participating in the interdisciplinary project WibQuS funded by the german ministry of research.

Peter Szczurko studied computer science and medical informatics at the Technical University of Aachen, Germany, where he is currently employed as a doctoral student and research assistant in the Information Systems group. In his research, he investigates the use of knowledge-based technology in quality management for distributed organisations, and has been participating in the interdisciplinary project WibQuS funded by the german ministry of research, as well as in projects concerning workflow management and quality control in medicine and chemical engineering. Since 1994, he is co-chair of the regional group Aachen within the German computer society, GI.

Matthias Jarke is professor of Information Systems and chairman of the computer science department at the Technical University of Aachen, Germany. After obtaining a doctorate from the University of Hamburg, Germany, in 1980, he held faculty positions at New York

University and the University of Passau prior to joining Aachen. His research interests lie in the development and usage of meta information systems for design applications.He has been coordinator of two European ESPRIT projects in this field, DAIDA (knowledge-based information system environments) and NATURE (requirements engineering environments), and was principal investigator in collaborative projects concerning IS applications in mechanical engineering (WibQuS) and medicine. He is editor-in-chief of the journal 'Information Systems'

Manfred Jeusfeld is currently a visiting professor at the Hong Kong University of Science and Technology. After obtaining his doctorate from the University of Aachen, he was employed as assistant professor at the Information Systems Group at the University of Aachen. During the ESPRIT projects DAIDA and COMPULOG (Computational Logic) he was a main developer of the ConceptBase system. He also was a main researcher in collaborative projects concerning IS applications in mechanical engineering (WibQuS) and medicine.

# 8

# A support environment for the disclosure of heterogeneous systems documentation

*D.H. Fijma, T.F. Verhoef, G.M. Wijers*
*ID Research*
*Kastanjelaan 4, 3833 AN Leusden, The Netherlands.*
*Tel. +31 33 951416, Fax. +31 33 945845.*
*E-mail: {DFijma, DVerhoef, GWijers}@idr.iaf.nl*

**Abstract**

It is difficult to support the reuse of system components satisfactorily. This holds in particular for organisations in which responsibility for systems and system components is distributed over the organisation and in which many different systems documentation techniques are used. For those organisations, it is important to dispose of a support environment for the disclosure of heterogeneous systems documentation, which is characterised by flexibility and distribution. The requirements of such support environments are discussed. Based on these requirements the concepts and functionality of a prototype of such an environment are presented. Finally, it is discussed how different types of systems documentation from various sources can be handled by the prototype.

**Keywords**

Systems documentation, information distribution, decentralisation, reuse.

## 1. Introduction

Reuse of system components (Biggerstaf, 1989) has been widely recognised as a means to improve productivity of IT departments and, by consequence, to control the costs of systems development and especially of systems maintenance. In practice however, reuse of system components has proven to be a difficult goal to achieve, due to many different reasons. In this article, we point out two of those issues and deal with them:

- **Lack of standards** If an organisation lacks well defined standards for the documentation of the systems developed and their components, many different techniques are used. This hinders the reuse of system components across organisation units.
- **Decentralisation of responsibility** While being advantageous in other aspects, an organisation structure with a high degree of decentralisation poses problems with respect to reuse. Responsibility for systems and system components is distributed over the organisation. Efficient communication of the documentation of available components becomes an important issue.

For organisations which are characterised by these two elements and which are willing to stimulate reuse of system components at the same time, it is important to dispose of a support environment for the disclosure of heterogeneous systems documentation in a way that is transparent with respect to the structure of and responsibility for the documentation contained in it.

In the literature, different environments have been described that support these requirements partially, e.g. (Arnold, 1987), (Brorsson, 1991), (Helm, 1991), (Garg, 1990). The flexibility of the environments described is not high enough for our needs. They offer only one, fixed, information model, to support a specific type of user documentation. Also, some of the environments support only a specific system development technique.

Naturally, the issues of flexibility and distribution in relation with systems documentation are discussed in literature. The environments described in (Freitag, 1994) and (Constantopoulos, 1992) both offer a variable document structure that can be used to define the specific documentation forms needed. Distribution is offered in the environment discussed in (van Oosterom, 1993). The particular combination, however, of the requirements of flexibility and distribution on an environment for the disclosure of systems documentation, has not been dealt with satisfactorily.

As an alternative to using specialised support environment for systems documentation, CASE tools could be considered. CASE tools that support flexibility are available (so-called CASE shells). Controlled distribution is a weaker point of CASE tools. As far as this is supported, the tools lack possibilities to communicate documentation across different organisational units, particularly if these groups use different techniques for systems documentation. The current generation of support environments does not support distribution *and* flexibility satisfactorily at the same time.

The problem situation sketched above has shown to be actual in a large Dutch governmental organisation. In the IT department of this organisation, reuse of system components is one of the major goals to be achieved as part of the overall strategy. Therefore, the organisation has initiated a project in which a prototype has been developed to demonstrate the functional possibilities and restrictions on a support environment for decentralised and flexible maintenance of heterogeneous systems documentation.

In section 2, we identify the exact requirements such an environment should meet. In section 3, we discuss the concepts underlying such an environment, and the functionality of a prototype that fulfils these requirements. In section 4, it is discussed how systems documentation from different sources can be handled in the environment so that it supports both the concrete documentation type at hand and an abstract, reuse maximising meta-model.

To conclude, in section 5, we discuss the lessons from the design of the environment and its benefits for future work.

## 2. Requirements

The two most important aspects of the requirements of the support environment pointed at are:

- **Distribution**. The distribution of systems documentation is needed to enable the reuse of components throughout the organisation.
- **Flexibility**. In the organisation, many different tools and techniques for system development are used. The environment must be able to deal with the resulting variety of systems documentation.

*Distribution* as meant here is logical distribution. We do not require the data to be physically stored in a distributed fashion. Naturally, from an implementation point of view, this may be a well suited option. Here, it is more important that the ownership of the systems documentation is distributed. In the envisioned environment, there is no centralised responsibility for the administration of some particular variety of documentation. If, for example, the set of entities is documented for various systems, these sets are owned and maintained by the organisational group that is responsible for the system concerned.

*Flexibility* is needed because of the wide variety of types of systems documentation. The structure, or meta-model, according to which the documentation is to be stored, must therefore not be fixed. The environment must be able to operate with the different meta-models related to different tools and techniques in use, both current and future. On the other side, flexibility should be controlled. After all, the information stored should enable the reuse of system components across a diverse organisation. The abstraction level of the structure of documentation must therefore be chosen carefully. If too abstract a meta-model is chosen, the documentation retrieved from the system does not offer enough information to enable actual reuse. If the meta-model is too concrete, the documentation will only be of use to persons or groups of persons that use the same techniques and tools as the owner of the information. Ideally, the environment offers means for retrieving the same documentation on different levels of abstraction.

The required functionality of the support environment is illustrated in figure 1. At the basis of the environment we find a document management facility. Around this kernel, specific functionality is partitioned over the different types of users of the environment. We distinguish three groups of users: system developers, system managers, and the controller(s) of the environment itself. To support these different types of users in the presence of the flexibility sketched, the environment should offer personalised work spaces. A user must be able to state the source and type of the systems documentation he is interested in, according to which structure or meta-model the documentation is viewed and which tools are used to access that documentation. In the remainder of this section, more specific requirements to the envisioned environment are discussed, for each of the three target audiences individually.

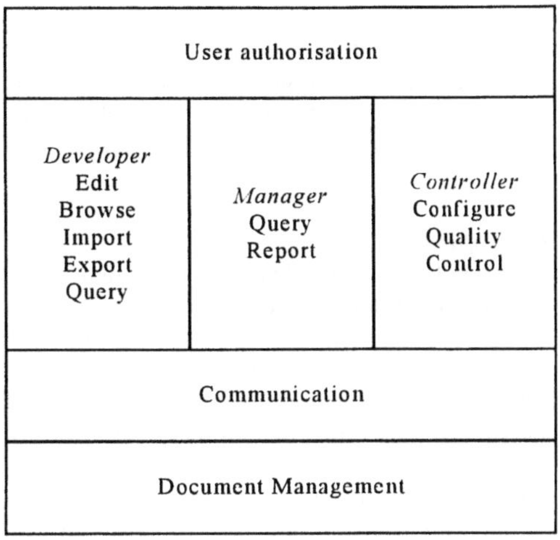


**Figure 1** Functionality of the support environment.

## *Support for system developers*

The *system developer* has to be supported by powerful tools to store and retrieve information. He needs easy access to the environment, preferably directly from his desktop workstation. The tools offered for retrieving information must support the following two tasks.

Firstly, the developer needs a query mechanism for finding reusable system components. Many different types of conditions on such components must be expressible, like their principal function, implementation platform and possible interfaces.

Secondly, it is the task of the developer to explore the exact properties of the system components found earlier. For this task, one does not only need information on the selected component itself, but also on related components. This is, for example, important while exploring the possibilities for interfacing the selected component with other components.

Developers probably maintain systems documentation outside the environment, either by using some CASE-tool or manually. The effort of maintaining the documentation within the support environment must be minimised by offering interfaces between the developers' native documentation tools and the support environment. It must be prevented that a developer has to enter the same information twice during the development process.

## *Support for managers*

*Managers* need less detailed information on system components than developers. Instead of detailed information on a single component, this type of users need a means for generation of summarising reports. Some of these reports are needed periodically, for example to gain insight in the growth of the number of available reusable system components the support environment offers.

### *Support for the environment controller*

The *controller of the support environment* does not manage or own the systems documentation stored. However, he is responsible for maintaining the meta-information of the support environment. For managing this information, the controller needs tools for creating and configuring users, groups of users and the meta-model according to which information is stored.

### *User type independent support*

Two requirements are illustrated in figure 1 that are independent of the type of user. Firstly, the environment has a mechanism for authorisation.

The support of (electronic) communication is the second user independent requirement. Providing an easy way for communication between the different users of the support environment is important for the co-ordination of the disclosure of the distributed systems documentation. Preferably, the services provided are integrated with the existing systems for electronic mail.

The development of the environment according to the requirements above and its introduction in the organisation has several consequences. Beyond the technological consequences related to the development of a tool, we recognise both organisational and methodical consequences. Organisational consequences are considered to be important. The introduction of the environment aims at the maximisation of reuse. People will have to be stimulated to use the support environment and to reuse system components.

Equally important are the methodical consequences: how is the systems development process to be organised and, as a more direct consequence for the support environment, according to which meta-model is the systems documentation stored from various sources?

In this article, we focus on the environment itself. We discuss a prototype of an advanced support environment for the disclosure of heterogeneous systems documentation.

## 3. A prototype

A prototype of the envisioned support environment has been built in Smalltalk/V for Windows. The prototype was meant mostly as a vehicle for researching the possibilities and requirements for the support environment itself. The prototype further provides an illustration to future users of the possibilities to meet the requirements and the clearness of the concepts used.

First, we show how the various requirements discussed above are translated into a series of concepts the prototype deals with. Also, we give an overview of the actual functionality it presents its users.

### *3.1 Concepts*

The concepts underlying the environment are discussed subsequently. Firstly, the concepts which are related to the core of the environment: object management, are discussed. After that, the concepts which are related to the requirements of distribution, flexibility, and co-ordination are presented.

## *Object management*

The basic functionality of the prototype is to manage information in the form of systems documentation. Therefore, at the center, we identify an object management system (OMS). This OMS keeps track of the various classes or *types* of elements identified in the systems documentation to be stored.

The concepts implementing the OMS are illustrated in figure 2. Each circle in the figure presents a concept. The straight lines represent relations between concepts. Arrows denote a sub-type relation between concepts. As the figure illustrates, the OMS maintains information at two levels. At type level it keeps track of a set of *object types*. At instance level, it controls the actual *objects*, which are instances of a certain object type. An object is a single unit of systems documentation that is stored and manipulated in the prototype. For example, we could create object types such as 'table' and 'column'. Typical instances of these types would be 'school' or 'student' for the object type 'table' and 'address' and 'date' for 'column'.

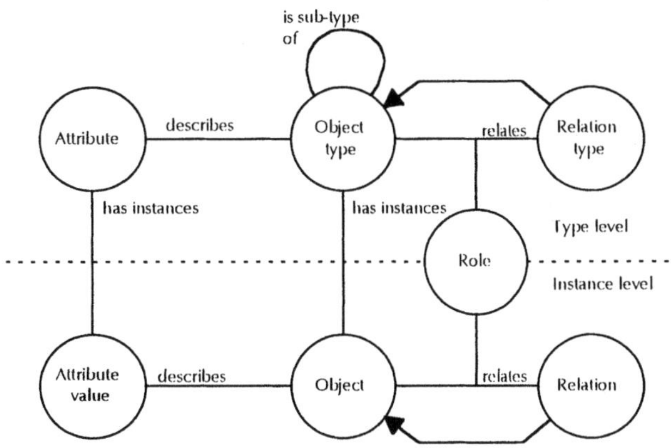


**Figure 2** Structure of the Object Management System.

*Attributes* are related to object types. They constitute the basic values that describe instances of object types. As figure 2 illustrates, the OMS supports sub-typing. Any object type can be a sub-type of any number of object types. For example, we could create the object type 'information element' that is a super-type of both 'table' and 'column'. Information that is maintained for both tables and columns, can be handled uniformly through this generalising construct. Super-types are not abstract. That means, super-types can have instances that are not instances of any of its sub-types. This prevents the need for unwanted over-specialisation in the case of incomplete information. For example, in the absence of the knowledge whether something is a table or a column, we could store that something as an 'information element', without making unjustified assumptions about its actual concrete type.

Relations between object types are registered through *relation types*, like 'table has column' in the example above. Instances of relation types are *relations*, like 'school has address'. Because relation types are a special kind of object types (and relations a special kind of objects), everything that is possible with object types also applies to relation types. Most notably, relation types can have attributes. For example, the relation type 'student is registered at school' could have the attribute 'year of registration'.

The cardinality of relations is not restricted. A relation type can be associated with any number of object types. The concept of *Role* is used to keep track of the roles each object type plays in the relation type. The definition of roles is to be made clear at both the type and instance level.

### *Distribution*

Directly related to the object management system a concept is identified that implements the basic requirement of distribution as formulated in section 2: *context*. 'Contexts' implement the distribution of ownership and responsibility for the systems documentation stored. This concept is illustrated in figure 3. A context is a grouping mechanism by which responsibility can be given explicitly to project teams and departments in the organisation. Users have access to certain contexts. If an actual user belongs to a certain group in the organisation, he will have access to the context that represents that group. Objects, and thus systems documentation, are owned by a context. That means that the responsibility for maintaining information contained in an object lies with (the members of) a context. Objects can only be created, changed and deleted by their owners. Objects are not owned by individuals directly. Information on individual users is included only to control access to the environment and the contexts defined.

A context can have two kinds of relations with other contexts. Both these relations are used to control the distribution of information throughout the organisation. Firstly, a context can give access to its information to other contexts. In this way, a group can give other groups read-only access to its documentation. Secondly, a context can be a sub-context of another context, giving rise to a hierarchy of contexts. Sub-contexts inherit properties of their super-context: if an user has access to a context, it has access to the sub-contexts of that context. Note that the 'is sub-context of' relation implies the 'has access to' relation.

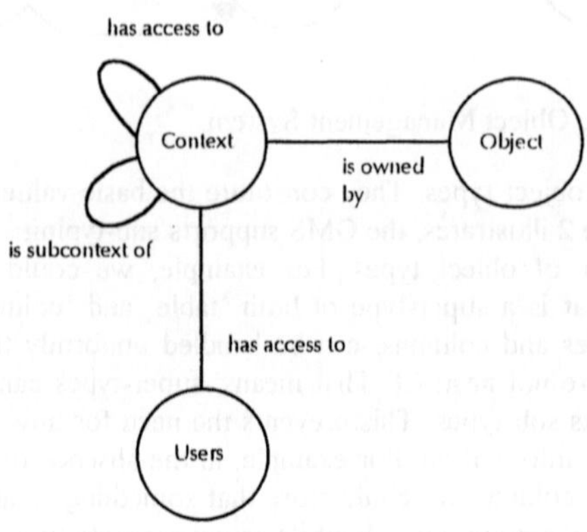


**Figure 3** Contexts, access and ownership.

### *Flexibility*

The general requirement of flexibility is realised by the concepts of *view* and *browser*. A view controls *what* information is visible from a certain context and *how* that information is presented to the users within that context. Browsers are the actual tools used to access the systems documentation stored. The concepts of views and browsers are illustrated in figure 4.

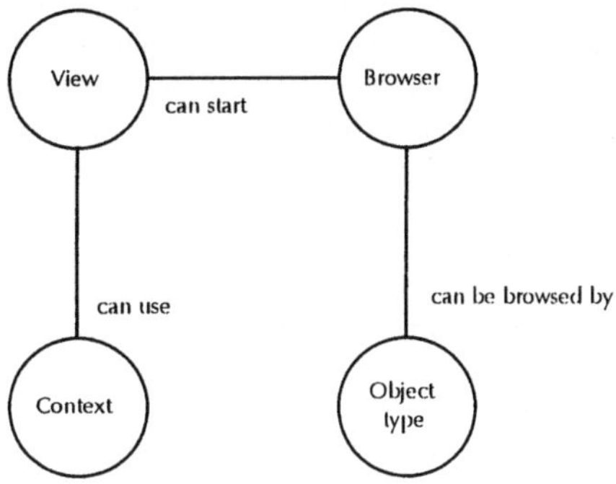


**Figure 4** Views and browsers.

A browser is defined for a specific object type, for example a brower can show tables, or entities, or processes, etc. A browser can be used to create, delete or change instances of its related object type. Also, browsers implement the querying capabilities of the prototype. The functionality of browsers is discussed into more detail later. Here, it is important to understand that a browser is fit only to access the instances of one certain object type (and its sub-types). In the design of the browser it is determined which associated attributes and relation types of the object type are visible in the browser. A view is a set of browsers. The controller of the environment can configure the various contexts so that they can use the views they need for their documentation jobs.

### *Co-ordination*

The last concept discussed here implements the requirement of co-ordination. The prototype offers the possibility to exchange electronic mail between users and contexts. Primarily, the mail system is based on users. However, it is possible to send a message to all users that have access to a certain context. The concept of electronic messages is illustrated in figure 5.

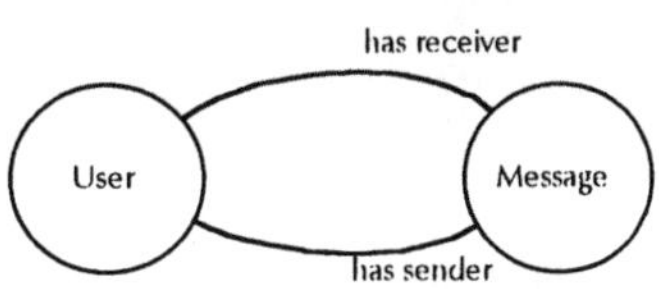


**Figure 5** Electronic messages between users.

## *3.2 Functionality*

Three types of users were identified in section 2. In the prototype as it is, this has led to two different working environments. Developers and managers are served by the same working environment, that satisfies both their needs. For the controller of the environment, a separate working environment has been designed. As this environment presents rather straightforward tools for the configuration of the environment, the functionality of these tools is not discussed further here. For the developer's and manager's working environment we first discuss the facilities to set specific working options. After that, the basic functionalities with regard to browsing, navigation and querying are discussed.

### *The entry of the system and how to set specific options*

The user has to login to the system. After having logged in using his user name, his password and the name of the context he wishes to enter, the user is presented the 'session window'. The session window is the main window for developers and managers. In the session window, see figure 6, the user can set options for his working environment and start browsers to access the systems documentation contained in the support environment.

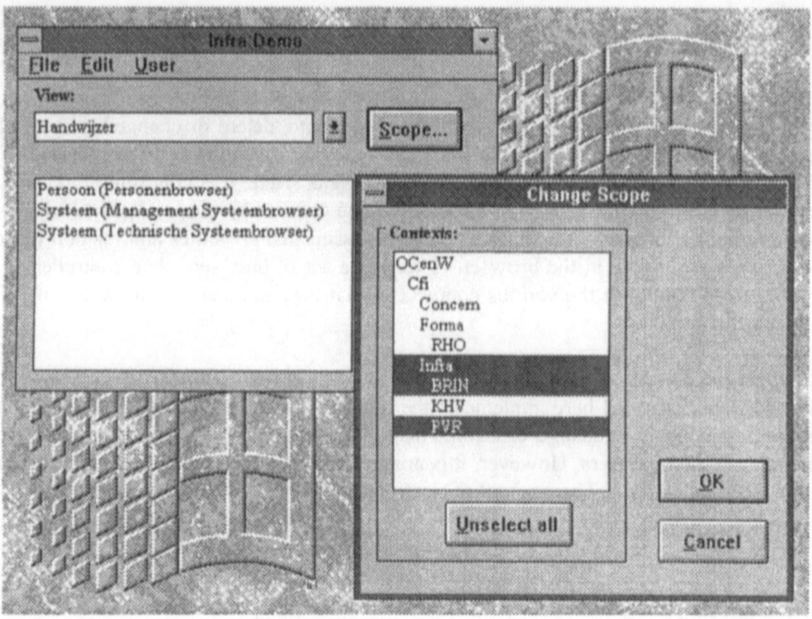


**Figure 6** The session window and the definition of the scope.

After selecting the appropriate view, the user can start one or more browsers from the presented list. The functionality offered by the browsers will be discussed below. Access to other contexts than the one used to login is provided via the concept of *scope*. The scope is basically a set of contexts. A browser only displays those objects that are element of the contexts within the scope defined (see also figure 6). Naturally, to add a context to the scope, the context selected at login must have access to that other context (as discussed in section 3.1).

The session window offers access to the electronic mail system. This option starts a relatively standard mail tool, that is not discussed further in this article.

## *Browsing and navigating*

Browsers implement the functionality to browse, change, retrieve and query the systems documentation. At any time, many browser can be open, thus giving access to different types of information at the same time. An example of an browser is shown in figure 7.

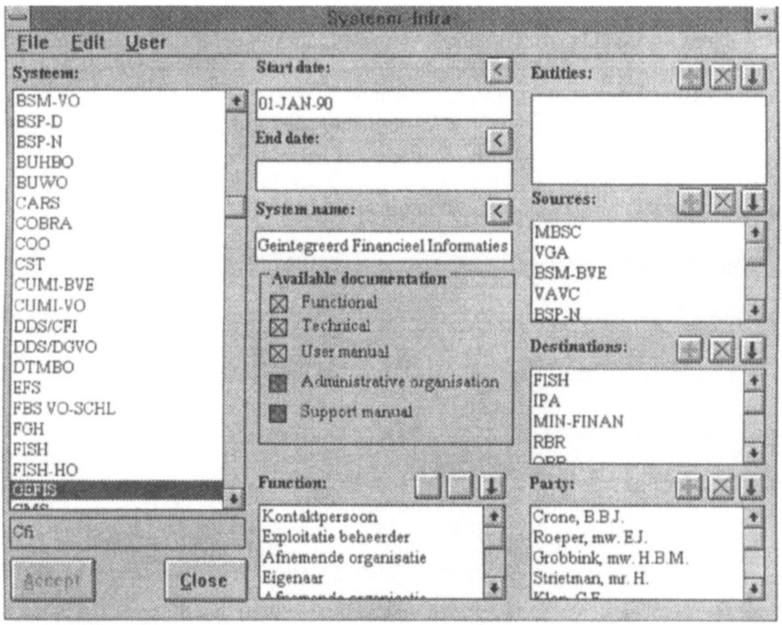


**Figure 7** A browser.

As stated before, a browser always operates on one specific object type. At the left side of the browser window, a list of instances of this specific object type is shown. This list contains only the set of instances which are within the scope defined before. At any time, one of the objects in the object list is the *current object*, as shown by the selection bar in the list. The remaining fields and lists of the browser show the attribute values and relations of the current object.

Attribute values can be edited by simply clicking and typing in the appropriate field. For relations, buttons are provided to add, remove or modify related objects. The user can navigate through the contents of the environment by double-clicking in relation lists. A new browser is opened after clicking a related object, revealing more information about that object.

## *Querying*

The type of search process sketched above, i.e. navigating through objects displayed in the browsers, is intended mainly for retrieving information or documentation about an already selected object. The query mechanism in the prototype enables the user to *find* new objects by specifying conditions for them.

The query mechanism does not require new user interface elements in the prototype. Queries are composed and executed from within the same browser that is used for displaying information about objects. After the user has composed a query, the browser automatically restricts the set of objects displayed to those that satisfy the conditions specified in the query. Figure 8 shows the same browser as figure 7, now showing the composition of a query.

Conditions on relations are composed by clicking on a number of objects to which the main object has to be related. Conditions on attribute values are entered using a simple expression language. This language offers the usual comparison operators, that can be used to compare the attribute to a value or another attribute.

This concludes the discussion of the functionality offered by the prototype. Reporting is an important aspect of the support environment that is to be implemented yet. Such functionality could be added by offering the possibility to display or print a selection of attributes and relations of the objects resulting from a query.

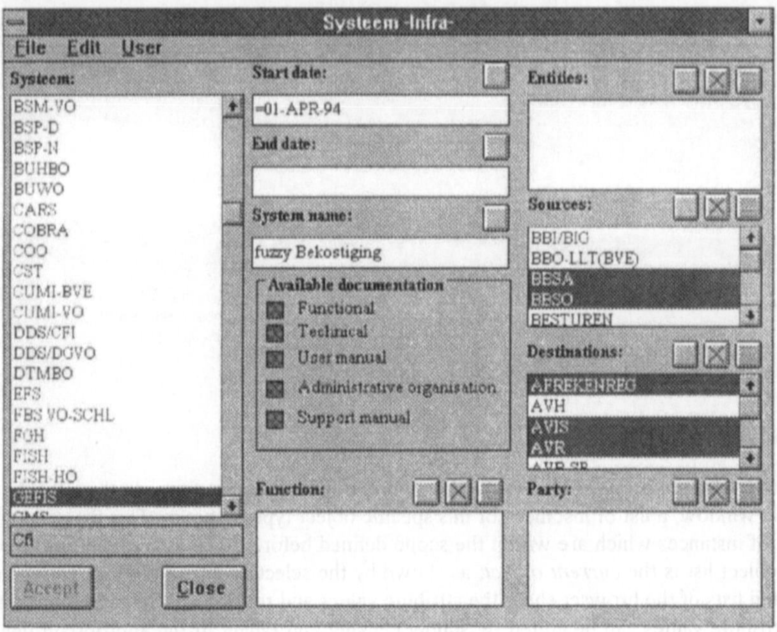


**Figure 8** Composing a query.

## 4. Contents of the Environment

The functionality of the prototype created has been evaluated by filling it with three different types of systems documentation. We have selected documentation from the following three sources:

- **SDW**. SDW (System Development Workbench), is the leading CASE-tool in The Netherlands. Based on a general repository, this CASE-environment offers different modules, supporting different techniques for systems analysis, design and documentation. From the repository, we selected the documentation of three smaller systems used in the target organisation. The documentation was created originally using the DFD (data flow diagram) and ERD (entity relationship diagram) techniques as supported by SDW.
- **Oracle**. From the dictionary of the Oracle RDBMS, we took table definitions, with associated packed procedures, of a large registration system used in the target organisation.
- **APA**. APA stands for A Parameterisable Application. APA is a customisable Oracle application to support one of the main tasks of the organisation, i.e. funding other institutions. This funding business process is dependent on ever changing rules and regulations. APA is capable of calculating the correct funds for these institutions based on a formal representation of the current calculation rules.

The first task in including the data from these three sources in the prototype has been to create a meta-model for each source. However, in order to really maximise the potential reuse, we also developed an abstract meta-model that is capable of handling all three types of systems documentation in a single format. As it has been discussed in section 2, that last model must be abstract enough to contain the different types of information, which are mutually very differing, yet still be concrete enough to offer sufficient information for developers looking for reusable components.

Because of the flexibility of the prototype of the environment, the abstract model could be included in the environment at the same time as the concrete models for the three types of

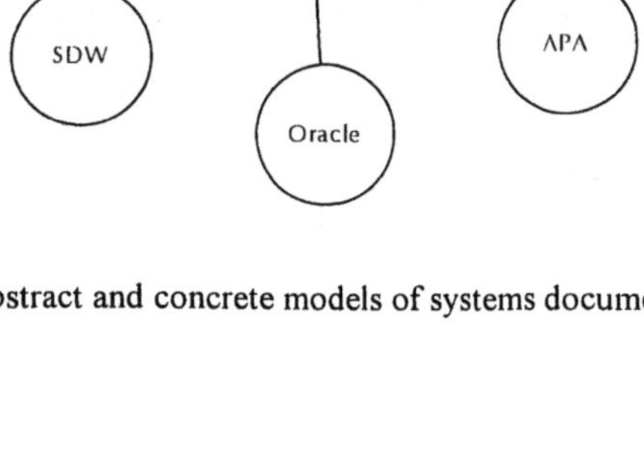


**Figure 9** Abstract and concrete models of systems documentation.

systems documentation. This is illustrated in figure 9. In this way, the information stored can be used to enable reuse across different groups or projects in the target organisation, while at the same time satisfying specific needs of developers working in different implementation platforms.

The construction of the abstract meta-model has been an independent sub-activity in the project (Verhoef, 1995). A discussion of the complete model is beyond the scope of this paper. Here, we discuss its principal structure and the way the three types of systems documentation have been mapped onto this meta-model. A simplified version of the abstract meta-model discussed below is illustrated in figure 10.

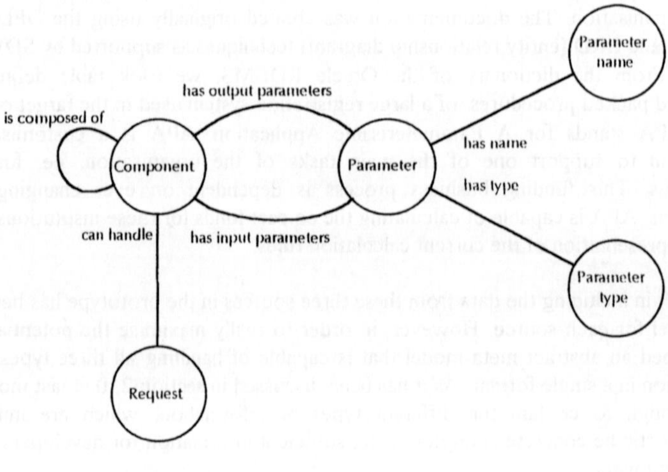


**Figure 10** The meta-model of components.

In its essence, the meta-model consists of the object types *component* and *parameter*. Two relations are identified between components and parameters. For each component the input and output parameters are kept track of. Components can be selected for reuse on the basis of attributes such as 'application domain', 'implementation platform' and 'basic functionality' that describe the functionality of the component both formally and informally. A parameter has a *parameter name* and a *parameter type*.

Components can be constructed using other components. The exact composition of a component is expressed using a formal construction language. A construction expression is parsed to populate the 'is composed of' relation that is included in the meta-model (and therefore is stored in the OMS).

One more concept of the meta-model discussed here is the object type *request*. A request corresponds to a single unit of basic functionality of a component, similar to a procedure in a module or a query to a database handler. For each request, it is recorded which input parameters are needed. It is also registered which output parameters are the result of the request after the component has finished its activity.

## 5. Epilogue

We have discussed how general requirements for the disclosure of variable and distributed systems documentation can be translated into a small but powerful number of concrete concepts.

The actual prototype showed the practical significance of the concepts underlying the envisioned support environment. The object management system, based on object types, is flexible enough to capture the different forms of systems documentation. Views allow the usage of several meta-models at the same time in a controlled way. The concept of context can be used efficiently to distribute systems documentation.

Experiments with diverging types of systems documentation have shown that with the prototype based on these concepts, it is possible to support co-ordination and flexibility in document management without losing too much information due to abstract meta-models. That is, the different types of systems documentation are stored in a uniform manner, while still being of practical use to the developer that wishes to reuse components of the systems documented.

The prototype as it is, however, can be improved on several points. At the functional level, capabilities for printing reports lack. As for the implementation, the prototype is not optimised for speed. Especially the object management system can be optimised much further in both time and space usage. However, the prototype did a good job in clarifying the way systems documentation environments could look like. The result will be valuable input for the actual further development of the support environment.

More challenging than producing a smaller and faster environment is its introduction in the target organisation. An organisation with distributed, heterogeneous documentation that aims at maximising reuse differs well from a classical organisation, in which wheels are reinvented everyday and, worse, are redocumented in many different languages. Practical lessons learned from using the prototype in actual development projects will be valuable in this reorganisation process.

## 6. References


Arnold, S.P. and Stepoway, S.L. (1987) The reuse system: cataloguing and retrieval of reusable software, in *Software Reuse: Emerging Technology* (ed. W. Tracz), 129–137.

Biggerstaff, T. and Perlis, A. *Software Reusability*, ACM Press, 1989.

Brorsson, M. and Kruzela, I. (1991) Museion-a reuse support system for design of service features, in *Proc. of the 10th Annual International Phoenix Conference on Computers and Communications*, IEEE Computer Society, Scottsdale, Arizona.

Burton, B.A., Wienk, R.A., Bailey, S.A., et al. (1987) The reusable software library, *IEEE Software*, **4** (7).

Constantopoulos, P. and Pataki, E. (1992) A Browser for Software Reuse, in *Proc. of the 4th Int. Conference on Advanced Information Systems CAiSE'92* (ed. P. Loucopoulos), Manchester, UK, Lecture Notes in Computer Science no. 593, Springer-Verlag, 304–326.

Freitag, B. (1994) A hypertext-based tool for large scale software reuse, in *Proc. of the 6th Int. Conference on Advanced Information Systems CAiSE'94* (ed. G.M. Wijers), Utrecht, The Netherlands, Lecture Notes in Computer Science no. 881, Springer-Verlag, 283–296.

Garg, P.K. and Scacchi, W. (1990) A hypertext system to manage software life-cycle documents, *IEEE Software*, 7 (5).

Helm, R. and Maarek, Y. S. (1990) Integrating information retrieval and domain specific approaches for browsing and retrieval in object-oriented class libraries, *OOPSLA '91*, 47–61.

Oosterom, N.E. van, Florijn, G., Hofstede, A. ter, et al. (1993) Gegevensdefinitiebeheer in een gedecentraliseerde organisatie, *Informatie* **35** (2), 128–139 (in Dutch).

Verhoef, T.F. and van der Weide, Th. P. (1995) *Gerichte ondersteuning voor systeemontwikkeling met bouwstenen*, Note CSI-N9501, University of Nijmegen, The Netherlands (in Dutch).

## 7. Biography

### *Dr. Duco H. Fijma*

Duco Fijma is a research consultant at ID Research. In 1994, he obtained his Ph.D. degree at the University of Twente, The Netherlands. The central theme in both his Ph.D. research and his current activities is the theory and practice of programming languages and environments. A particular interest within this area is formed by techniques for the (automatic) analysis of both programs and documentation, as applied in, for example, reverse engineering and system renovation. In the project covered by this paper, he concentrated on the design and implementation of the prototype of the support environment discussed.

### *Dr. T.F. Verhoef*

Denis Verhoef has obtained his Ph.D. degree at Delft University of Technology, in 1993. His Ph.D. study has covered the diversity of information modelling practices, and, consequently, the adaptability of support environments to those different practices. Currently, he is employed as a research consultant at the company ID Research. Particular interests include conceptual modelling, workflow, and Euromethod. Within the project described in this paper, his particular focus has been the development of an abstract meta-model for software components, and the mapping of specific systems documentation types onto that meta-model.

### *Dr. Gerard M. Wijers*

Dr. Gerard M. Wijers is director of ID Research, Leusden, The Netherlands. In 1991 he finished his PhD study on method engineering and adaptable CASE technology (with honour). For a number of years he has worked at the Software Engineering Research Centre, The Netherlands, as project manager 'Methods and Tools'

ID Research is an independent consultancy firm for large IT departments on IT-innovation and research. ID Research is specialised in customer specific market surveys, selection procedures and pilot and prototyping projects. Dr. Wijers is Technical Co-ordinator within the Euromethod Programme Management Board. His personal interests are IS development methods, CASE, software quality and metrics, object-orientation and method engineering. He has published many national and international articles and books.

9

# Modelling Business Relationships in a Non-Centralised Systems Environment

*I.G. Macdonald & R.A. Veryard*
*TI Information Engineering Ltd., Wellington House, 61-73 Staines Road West, Sunbury-on-Thames, Middlesex TW16 7AH, UK*
*Tel. + 44 1784 245058 Fax + 44 1932 770142*
*e-mail 7188581@mcimail.com and 5913301@mcimail.com*

**Abstract**

Systems development is now occurring in a range of environments ranging from those that are simply de-centralised to those that are open and distributed. Forms of federated development activity are beginning to emerge between heterogeneous organisational units. A clear understanding of business relationships is critical for success in such situations. A Business Relationship Modelling methodology is introduced that allows both the organisational and technological issues to be properly explored and resolved. Its use is illustrated through a case study based on video on demand.

**Keywords**

Business relationship modelling, enterprise modelling, open distributed processing

## 1 INTRODUCTION

### 1.1 The move to openness and federation

It is a commonplace observation that organisations are tending to move away from structures that are centralised and control-oriented towards those that are more decentralised and dependent on clear levels of empowerment. Centralised, hierarchical structures drew much from traditional military forms of organisation; much corporate thinking, with its focus on strategies, tactics, campaigns, objectives and even warfare (Ries and Trout, 1986), remains steeped in military jargon.

The traditional military model can be very effective in controlling large organisations. However, in situations where rapid response to changing circumstances is necessary and organisational flexibility is at a premium it can be found wanting. There are now many examples of how difficult the formal military structure finds it to deal with small bands of loosely coordinated guerrillas.

Equivalent difficulties exist in the corporate world. Increasingly, corporate giants are being put under pressure by smaller organisations and by the rate of change in their marketplaces. In the past, only companies with a world-wide physical presence could be viewed as players in the world market. Now, improvements in communications technology and the dawn of the information superhighway make it easier for small organisations to get their message out to the world. The overhead cost of a global infrastructure is no longer a significant barrier to becoming a global player.

Large organisations are responding to this challenge. Many accept the spirit of "small is beautiful" (Schumacher, 1974) and are seeking, not to become small, but to relearn how to behave like small organisations – particularly in terms of responsiveness, flexibility, and entrepreneurial initiative. Organisations are being flattened and decentralised; empowerment (Bowen and Lawler, 1992) and teaming (Katzenbach and Smith, 1993) are replacing command structures; networking is replacing hierarchy. It is now possible to envisage an organisation managed through a federation of teams, as in Figure 1.

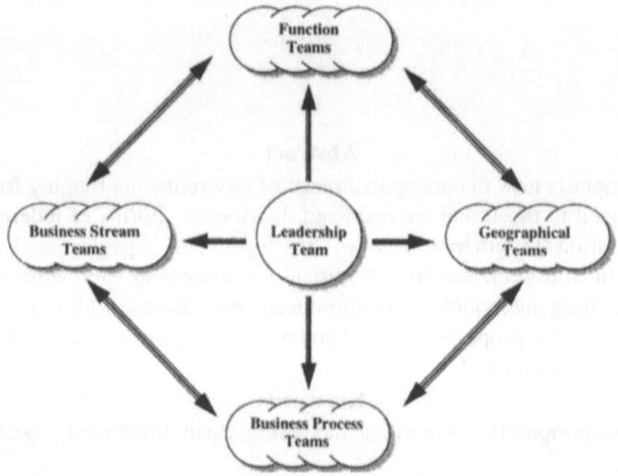


**Figure 1** Networked management teams.

Information technology promises to force the pace yet further. 'Openness' is increasing and it is now possible to look forward to widespread availability of open distributed processing – possibly of the kind envisaged in the ODP Reference Model standards (ISO 10746, 1993). As expected from its name, open distributed processing combines the technological concepts of openness and distribution.

The notion of open distributed processing also carries with it an implied promise of openness and federation for business management. This may be divided into two levels: internal (concerning the structure and management of a large organization), and external (concerning market opportunities and business alliances), (Veryard and Macdonald, 1994). Table 1 shows a characterisation of each level.

**Table 1** Levels of openness and federation

| | *Openness* | | *Federation* | |
|---|---|---|---|---|
| **Technical** | Portability | The capability of implementing programs without change on different computer systems. | Heterogeneity | Multiple system platforms<br>Multiple system design authorities |
| | Interconnection | The ability to move information between computing systems using communications. | Brokerage | Autonomous agents trading objects and services |
| | Interoperability | The ability of joint working between interconnected computing systems. | | |
| | Distributability | Extends the interoperability idea to allow processes and information to be provided and migrated automatically to the most convenient point of an interconnected set of computing systems. | | |
| **Organizational / Managerial** | Evolution | The ability of an information system to be maintained to respond to changing requirements. Software engineers such as Lehman (Lehman, 1980) have encouraged us to consider the information system, across its operational life-cycle, as an evolving object. | Decentralisation | Horizontal coordination and problem-solving |
| | | | Service culture | Negotiated relationships (service level agreements) between parts of the organization. |
| | Unboundedness | The absence of barriers to the provision of information and services for the end-user. The ability of unexpected information, from unexpected sources, even in unexpected formats, somehow to enter the system. | | |
| **Market / Entrepreneurial** | Low entry barriers | The ability of new competitors to 'freely' enter a market. | Business Alliance | Business process chains that cross enterprise boundaries |
| | Low exit barriers | The ability of competitors to 'freely' leave a market. | | |

Technological openness and federation allow the use of components from various suppliers in the design and development of information systems, using common standards to achieve economic benefit.

In the organisational/management sense, business information systems have always been open, to some extent. Most attempts to centralise and homogenise information systems have fallen short of complete integration and closure (Veryard 1994). Decentralisation may be viewed as an early step towards open distributed processing, with full conformance to open system standards being positioned at (or at least towards) the fully open end of the spectrum. Openness also connotes flexibility, the ability of organisations to evolve in ways not predicted or controlled by top management (Kelly 1994).

Market openness is often referred to as the 'level playing field'. Barriers to entry and exit are partly technological and partly socio-political and there are few markets where it would be appropriate or possible to wholly eliminate barriers to entry or exit. Partly, this is to do with the acquisition of obligations as a consequence of contractual or co-operative relationships.

Open distributed processing also contains the notion of technical federation. In parallel to this technical concept of federation, we believe that the availability of technological capacity that fully supports openness and distribution will act as an enabler or as an inducement to organisational federation and other forms of co-operative management. Federation is therefore relevant both as a management concept and as a technical concept.

Federation can be seen as an organisational extension of the notion of distribution; it is the distribution of management authority. Either by coincidence or design, federation is currently a hot topic both in management science and in information science. Eloquent arguments for federated management structures appear in Sloan and Harvard business reviews (Davenport et al, 1992; Handy, 1992), while the development of the technical concepts of broker and trader (ANSA, 1991; OMG, 1991) support technical federation across computer networks.

The vision of open distributed processing as it appears in the ISO standards is of heterogeneous distributed systems that cross the boundaries of traditional organisations. The Business Relationship Modelling methodology has therefore been designed to cope with inter-organisational as well as intra-organisational developments. It explores the topology of business relationships in parallel with technological relationships and in a market context as a means of encouraging a coherent approach to systems definition.

## 1.2 Difficulties of designing in an open world

Full openness can be viewed as the natural state of all systems, with decentralisation being a special, constrained case in moving towards it. We are, however, used to designing for such special cases and, in particular, to working within the narrow confines of centralisation.

Openness may also lead to open-ended, incrementally developed and continually evolving systems (Hewitt and de Jong, 1984) that are created even by multiple organisations. The principal difficulty in such a relatively unbounded situation is that there may be a different design process – where the process is itself distributed. Conflicts can arise because parts of the system derive from different sources and are created under different regimes. There are then issues over the consequent need for maintaining and making available specifications and reasons for particular design choices. (Veryard 1995a)

When system components and information about them are passed across organisational boundaries obstacles appear that are partly technical, partly human, and partly a consequence of the way in which capability is procured. Wood and Sommerville (1988) point out that the human problem is a result of the fact that reuse involves a kind of de-skilling of what are seen as highly skilled developers. There are economic problems associated with deciding who owns a complex object which has been built by X for Y, using components developed by Z. Technical problems are associated with the difficulty of developing reusable components – deciding whether a component is actually reusable; the absence of effective catalogues which can be searched effectively; the absence of agreed quality criteria for reusable objects and their interaction with other objects.

There are many other differences on either side of each organisational boundary:

- No common purpose; different organisational entities often lack a common purpose, especially if boundaries lie between dissimilar industries.
- No trust; this is inherent between different organisational entities. It is vividly reflected in uncertainties about the quality of software components obtained from elsewhere.
- No common economic framework; where components are provided by one organisation and used in another there may be a need for payment. There is no defined market for software components or information about them, neither is there a clear idea of how to charge for either use or ownership.
- No common legal framework; software components may be of inferior quality, or the information about a component may be inaccurate. It is unclear what, if any, legal framework applies in these cases.
- No common meaning and representation; there is little agreement about the languages which should be used for the description of software components. Misunderstandings can arise despite the presence of comprehensive descriptions.
- No common quality standards; the agreed measures for software component quality have been derived from those suitable for hardware components (e.g. MTBF, MTTF). Software quality of service is often better expressed in application dependent terms, such as mission time (the time during which a component is to stay operational with a precisely defined probability of failure for instance) (Siewiorek and Swarz, 1992).
- No support for distribution; this is a problem which requires the application of distributed processing technologies.

These organisational issues should be solved within the business process of producing new features for systems to support novel business services. They are part of a business process reengineering activity (Hammer & Champy, 1993) in which several organisations may wish to become engaged.

## 2 METHODOLOGICAL ISSUES

Establishing a clear definition of business relationships is a primary issue as we move from decentralisation to greater openness – otherwise solutions to other issues are in constant jeopardy of failing at the implementation stage through confusion over the execution of necessary obligations. For most organisations, to whatever extent they promote decentralisation, there remains a concern over the means of retaining some form of management control over what is going on (Goold, 1991; Hammer and Champy, 1993; Iggulden et al, 1993).

Put simply, we need to establish **who** is involved
**what** responsibilities they accept
**what** consequent obligations they agree to fulfil
**where** authority for resources lies.
**where** accountability for execution is invested

In our view, without a proper understanding of these, it will be difficult to achieve success in the major activities whose importance is accentuated by increasing decentralisation and openness. We therefore need to deal with:

- suitable concepts for modelling business relationships
- requirements determination
- business case formulation (supporting investment and/or procurement decisions)
- flexibility and coordination in design.

## 2.1 Concepts in business relationship modelling

We are interested in the rules of engagement for business activity. In Ackoff's (1972) classification, our view of business enterprise is of *purposive, multi-goal-seeking systems*. These are systems that pursue different goals with the common property of a shared system's purpose. Goals are selected for such a system (for example by strategic planning), which then chooses its own means of pursuing them.

Various styles of modelling exist to support the purposes outlined in the previous section. Our starting point has been to identify some of the concepts that recur in many of these styles, and our perception is that the notions of agent, activity and resource (Veryard and Macdonald, 1994) can provide the hub of a unified business relationship modelling language.

Agents have various intentions, expressed through such means as plans, policies, objectives and strategies. These are best understood in the context of the responsibilities and obligations held by the agent (Strens and Dobson, 1993). Obligations may be bundled into contracts or agreements (e.g. service level agreements).

Responsibilities and obligations are relationships between agents. An agent has a responsibility to another agent to maintain some desired state-of-affairs; an agent has an obligation to another agent to perform some activity.

In actual organisations, we typically find mismatches between the distribution of responsibility (R) and the distribution of authority (A), as well as with the distribution of expertise (E) and work (W). An analysis technique designed to identify and resolve such anomalies is known as RAEW analysis (Crane, 1986; Texas Instruments, 1990).

Distribution also entails some coordination activity. One of the difficulties of coordination is that in any reasonably large system, there is a very large number of things that *could* be coordinated. A good coordination methodology therefore needs to identify the things that *must* be coordinated (Veryard, 1994).

To model this aspect of the enterprise, we introduce the concept of *interaction distance* (Veryard and Macdonald, 1994). This is a logical concept, and is only metaphorically related to geographical distance. We can appreciate informally what is meant by saying that an Apple Macintosh in London running Claris Works is closer to another Apple Macintosh in California with the same software configuration than it is to a PC in the same room running Word for Windows. This captures the concept of interaction distance.

For two activities or departments or whole companies that need to be closely coordinated, we can work out the required interaction distance, and compare it with the distance in the current technical environment. This comparison is used to cost-justify both organisational changes and IT developments that reduce or bridge the distance, thus improving coordination.

The need for close coordination can be derived from a model of the enterprise that indicates where resources or decisions need to be shared (over some interaction distance). This in turn is derived from an understanding of responsibilities and obligations, as discussed above.

This leads to an identification of specific *exchanges* between agents (or between activities) concerned with: *sharing of resources*, *communication between agents* and the *coordination between activities* .

These exchanges are carried out across a measurable interaction distance. Thus if we are going to acquire and use technology to bridge these distances, we need to understand, estimate or determine two things:

- what is the business value of such bridges
- what are the specific requirements.

## 2.2 Requirements determination

Systems design is a process that produces a solution to a given requirement using the available technology. Technological advance therefore alters the design process; as the technological constraints on information technology systems are reduced, the choices available to the system designer are increased.

With increasing openness, the designer has new topologies to choose from, new mechanisms (including control mechanisms), and new styles of interfacing and inter-working. These new choices demand resolution by reference to the statement of requirements. This therefore places new demands on the requirements determination process. These need to be addressed by the business relationship modelling methodology.

To begin with we have to ask:

*Whose requirements are they?*

In trying to answer this question we find two complicating factors that become exaggerated as openness increases:

1. the developing nature of the requirements owner
2. multiple owners.

### *Owner development*

During the requirements formulation process, the requirements owner is himself transformed: from a 'naive' client who articulates an infinite (imaginary, fantasy) demand for a magic solution, into a 'mature' client who articulates a moderated (symbolic, formal) desire for a realistic solution. This can be illustrated in a Z-shaped schema, which shows how the development of the requirements is paralleled by the development of the client.

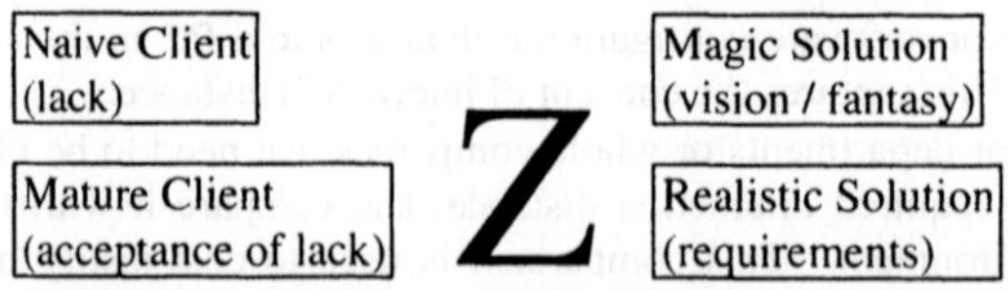


**Figure 2** Parallel development of requirements and client.

This maturing of the requirements owner is a developmental process of which the requirements engineer needs to be aware, as it affects the relationship with the client, and may also well affect the nature of the contract – at least for the next system, if not for this. Organisational learning as an outcome of a requirements process is one that is often unrecognised. However, it is part of any engineering discipline to suggest and incorporate organisational learning improvements into the processes of that discipline (Veryard, 1994).

## *Multiple owners*

What happens when (as is usual) there is more than one requirements owner?

The requirements formulation process may start with a collection of separate requirements owners, with overlapping and conflicting requirements. The goal of the process (not always reached, of course) is a transformation of this collection of separate requirements owners into a reasonably coherent 'we' – a group identity with a shared set of requirements. This does not imply that all conflict within the group has been resolved or suppressed, but that a sufficient commonality of purpose across the group has been forged.

There seem to be two distinct situations, which will need different contract models (Smith and Berg, 1987):

1. The stakeholders come to the group accustomed to playing parts in a larger whole. They therefore have a basis (or 'frame') for communication, negotiation and agreement. Conflicts between stakeholders exist, but can be 'contained' within the frame. Such frames typically exist long beforehand and long afterwards.
2. The stakeholders come to the group as independent wholes, with no larger entity to which they owe allegiance. There is no pre-existing frame, and the stakeholders must create one for the purpose of this project alone. Such frames usually do not outlast the project. Conflicts are not easily contained, and are at best only temporarily suppressed.

In the former case, a group of stakeholders is likely to be able to achieve a reasonable level of commonality of intention, and can for some purposes be regarded as a single system. In the latter case, typical of an open situation, any commonality of intention may be illusory.

Where we have multiple owners, what is at issue during requirements formulation is the establishment of a collective identity: 'we'. The aim then is to develop requirements statements that can be expressed in the form 'We Require This'. Such a statement contains three components, but requirements engineering usually fails to address them all.

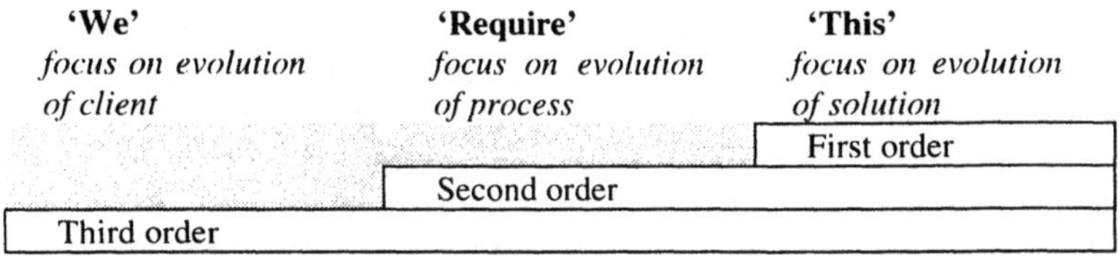


**Figure 3** Third order requirements engineering.

Most approaches address only the solution, and take the process (including procurement) for granted. These can be described as 'first order' requirements engineering. Some approaches (notably the soft systems methodology (Checkland, 1981) and the ORDIT approach (Dobson et al, 1994)) address both the process and the solution and can be referred to as 'second order' requirements engineering.

Both first order and second order requirements engineering consider the identification of the client to be merely a matter of correctly naming all the stakeholders. The development of the group identity of the requirements owner (as well as other participants in the requirements engineering process) is only properly addressed by 'third order' requirements engineering (Veryard and Dobson, 1995).

## 2.3 Business case formulation

One of the key components to a methodology for open distributed systems is a process for formulating and agreeing the business case for development and change. Both investment and procurement decisions are supported by such a business case, which shows benefits (tangible and intangible) outweighing costs, on some scale to be agreed. The business case formulation process, which is iterative and requires negotiation between stakeholders, needs to be fully integrated with the development and change processes.

Existing information systems development methodologies typically gloss over this area. Business case methods exist in management science and operations research, but are seldom integrated into systems development methods (Symons and Walsham, 1988). Open distributed processing also raises new issues for business case formulation. Most approaches to investment and procurement assume a central design and funding authority, but with decentralisation and federation we have to abandon this assumption. Openness introduces a problematic element to the scope of the business case and to assessing the nature of value chains in the open environment (Benjamin and Wigand, 1995).

To understand benefits, we need to recognise that benefits are distributed in three ways:

- over time
- over multiple stakeholders
- over different future scenarios, with different levels of probability.

Traditional business case methods collapse these onto a single value, assessed from a centralised decision-point. Since the distribution of benefits is three-dimensional, it follows that there are three dimensions to this collapse:

- Accounting techniques of discounted cash flow reduce the future to the present. (This is known to have some distorting effect, but the techniques are still widely used.)
- Stakeholder weighting techniques reduce multiple stakeholders to a single (virtual or abstract) stakeholder. Sometimes multiple stakeholders are just ignored or overruled.
- Uncertain benefits are converted into benefit expectations, using probability theory. This collapses branching future scenarios onto a single probabilistic future space.

With inter-organisational systems, and even within most large corporations, this notion of a centralised decision-point is a dangerous myth. There are many important issues.

- Who counts as a stakeholder?
- How do we cope with conflicts of preference between stakeholders?
- How do the costs of shared infrastructure get distributed between the beneficiaries?

If the decision-making is distributed – each stakeholder acquiring local technology in order to connect to a network – we may need to depart from the traditional business case methods, towards one that looks at critical masses (Markus, 1990).

The business case methodology therefore needs to support a range of decision-making styles:

- Central decisions require benefits to be collapsed to a single perspective.
- Central policies (especially where these do not have mandatory force, but aim to achieve a critical mass of a certain technology within an organisation or consortium) need to be analysed in terms of a dynamic take-up model. We can look at other communication technologies such as fax and EDI to help us build this kind of model.
  This kind of analysis also supports analysis of market opportunities by service vendors.
- Local decisions may be taken in isolation, but are also likely to be coordinated/negotiated. The business case methodology needs to support negotiation between autonomous or semi-autonomous agents, by predicting the costs, benefits and risks of particular infrastructure to each stakeholder, and therefore helping them agree on a fair basis for co-operative acquisition or development.

## 2.4 Flexibility and coordination in design

Key methodological issues arising from these problems are the needs to ensure that the design process provides for flexibility and coordination in the resulting systems.

### *Design for flexibility*

Designers need to specify **flexible** yet **integrated** solutions. With closed technology, flexibility and integration were often opposed goals: the more you had of one, the less you had of the other. Openness helps the designer reconcile these goals. Flexibility is promoted by the following design goals, which are supported by business relationship modelling:

| | |
|---|---|
| Design for diversity | • The business relationship model indicates where multiple agents may provide variant services. |

| | |
|---|---|
| Decentralise control subsystems | • Relieve bottlenecks of command and control, in which opportunities for parallel operations are frustrated by central (decision-making) authority and lack of local empowerment. |
| Design systems by composition from smaller units. | • The business relationship model shows ways in which an enterprise may be decomposed and also shows ways in which the parts may gain by being connected. |
| Improve the overall robustness of a system by improving the robustness of individual components. | • The model may indicate particular areas of uncertainty where early commitment may be unwise. |
| Use responsibility clustering to divide a system into subsystems. | • The business relationship model clarifies the intentions of the various agents and supports a search for those groupings of agent's that will give high internal cohesion of responsibilities and low external coupling. |

*Design for coordination*

Coordination is promoted by supporting the following design goals:

| | |
|---|---|
| Federate, as a cheap way of reducing interaction distance between heterogeneous systems. | • The modelling provides a means of determining current interaction distance by analysing relevant exchanges and then determining a desired interaction distance by analysing relevant intentions. |
| Give agents the necessary authorisation to enable them to access the resources needed to fulfil their responsibilities and discharge their obligations. | • Business relationship modelling of responsibilities and obligations is used to clarify or establish new responsibility relationships between the (pairs of) agents involved. A chain of responsibility relationships can be defined for agreement by showing how obligations pass from one agent to another. |
| Ensure that conversation parties have agency over the related policies. | • The modelling is used to clarify the responsibilities for **making** policy versus **executing** policy, of the parties to conversations in the conversation hierarchy. |

# 3 THE MODELLING METHODOLOGY

## 3.1 Structuring principles

The Business Relationship Modelling methodology describes a number of components of a solution to the problem of modelling an open information system development project. It does this by defining tasks which have to be undertaken in such a development and showing the role and nature of the models which need to be employed during each of these tasks.

The perspective adopted for the Business Relationship Modelling methodology is models of organisational structure and boundaries. This is an important perspective since openness is not just about heterogeneity of network infrastructure, but about federated computing across organisational boundaries (which is what may have given rise to the network heterogeneity in the first place). There is quite a lot of evidence that many difficult problems and failure modes of information systems arise where these systems cross organisational boundaries.

The Business Relationship Modelling methodology has a view of the information systems development process that was adopted from the ORDIT model of requirements capture (Dobson, 1993) then adapted. It consists of activities in four **zones** (derived distantly from the four dialogues of Lacan (Bracher, 1994)), as shown in Figure 4 below:

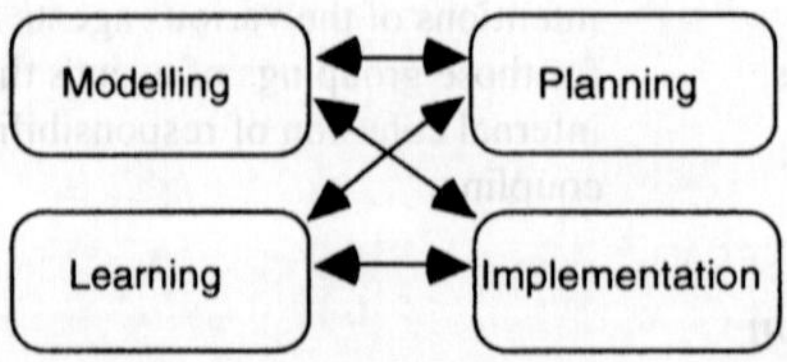


**Figure 4** Four zones of organisational intervention.

Each of the four zones corresponds to a distinct set of activities which normally are performed by separate groups, or perhaps separate enterprises, involved in a development project. They form a natural division between separate domains of ownership or management.

In the **modelling zone** we seek understanding and develop models of business relationships. Within this zone, there are four sub-zones: scoping, (re)presenting, opting (preference structures) and prototyping.

In the **planning zone** decisions are taken over action and are translated into plans, for example, scoping plans, design plans, investment plans, evaluation plans, and action plans. The models and the understanding they promote serve to provide a basis and support for the planning.

In the **implementation zone** we seek to achieve practical change to address identified issues and gain tangible value from the change. This is where plans are put into effect; systems are built, tested and commissioned; people are trained, and new skills are deployed.

In the **learning zone** organisational learning emerges as well as general improvements in the 'state-of-the-art'. It may include comparative research, reviews of experiences and successes, selection and synthesis of findings and dissemination of relevant knowledge.

These zones correspond to separate sub-processes which occur generally in any form of system development. These sub-processes are essentially asynchronous and iterative in nature. There is no linear ordering either of the sub-processes themselves or of the component tasks within each sub-process. A complete development project will visit each zone several times, in an order which will vary from project to project.

Each sub-process will consist of some number of asynchronous tasks, the details of which will also vary according to the development project. The Business Relationship Modelling methodology and the case study provides one description of these tasks.

The methodology itself is not prescriptive about the order in which zones are visited or tasks performed, since this depends on the context of the problem, the project, and contingent features of the situation such as the development contract. However, the methodology does suggest a default approach which can be used when there is no good reason to adopt an alternative one. The choice of a route through the maze is made easier by experience, judgement and sensitivity to a problem.

Finally, a comment should be made on managing a project using the Business Relationship Modelling methodology approach. Because of the asynchronous nature of the sub-processes and tasks, it is important to define the synchronisation points between them. This is a management task, but because development of a non-centralised system will involve several management domains, these synchronisation points need to appear at well-defined interfaces between these domains. It is a frequent observation that this leads to inefficiencies in the process, for example, delays in scheduling meetings, delays in the production of documents and the meetings themselves. There is still no easy solution to dealing with these sources of inefficiency, but one of the benefits of our approach is that it allows prediction of where and when these inefficiencies are likely to arise, so that an alternative allocation of tasks to the management domain can be considered if one is found that is both desirable and feasible.

## 3.2 Business relationship modelling methodology task structure

The following diagram shows the overall task structure of the modelling and planning zones. Details of the application of these tasks to a video-on-demand scenario are presented in the remainder of this paper. Task structures for the implementation and learning zones are outside the scope of this paper, though some comment on implementation is provided.

Since the Business Relationship Modelling methodology is not a linear methodology, it is important to stress that the actual sequence of activity need not follow the numbers assigned to the tasks. This fact is illustrated by our video-on-demand case study, in which we started with task 2, and continued with task 4 before tackling task 1. Furthermore, we only made a quick and dirty stab at task 5 before attempting tasks 6, 7 and 8, and then returning for a second go at task 5.

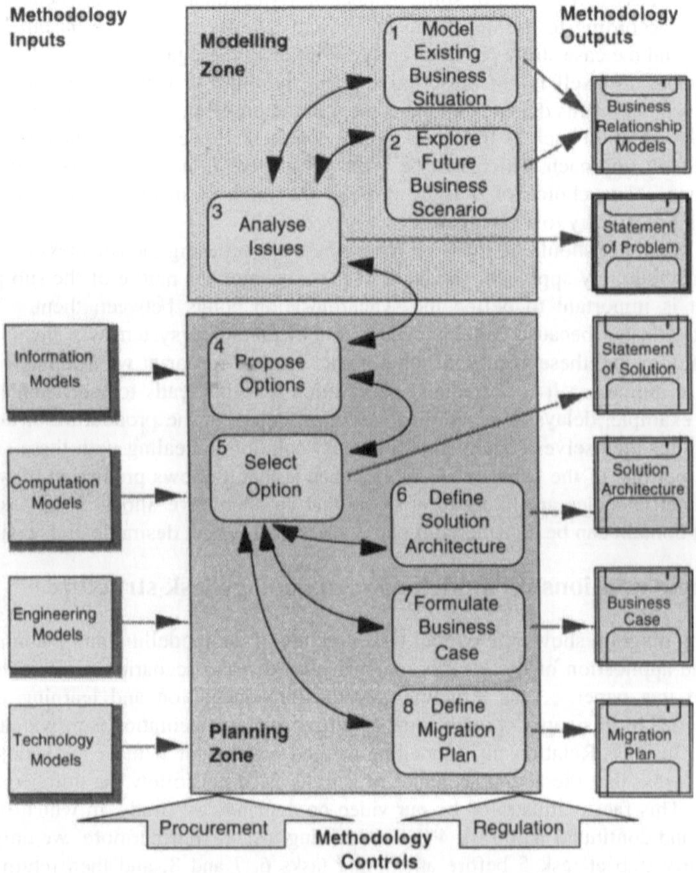


**Figure 5** Business relationship modelling methodology tasks.

# 4 VIDEO-ON-DEMAND CASE STUDY

## 4.1 Introduction

Video-on-demand is a service by which a consumer can electronically order a video at any time of the day or night and have that video screened immediately or at any other time chosen. It eliminates trips to a video shop and any tape handling, but otherwise offers the same functions available from a video player via a remote control.

The scenario for the case study, in figure 6, assumes relatively conventional terminal equipment. At this stage, organisational boundaries have been imposed on this technical structure in a, perhaps, arbitrary manner. Links to accounting, billing and payment systems will inevitably be part of such a system, but for simplicity they have not been included.

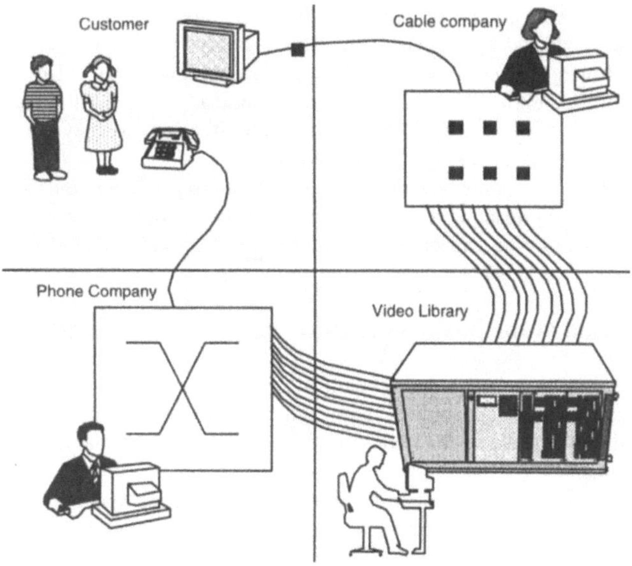


**Figure 6** Basic video-on-demand equipment.

Telephone is used for conveying the wishes of the consumer to the service provider. A wide-band medium (offered via a local cable operator) is used to serve the customer (with video in this case). In the short to medium term this is economical since much of the infrastructure is already in place. Also, terminal equipment at the customer site is cheap, resulting in better take-up of new services.

A typical customer family has phone and cable connections. They possess a decoder and a television and an interest in particular types of video films. To protect their children they want to be able to block the screening of video nasties; to help manage the household budget they want to have access to their account to see how much is owed at any one time.

There are many different video-on-demand services available. The only way our customer can find out about differences between their requirements and those on offer, is by being informed about other services. Information provision takes the form of (unsolicited) advertising and (solicited) browsing amongst the services available.

Once our customer family has become a subscriber they will want to negotiate the particular films to be shown. For this they use the telephone to contact the video library and to direct searches through the title index. The titles and other information are displayed on the television screen.

Once a film has been selected, it can be watched from beginning to end (the phone connection being no longer needed). If the customer wishes to interact with the player, several scenarios exist concerning, for example, replay, pause, slow motion, stop. Depending on the technology supplied, these signals can be processed locally or remotely.

There is an obvious connection between the technological solution and the business issue of being able to obtain a copy of a film on tape. A tape may be replayed several times, possibly with different audiences, hence devaluing the video-on-demand service.

Both video library and customer will do some accounting. The video library will track usage of its films and either charge upon use or periodically send a bill. The customers will keep information as to what use has been made and either pay as they watch or as the bill arrives. A receipt for payment may also be needed.

The issues of what is being charged for, how accounting is done and how payments are made have a profound impact on technology and the way in which services are used. Another important issue is how the carrier companies (Phone Co. and Cable Co. are paid for the service of transporting the signals.

## 4.2 Application of the business relationship modelling methodology

In providing a service, such as video-on-demand, there are many design trade-offs each with associated organisational, economical and technical issues. The Business Relationship Modelling methodology allows the trade-offs to be examined such that rational decisions can more easily be made.

The methodology is always applied from a particular **perspective** and results in a model which is valid from that perspective. We have analysed video-on-demand from the perspective of the **video library**. This allows us to explore opportunities for the video library to use the video-on-demand notion to offer new products and services to its customers, and to enter new markets.

Several aspects of the scenario are not covered in detail. Payment is mentioned only in passing; regulation is referred to, but its precise nature is kept outside the scope; registration of video on demand services is not covered; complaint handling is not explicitly covered.

The methodology enables questions to be raised which help both to elucidate requirements and to achieve a suitable solution architecture. Some of these questions are left unanswered since even without them the use of the methodology is sufficiently demonstrated.

## 4.3 Task 1 — Model Existing Business Situation

### *Agents and interactions*

Two current ways in which video signals enter the home were identified as: (1) Video Hire and (2) Cable/Satellite & Broadcast.

Later we decide that the Video Hire system is the one we want to improve and replace. The nature of the methodology is however to initially cover a wider area so as to ensure good understanding of the context in which new opportunities will be analysed.

For this broad context we identified the following **agents**:

a) Video Hire: Customer, Viewer, Video Rental Shop and Video Library.

b) Cable/Satellite & Broadcast: Customer, Viewer, and Broadcaster (e.g. Cable/Satellite/Terrestrial)

There are also regulatory bodies which act as agents in one or both systems, such as film regulator, broadcast regulator and cable regulator.

The sets of agents overlap as follows:

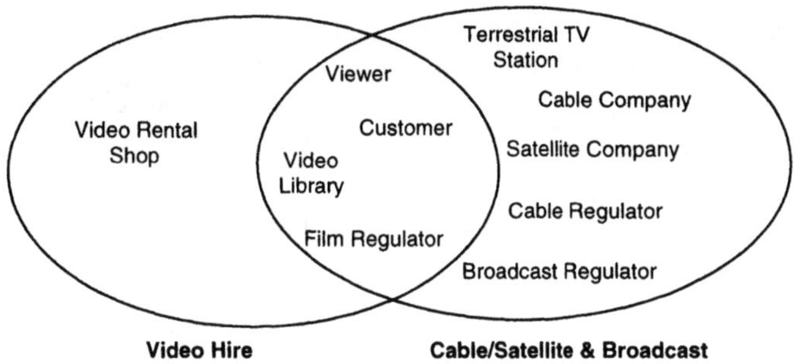


**Figure 7** Overlapping sets of agents.

Principal **interactions** were then identified. Interactions are represented in Figure 8 within, a) the Video Hire system and b) the Cable/Satellite & Broadcast system.

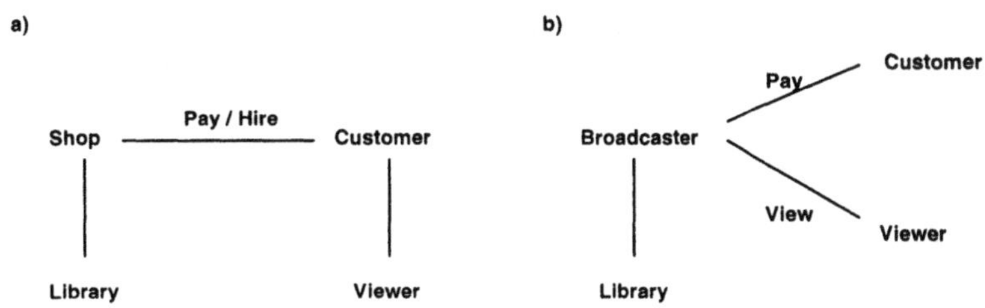


**Figure 8** Interaction structures.

Note how the payment and delivery subsystems are differently linked in the two systems. In both cases signals are paid for. In Video Hire, a straightforward hire charge is made (perhaps in addition to a library membership fee). Cable/Satellite systems may charge for signals by providing decoders in exchange for payment. Broadcast most frequently relies on the collection of TV license moneys or is paid for by advertising.

Regulators are omitted from the picture because they do not have specific interactions with other agents and only intervene on an ad hoc basis to police adherence to regulations.

### *Analysis of Interactions*

Once identified, each interaction is characterised in terms of its mechanism, interaction distance and availability. It is then analysed in detail by considering its characteristics of service provision and consumption. For instance, the Library offers a service to the Shop, the Shop offers a service to the Customer and so on. Each service provision is analysed in terms of service delivery and quality.

**Characterisation**

**Table 2** Example of interaction characterisation

| **Shop/Broadcaster – Customer Interactions** | | |
|---|---|---|
| System | Video Hire | Cable/Satellite & Broadcast |
| Mechanism | Physical Tape<br>VHS format | Cable/Satellite broadcast<br>Broadcast analogue (625) |
| Distance | Physical trip to the shop to collect and return tape | If satellite it is via a dish<br>If cable it is via wiring to the home.<br>Hybrid solutions also exist, whereby cable companies re transmit satellite and terrestrial signals to customers via cable |
| Availability | When the shop is open | 24 hour transmission but only according to a schedule |

Particular emphasis is placed on characterising interaction distance since this will play an important part in making the business case. *Interaction distance* can be illustrated as follows:

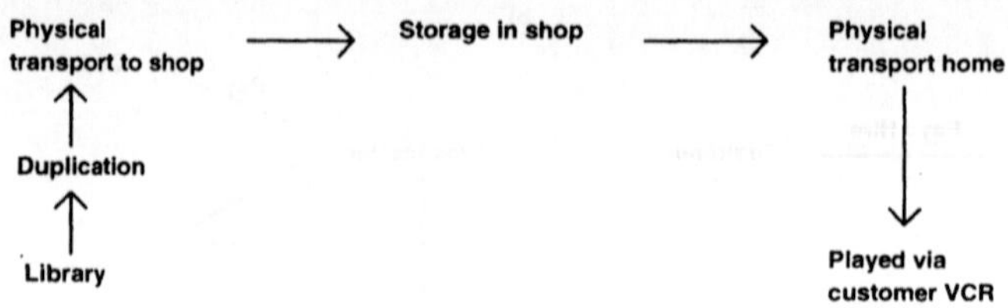


**Figure 9** Interaction distance elements in Video Hire.

Each step implies:

| | |
|---|---|
| Cost: | carrying video tapes to shops is expensive and involves people and trucks |
| Inconvenience: | mostly for the customer, who will have to visit the store to select a tape |
| Delay: | latest videos cannot be stocked in sufficient numbers to satisfy demand |
| Risk: | the risk of loss of material at any stage in the path between the library and the viewer is considerable (there are few checks along the way). |

These issues indicate that the interaction distance is too great in the conventional video hire model and highlight one area for potential improvement in the existing system.

**Service delivery**

The analysis brings out a number of issues that might need to be clarified:

**Table 3** Issues in the Video Hire scenario

| Formal Contract(s) | *Things which need to be clarified* |
|---|---|
| Library –> Shop | Does the shop purchase the tapes outright OR<br>Is there a royalty payable for each rental? |
| Shop –> Customer | Quality of physical tape e.g. first generation copy, clean tape |
| | Payment, deposit |
| | Prompt return of tape and deposit |
| **Informal Social Agreement** | *Things which need to be clarified* |
| Customer –> Viewer | Customer could be the viewer, the parent of the viewer, the host for several viewers etc. |

**Table 4** Issues in the cable/satellite and broadcast scenario

| Contract | *Things which need to be clarified* |
|---|---|
| Library –> Cable/Satellite Co. | Does the cable company purchase material outright? |
| | Payment per showing |
| Cable/Satellite Co. –> Customer | Payment for connection/de scrambler |
| | Payment per view |
| | Payment by advertising |

**Service quality**

Another set of issues can be found by examining the quality of each interaction. Some issues that might need to be clarified were identified as:

- Actual quality of rented tapes:
  Poor copies – third generation
  Dirty tapes – breaks, cracks
- Actual quality of satellite & broadcast:
  Interference
  Tuning

Note that these are "technical quality" issues. We might also have considered more subjective issues related to satisfaction with service and also issues relating to registration, regulation, payment and complaint handling.

### *Agree model of existing situation*

At this stage it is necessary to agree on the actual model for the existing system. Much of the task so far was to do with exploring the context for this model.

We decided to concentrate on a system from the Video Library perspective, not the Cable/Satellite & Broadcast perspectives. Other possibilities rejected included Interactive Video. Video-on-demand combines the benefits of both Cable and Video Rental.

## 4.4 Task 2 — Explore Future Business Scenario

### *Agents*

Before going into further detail in determining the agents in a notional video-on-demand system, it is necessary to identify the level of analysis. Three possible levels are identified:

1. Commercial
2. Information
3. Technological and/or Engineering.

A diagram can then be produced to identify agents within each level:

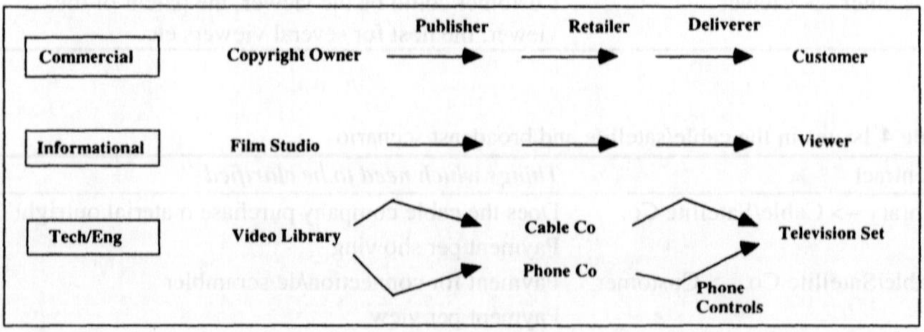


**Figure 10** Three levels at which video-on-demand could be considered.

The intention is to consider one level at the time. However, the three levels are not independent. For instance, the choice about the delivery mechanism at the home (a technical question) may enable a customer to make copies of video material on a home video recorder.

Task 6 examines the relationships between the levels further. Since we are concerned with relationship modelling, it is appropriate to start by concentrating on the agents at the commercial level. The crude identification in the diagram above requires further refinement. This can be done by asking the following key questions:

*What are the roles at the commercial level?*

The agents that would be involved in a notional video on demand system are as follows:

Customer, Viewer, Phone Co., Billing Co. and Cable Co., and various regulatory bodies.

If video rental shops were used then they would be classed as agents, and would need to be included in the model (in the role of "allies" and not "competitors").

*Who is developing the key technologies?*

The key technological components of video-on-demand are being developed by the telecommunications companies. This makes them an important agent in the new system, both as suppliers of the technology, as well as participants in the delivery of the new service.

Telecommunications companies will see the revenue they can earn from the provision of basic interconnection services drop as the technology becomes cheaper. This must be a major driver for them to diversify into service provision across the interconnection services under their control – in this case, to provide video library capability.

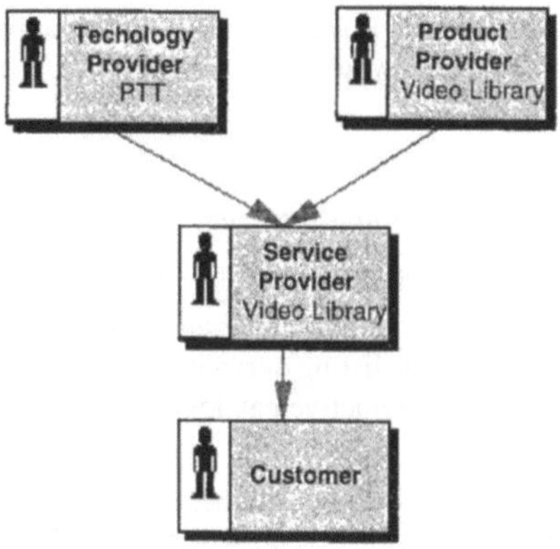


**Figure 11** Service = Product + Technology.

## *Interactions*

Interactions between the proposed agents are analysed next by asking the following key questions:

*What are the options for payment flow?*

How is payment dealt with? Electronic payment is ruled out in the short term, because the technology is not yet sufficiently mature. However, does the video library make use of well developed accounting and billing services which could be provided by either the telecommunications service provider (Phone Co.) or the cable company (Cable Co.)? Is payment by credit or is there a pay as you view policy? Is a credit card company involved?

*What are the payment/service obligations?*

Who pays, and for what. What rights are obtained over what from the exchange of money? If a customer pays to view a film then the video library has an obligation to screen that film with agreed quality characteristics. There are obligations on the customer and the viewer as well. Viewing a film is not the same as being able to record it and show the recording to friends. A customer has an obligation to look after the terminating equipment and not connect other equipment which is not approved by the phone or cable companies.

*What other information flows are there?*

The video signal itself can be regarded as information with a certain value. Similarly, if a video catalogue is part of the service then the information it affords has a value.

## *Identify future scenarios*

Two scenarios are possible. One ignores the existence of high street video rental shops, the other uses these facilities to promote a video on demand service. The two business models which emerge from this are quite different.

The idea of including (parts of) several existing enterprises in a new enterprise raises the key question:

*Do we need to consider the possibility of mergers and acquisitions?*

For example, video libraries might merge with rental shops, cable companies might merge with telecommunications companies. This would affect both the business cases and the migration plans in tasks 7 and 8.

A further question is:

*What are the opportunities for new agents/services to interpose?*

The titles catalogue is one example of an opportunity for a new agent in the system.

In broadcasting, listings are widely distributed on paper and via teletext, prestel or minitel. A video on demand service requires a similar listing service, targeted at its customers alone. This service could be made available as an interactive catalogue and could include video clips (trailers) and other advertising material.

The video title catalogue could be modelled as a resource, which might be controlled by an existing agent (such as the video library), or as an agent, which might be owned/controlled by the video library, or spun off as an independent company. This opportunity is easily spotted by distinguishing between the video catalogue resource and the agent which makes that resource available as a service.

## *Agree future model*

Examining issues helps in exploring the possible configurations of agents, activities and resources, which might make up the proposed enterprise. A migration path from the existing situation to a possible new situation can now be plotted.

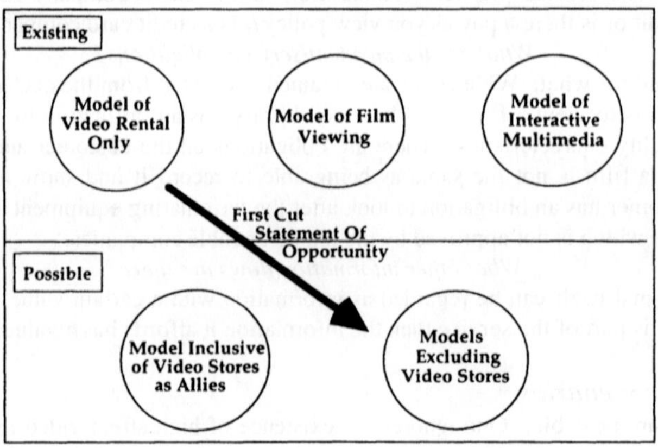


**Figure 12** Existing versus Possible scenarios.

The perspective from which this migration is proposed is of the stakeholders in a video library.

## 4.5 Task 3 — Analyse Issues

The existing and available systems (derived and described in task 1) and the possible systems which could emerge (analysed in task 2) can be compared and contrasted. This is best done by analysing problems associated with each of the systems and options under discussion.

Perceived issues or current problems can be identified through the many sources of complaints within the Existing system. These were identified in task 1 as:

- tape quality
- inconvenience: the shop is too far
- waiting time for new releases.

The New system will also display a number of challenges, some of which may become the source of complaints. These are projected to be:

- Synchronisation between Phone Co. and Cable Co. – for quality of service and predictability of delivery
- Transmission quality – dependent on encryption and compression techniques, and source quality.
- Payments – which can be better tailored but may be more prone to disputes.
- Control over viewing – in terms of authentication of viewer, the material which is delivered and the time at which certain materials may be delivered.

A comparison of the existing and new models will show up differences. These are potential issues. Differences can occur when agents either gain or lose roles in moving from one model to another. Here, a difference has been discovered in that there is no role for the Phone Co. in the old system and a dubious role for the Video Shop(s) in the new system

Most of the current problems are the consequence of the large interaction distance between the library and the viewing station. This problem is addressed by the new system, so our simplest option at this stage is to agree an appropriate project objective, e.g.:

*"To find a way, using video-on-demand, of reducing the interaction distance between the library(s) and the viewing station(s)"*

## 4.6 Task 4 — Propose Options

The analysis of existing and potential issues is more wide ranging than the anticipated final scope. Task 4 is about delimiting the scope of the solution and gives responsibility for identifying choices and propositions to the analyst. In task 5 there is a shift to the problem owners, who make choices and select from the options put in front of them.

The first question here is which issues and problems are or can be fixed? From those identified in task 1 the following were selected:

- Poor tape quality
- Inconvenience.

The first was a result of tape as the medium, the second a consequence of the interaction distance between the source of the video material and the place of delivery (the home).

The objectives for any resolution are then:

- Improve viewing quality (move from tape to mono/multicast)
- Reduce inconvenience (remove visit to shop to hire/watch videos; do it from home).

These are achievable through video-on-demand but still leave us with one major service issue – which agent has the prime contract with the customer? There are 4 options:

- Option 1 – Video Library
- Option 2 – Phone Co.
- Option 3 – Cable Co.
- Option 4 – Video Retailer.

The key question that needs answering here is:

*Does each option satisfy our objectives for viewing quality and convenience?*

This question is addressed in task 5.

## 4.7 Task 5 — Select Option

One of the proposed options from task 4 is selected in this task. Responsibility for making this choice shifts away from the analyst to the problem owner, and the task attempts to shed light on the nature of the choices which have to be made. Specifically we must address the issue of which agent has the prime contract with the customer.

Selection criteria must be defined that reflect attributes of the video on demand service and the process required to implement it. These are the attributes necessary to achieve the solution objectives defined in task 4 and for this example, the following criteria were identified:

| | |
|---|---|
| Speed of implementation: | The service should be easy to implement and the implementation should be fast so as to beat potential competition at least in the short term. |
| Profitability: | The service should be profitable as soon as possible. |
| Simplicity: | The service should be easy to understand by customers. A simple system structure will also help configuration management and maintenance of the system in the field. |
| Risk: | Risks associated with the service, its implementation and operation should be as low as possible. |

Each option is then evaluated according to the selection criteria.

***Option 1 – Video Library:***

The Video Library depends on both the Phone Co. and the Cable Co. for delivering signals to the customer. Since this service is the main line of business for both companies, this option should be quick and simple to implement. The only complication is that cable tends to be a multicast environment, whereas video-on-demand requires monocasting. This is no problem given sufficient bandwidth.

There is a further dependency between Cable Co. and Phone Co. which affects the quality of control over viewing by the customer. Control signals which flow from the customer to the Video Library via Phone Co. wires need to be reacted to quickly enough (judged by the customer who expects some effect to be visible in the signal that gets passed from Video Library to the Customer via the Cable Co. infrastructure).

Both Cable Co. and Phone Co. will want to be paid for the data they ship. This option's profitability depends on the charging structures applied by the carriers so some risk is associated with a lack of control over data transfer pricing policies.

***Option 2 – Phone Co.:***

The Phone Co. may be keen to provide services which will encourage use of its network. Given the complexity of the network and the nature of local legislation it may be slow to implement this service.

The competition between Phone Co. and Cable Co. (who also may provide phone services) is likely to be fierce, ruling out co-operative ventures of the kind required. Where co-operation does succeed, the relationships could be quite complex and this complexity may against the interests of the customer of the video on demand service.

On the plus side, the Phone Co. does have advanced charging and billing facilities which could be a solid basis for the administrative part of the video on demand service. The Phone Co. also has a wide-spread network, serving a majority of households in developed countries.

***Option 3 – Cable Co.:***

Many of the issues mentioned under option 2, are also valid here. Speed of implementing the service and making it available to a large customer base depends greatly on the area observed. For instance, most cities and built up areas in the USA and certain countries in Europe (e.g. The Netherlands and Belgium) have been cabled with wide area networks. The installed bandwidth does vary enormously, however, and video on demand services can be introduced only where the bandwidth allows. In other developed countries, and in most rural areas, cable provision is patchy.

The criteria could, however, easily be met if this obstacle were to be overcome. The Cable Co. could provide a simple and virtually risk free service for its potential customers and could prove to be very profitable.

***Option 4 – Video Retailer:***

The Video Retailer has customers who rent videos but placing video provisioning services in the stores still leaves the problem of how to transport the signal to the home. The customer and the retailer would still have to rely on the phone and cable networks which lie between them. This is therefore little different from option 1.

Video retailers often occupy high street premises which are expensive to rent. Although a physical presence may be comforting to the customer, it is not required and will push up the cost to the customer.

From the above analysis it is straightforward to make a selection:

*The Video Library has the contract with the Customer.*

## 4.8 Task 6 — Define Solution Architecture

### *Analyse implications of solution*

Task 2 identified three levels at which agents could be identified – Commercial, Informational, Technological / Engineering – and concentrated on modelling the chain of interactions at the commercial level. In this task, ways in which the different chains impinge on one another need to be examined.

One way in which to discover some of the dependencies between commercial, informational and technical or engineering concerns is to consider the ways in which a proposed system might fail. This negative analysis often delivers results more quickly than analysis of the correct operation of a system.

The following possible component failures were identified:

- child (as viewer) getting access to unsuitable (adult, X-rated) video material - this would be interpreted as a failure of some selection mechanism
- interrupted delivery - this would be interpreted as a failure of some delivery mechanism.

The following possible consistency failures were identified:

- video catalogue referring to unavailable material - this would be interpreted as a failure to co-ordinate the catalogue with the video library store
- video catalogue referring to unsuitable (X-rated) material - this would be interpreted as a failure to co-ordinate the catalogue with the selection controls.

Only a few examples of possible failures are provided here. An extended analysis is needed in real world situations.

### *Define required components*

The following generic components were identified. These components would probably appear in any of the likely options:

- video catalogue
  - containing video titles, synopses, cast, ...
  - allowing on-line browsing, ...
- selection mechanism; a way to select some particular material from a list of possible materials
- delivery mechanism; a way to deliver the selected material to the customer or viewer
- billing/payment/collection mechanism; a way to monitor the use of a service, keep records, generate bills and account for the receipt of moneys.
- selection control mechanism; a way to control the extent to which selection can be exercised by the viewer, consistent with the wishes of the customer
- delivery control mechanism; a way to control the rate and time of delivery: for instance slow motion, fast forward or reverse
- display result ; the result of service delivery i.e. output to viewer's TV screen, perhaps not to a tape owned by the customer.
- authentication / authorisation mechanism; to validate Customers and to ensure that records of service use remain consistent with actual use.

These descriptions require refinement before they can be implemented as sensible technological components. Such decomposition forms part of the technical design of the system and only impinges on the business model when any of the concerns about the enterprise expressed here become invalid or are contradicted.

### *Define required contract*

The contract between the video library and the customer needs to include provisions for the following items:

- Who bears the cost of failure? For example, if the connection is lost while a viewer is watching a film, does the customer pay for the whole film, for the part watched, or not at all?
- What guarantees can/must be offered? For example, is delivery guaranteed at all times of the day or is there a visible bottleneck at peak viewing times (20:00 to 22:00).
- Proforma contract (standard terms and conditions). For instance, there may be standard consumer protection clauses which are enforced by a regulatory body.

Contracts may also specify other agents, such as service registration agencies and regulatory bodies, consumer rights and other references to the law, and complaint procedures.

### *Confirm architecture*

This sub-task can only be completed when other sub-tasks are done in more detail than is possible here.

The solution architecture is agreed between the problem owner and the analyst and as such forms part of the contract between these two agents. It has clear implications for any quality assurance process associated with the methodology.

## 4.9 Task 7 — Formulate Business Case

### *Identify stakeholders and decision drivers*

The key stakeholder from whose perspective the modelling is proceeding is the video library. However, other stakeholders include the agents of existing systems (task 1) and potential agents of the proposed system (task 2).

For each of these, an estimate of their likely decision drivers is included in the table below:

**Table 5** Stakeholder and Driver analysis

| *Stakeholder* | *Decision drivers* |
|---|---|
| Video library | Revenue growth |
| Cable Co. | Subscriber growth |
| Phone Co. | Revenue growth |
| High street shop | Survival against technological redundancy. Possible entry into niche markets. |
| Viewer | Ease of access, range of available material |
| Customer | Quality of service (value-for-money, control over use of Video on Demand service by viewer) |
| Regulatory bodies | Fair competition, national/Government interest, public morals and decency, |

Billing agents have not been included among the stakeholders. This is because their participation in the video on demand scheme can be taken for granted and many, such as card companies, provide a known, generic service.

### *Identify benefits, costs and risks*

For each stakeholder, it is important to estimate benefits, costs and risks. The video library is the case study's perspective but the estimated perspective of the others on the situation is nevertheless of relevance to any business case: *"what will the competition do?"* is an important question.

**Table 6** Stakeholder value analysis

| *Stakeholder* | *Benefits* | *Costs* | *Risks* |
|---|---|---|---|
| Video library | Increased utilisation of existing video stock | Hardware, software, network connection, administration, marketing | No take up of new service or conversely too many customers causing service degradation |
| Cable Co. | Increased utilisation of cable, increased traffic | Installation of switching capabilities | Few if any; lack of bandwidth provision or lack of take up of provided bandwidth |
| Phone Co. | Increased utilisation of network, increased traffic | Minimal | Minimal |
| High street shop | Possible short-term profit selling customer lists or customer recruitment service to video library. | None | Erosion of normal business |
| Viewer | Increased access to video | Minimal | None |
| Customer | Better value-for-money More flexible cost structure (you only pay for what you've seen). | Installation of terminal equipment; costs depend on charging structures and market conditions | Potential loss of control over viewed material & expenditure |

### *Analyse benefit/cost/risk distribution*

The analysis of benefits, cost and risks in ODP systems is no different from non-ODP systems. Some the questions that will need investigation are:

- How much can we charge the customer for the service?
- How does this need to get distributed between the various agents?
- How much is the infrastructure going to cost?

- How are these costs shared between the various agents?
- How are the risks shared between the various agents?

*Formulate investment / procurement plans*

It will be necessary to analyse whether each agent has a reason to participate in the video on demand system. This analysis is to be developed from the perspective of required investments and procurements. One important question will be:

*How quickly (if ever) will investments be recouped?*

This sub-task also cannot be completed until other sub-tasks are done in more detail.

The investment and procurement plans are agreed between the problem owner and the analyst and as such form part of the contract between these two agents. They too have clear implications for any quality assurance process associated with the methodology.

## 4.10 Task 8 — Define Migration Plan

*Define steps towards solution architecture*

- Advertise / pilot new service - this may involve service brokers or other mechanisms of information dissemination. Existing teletext services may be used and advertising in the daily or weekly press may also be needed.
- Identify components that can be used independently (e.g. video catalogue which is not on-line). These components can sometimes be separately tested. For instance an on-line programme listing service for satellite movie channels, available via prestel or teletext, is already a standard feature in broadcasting systems.
- Confirm technical capability; this can best be done with a pilot implementation, following naturally from a laboratory prototype.
- Confirm economics - verify assumptions contained in the business case; again, the pilot implementation can provide valuable feedback.
- Extend the service to cover ever wider geographical areas.

*Analyse migration risks*

Migration risks are best analysed by looking at the ways in which things can go wrong:

- What happens if the video catalogue starts losing information? What happens if the updates are insufficiently frequent? They will cause people to ask for videos that aren't there, leading to customer dissatisfaction, or will lead new videos not to be utilised, because nobody knows they are there.
- Risk of companies not fulfilling their contractual obligations or of going broke.
- Risk of tight coupling (synchronisation) between independent parallel activities - are there opportunities to decouple these activities?
- Risk of video shops having exclusive arrangements with video libraries, hence causing problems for access to material over a cable.
- Risk of the emergence of new technology which will leapfrog the current video on demand service proposal.

*Agree migration plan*

At this stage both the new and existing enterprise are well analysed and a plan for the migration from one to the other can be drawn up. This step has not been completed for the video on demand example since there are few ODP specific activities involved in these steps.

The migration plan is agreed between the problem owner and the analyst and as such forms part of the contract between these two agents. Once again it has clear implications for any quality assurance process associated with the methodology.

# 5 IMPLEMENTATION

## 5.1 General model for implementation

The authors, as practitioners in a commercial organisation, are conscious of the fact that many modelling methods have no clear link with implementation. We would argue that any apparent insights provided by such methods are flawed because they fail to provide understanding that can be acted on. The business relationship modelling methodology described and illustrated in this paper is connected with a zone of implementation (Figure 4). In this zone what we need is a general **problem-solving engine** for implementation and delivery problems. The structure of this engine is:

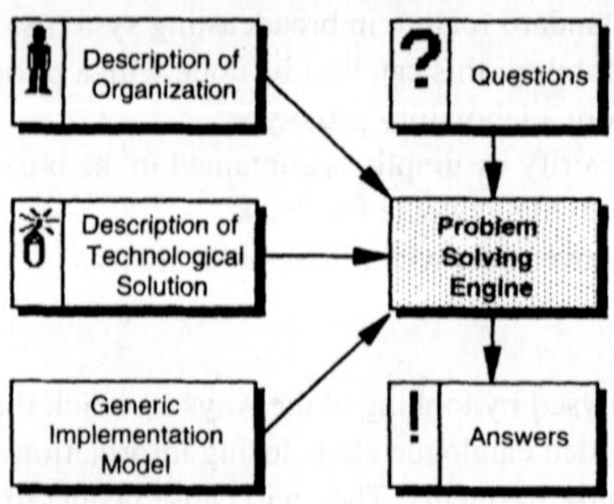


**Figure 13** Problem solving engine.

The kind of questions that this problem-solving engine can address are:

- Can this organisation, in this context, reasonably expect to implement this solution to this problem? To what extent is the intention to implement this solution compatible with other prevailing intentions? What are the implementation risks? What are the chances of achieving the desired benefits? What are the possible side-effects, and what are the implications of these side-effects to the stake-holders?
- How do we change the organisation (and its environment and infrastructure) to get the desired benefits from a given system?

- How do we design an implementable solution for this problem of this organisation in this context? How do we set an appropriate balance between risk and reward?
- How can we decompose a large complex and high-risk change, so that it may be effected in easier steps?

To answer such questions, the problem-solving engine draws on a generic model of the implementation process, together with context-specific models of the organisation (enterprise models) and solution (technology models). Such a model requires both theoretical and empirical grounding. Different theories (for example, Attewell's, (1992) view of technology diffusion through a knowledge barrier or Fowler and Rifkin's (1990) advocate/receptor model) could be incorporated into the model.

- A good theory may provide links between the characteristics of the organisation / context, and the factors affecting successful migration / implementation.
- Alternatively, a good theory may provide links between the characteristics of the solution / system, and the factors affecting successful migration / implementation.

Each theory may prompt consideration of particular aspects of the situation, and may even provide theoretical justification for further research on specific points. The model is then used to give recommendations and reassurance (directly or indirectly) to user organisations, as well as to vendor and third-party organisations.

A simple model would describe the implementation of a single integrated solution into a single integrated organisation. In reality, we usually have to deal with the concurrent implementation of several semi-integrated solutions into decentralised or federated organisations. Thus a more complex model would deal with the complications that arise from this concurrency.

## 5.2 Planning and managing change

The implementation of a solution by an organisation is likely to be more successful if it is explicitly managed as a change. This management should cover both accommodation and assimilation (Hundert, 1989).

- Accommodation of the organisation to the solution can be divided into two parts. The organisation needs to ensure that its plans and policies are geared to the exploitation of the solution. And the organisation also needs to ensure that it acquires the capability to exploit the solution effectively.
- Assimilation of the solution can also be divided into two parts. The solution will offer a set of tools and methods, which will usually have to be adapted and extended to fit the requirements of the organisation. And the solution will then have to be used for the purposes of the organisation, in which it will be applied in unique ways to unique problems and projects. Application of the solution includes interpretation (creating meanings) as well as use.

If we consider the two parts of accommodation, the two parts of assimilation, together with the overall management of the change, this gives us five implementation streams, as shown in the following diagram.

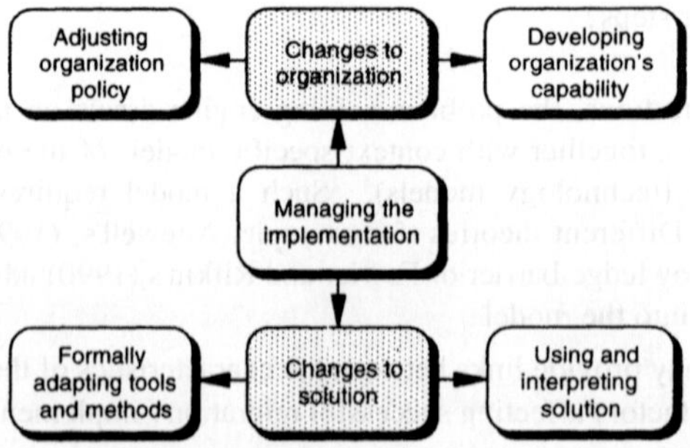


**Figure 14** Five streams of implementation.

When a sophisticated and complex solution is implemented into a large and socio-technically heterogeneous organisation, the effects cannot be completely predicted. Some of the changes can be planned, but there must be enough flexibility in the plan for what cannot be planned. However, a roadmap for implementation, based on a similar five stream approach, is already successfully in use within our organisation to manage the introduction of technology change in the integrated CASE tools market. This gives a degree of confidence that this model is soundly based.

For more discussion and analysis on implementation and delivery of IT solutions, see (Veryard 1995b).

# 6 CONCLUSION

As we decentralise and provide greater technological openness in the means of support to organisational activities we introduce more factors into our systems development decision processes. We need to be able to determine where to position systems within the complex web of business inter-relationships that will emerge on the Information Superhighway and through open distributed processing initiatives. We need to develop information systems strategies that support business strategies without them becoming locked together in ways that curtail organisational flexibility.

To satisfy these needs, there must be effective methods for modelling the business topology and the information technology topology in parallel: comparing them and supporting judgements about appropriate systems solutions. The business relationship modelling methodology described and illustrated in this paper is a step towards satisfying the needs.

## 7 REFERENCES

Ackoff, R.L. (1972) Towards a system of systems concepts, in Systems Behaviour (eds. Beishon, J. & Peters G), pp 83-90, Open University / Harper & Row, London, UK.

ANSA, (1991) *A Systems Designer's Introduction to the Architecture*, APM Ltd., Cambridge, UK.

Attewell, P. (1992) Technology Diffusion and Organizational Learning: the case of business computing, *Organizational Science*, **3** (1), February 1992.

Benjamin, R., and Wigand, R. (1995) Electronic Markets and Virtual Value Chains on the Information Superhighway, *Sloan Management Review*, Winter 1995, pp 62-72.

Bowen, D.E. and Lawler, E.E. (1992) The Empowerment of Service Workers: What, Why, How, and When, *Sloan Management Review*, Spring 1992, pp 31-39.

Bracher, M.(1994) On the Psychological and Social Functions of Language: Lacan's Theory of the Four Discourses, in *Lacanian Theory of Discourse: Subject, Structure and Society* (eds. Bracher, M. et al), pp 107-128, New York University, New York, USA.

Checkland, P. (1981) *Systems Thinking, Systems Practice*, J. Wiley & Sons, London, UK.

Crane, R.R. (1986) *The Four Organisations of Lord Brown and R.A.E.W.*, Doctoral Thesis, Kennedy-Western University, USA.

Davenport, T.H., Eccles, R.G. & Prusak, L. (1992) Information Politics, *Sloan Management Review*, Fall 1992, pp 53-65.

Dobson, J.E. (1993) Organisation Requirements Definition for Information Technology Systems, in *Conference on the Theory, Use and Integrative Aspects of IS Methodologies*, pp 295-308, British Computer Society, London, UK.

Dobson, J.E., Blyth, A.J.C., Chudge, J. and Strens, R. (1994) The ORDIT Approach to Organisational Requirements, in *Requirements Engineering: Social and Technical Issues* (eds. M. Jirotka and J. Goguen), pp. 87-106, Academic Press, London, UK.

Fowler, P. and Rifkin, S. (1990) *Software Engineering Process Group Guide*, Technical Report CMU/SEI-90-TR-24, Software Engineering Institute, USA.

Goold, M. (1991) Strategic Control in the Decentralized Firm, *Sloan Management Review*, Winter 1991, pp 69-81.

Hammer, M. and Champy, J. (1993) *Reengineering the Corporation*, Harper Business, Harper Collins Publishers, New York, USA.

Handy, C. (1992) Balancing Corporate Power: A new federalist paper, *Harvard Business Review*, Nov-Dec 1992, pp 59-72.

Hewitt, C. & de Jong, P. (1984) Open Systems, in *On Conceptual Modelling* (eds. Brodie, M.L., Mylopoulos, J., & Schmidt, J.W.), Springer Verlag, New York, USA.

Hundert, E.M. (1989) *Philosophy, Psychiatry and Neuroscience: Three Approaches to the Mind: A Synthetic Analysis of the Varieties of Human Experience*, Oxford University Press, New York, USA.

Iggulden, D., Dobson, J. & Veryard, R. (1993) Enterprise Computing: ODP as an Instrument of Hegemony, in Proceedings of ICODP 93, Berlin, Germany.

International Standards Organisation (1993), *Recommendation X.902: Basic Reference Model of Open Distributed Processing Part 2 Descriptive Model* and *Part 3: Prescriptive Model*, ISO 10746-2 CD and ISO 10746-3 CD.

Katzenbach, J.R. and Smith, D.K. (1993) The Discipline of Teams, *Harvard Business Review*, March-April 1993, pp 111-120.

Kelly, K. (1994) *Out of Control: The New Biology of Machines,* Fourth Estate, London, UK.

Lehman, M.M. (1980) Programs, life-cycles and laws of software evolution, *Proc IEEE*, **68** (1), pp 1060-1076.

Markus, M.L. (1990) Towards a "Critical Mass" Theory of Interactive Media, in *Organisations and Communication Technology* (eds. Fulk, J. & Steinfeld, C.), pp 194-218, Sage, Newbury Park CA, USA.

OMG (1991) *CORBA*: *Common Object Request Broker: Architecture and Specification*, Object Management Group & X/Open, USA.

Ries, A. and Trout, J. (1986), *Marketing Warfare*, McGraw-Hill Book Co., Singapore.

Schumacher, E.F. (1974) *Small is Beautiful*, Sphere Books Ltd., Penguin Group, London, UK.

Siewiorek, D.P. and Swarz, R.S. (1992) *Reliable Computer Systems, Design and Evaluation*, Digital Press, USA.

Smith, K.K. and Berg, D.N. (1987) *Paradoxes of Group Life*, Jossey Bass, San Francisco, CA, USA.

Strens, R. & Dobson. J.E. (1993) *Responsibility Modelling*, Department of Computer Science, University of Newcastle upon Tyne, personal communication.

Symons, V. & Walsham, G. (1988) The evaluation of information systems: a critique, *Journal of Applied Systems Analysis*, April 1988, pp 119-132.

Texas Instruments Inc. (1990) *A Guide to Information Engineering using the IEF™*, Second Edition. Texas Instruments, Plano TX, USA.

Veryard, R. (1994) *Information Coordination: The Management of Information Models, Systems and Organisations*, Prentice-Hall, Hemel Hempstead, UK.

Veryard. R. (1995a) How Business Relationship Modelling Supports Quality Assurance of Business Objects, unpublished paper.

Veryard, R. (1995b) IT Implementation or Delivery: Thoughts on Assimilation, Accommodation and Maturity, unpublished paper.

Veryard, R. and Dobson, J. (1995) *Third Order Requirements Engineering: Vision and Identity*, Proceedings of REFSQ 95, Second International Workshop on Requirements Engineering: Foundation for Software Quality, June 12-13, 1995, Jyvaskyla, Finland.

Veryard, R. and Macdonald, I.G. (1994) *EMM/ODP: A Methodology for Federated and Distributed Systems*, in Methods and Associated Tools for the Information Systems Life Cycle (eds. Verrijn-Stuart, A.A., and Olle, T.W.), IFIP Transactions, North-Holland, Amsterdam, Netherlands.

Wood, M. and Sommerville, I. (1988) An Information Retrieval System for Software Components, *Software Engineering Journal*, pp 198-207, Sept. 1988.

## 8 ACKNOWLEDGEMENTS

This paper derives from work done in the Enterprise Computing Project, a collaborative effort, grant-aided by the UK's Department of Trade and Industry under their ODSA programme. Important contributions towards the case study were made by Sally Jack of TI Information Engineering Ltd. and by Rob van der Linden of APM Ltd., Cambridge. This work has also benefited from the participation of David Iggulden and John Dobson.

## 9 BIOGRAPHIES

### Ian Macdonald

Dr. Macdonald is the Group Quality Director for the Texas Instruments' Software Business in Europe, presently known as TI Information Engineering. He was one of the founders of James Martin Associates (bought by TI in 1991 to become part of the Software Business). In 1983-84 Ian led the JMA team in developing the Information Engineering methodology for systems development. He was also involved in the initial specification of TI's Information Engineering Facility – the first integrated CASE tool. Recently he led the development and commercial launch of TI's IE\Q methodology – the first such approach for setting up and managing a quality system for the information systems function.

For the past 15 years Ian has managed consulting and training operations in CACI, JMA and TI. Prior to that he was a database specialist with Univac and ICL. He is a parasitologist, a quality auditor, a Chartered Engineer, a Fellow of the BCS and a member of IFIP WG 8.1.

### Richard Veryard

Richard Veryard is a Principal Consultant with Texas Instruments, and a member of TI Group Technical Staff. He has guided numerous large organizations through the implementation of sophisticated tools and methods; his experience in business information modelling, information coordination and technological change management has been captured in several books and countless articles. He has made a significant contribution to a number of recent methodological innovations within Texas Instruments, including IE\Q. He is a member of the BCS Requirements Engineering SIG, and of IFIP WG 8.6.

# 10

# Realization of a decentralized IS-strategy

*K. Axelsson*
*Department of Computer and Information Science*
*Linköping University, S-581 83 Linköping, Sweden*
*Telephone: 46 13 28 26 79, Fax: 46 13 14 22 31, karax@ida.liu.se*

**Abstract**

Today almost all organizations are dependent on information technology. It is therefore of great importance to structure the information systems in a satisfying way. Different strategies for structuring information systems, in order to create an information systems architecture, have been used for several years. This paper discusses an IS-strategy that enables each business function in a decentralized organization to co-operate with other functions, without losing their autonomy. The IS-strategy could be described as an activity-based, functional approach. Three case studies in different organizations, with the strategy in common, have been conducted. Experiences of success and failure with the strategy realization in these organizations are presented and analysed in the paper. The conclusions show that the IS-strategy can give a substantial support to decentralized organizations. To achieve this result user participation during system development can not be disregarded. Otherwise, problems with the distribution of responsibility for the information systems almost inevitably occur. In decentralized organizations it is of greatest importance to take such problems into serious consideration.

**Keywords**

Decentralization, information systems, information systems strategy, information systems architecture, case studies, responsibility, user participation

## INTRODUCTION

Most organizations have several information systems and the need to structure these systems accordingly is growing. Structural aspects are becoming more important when the coordination of the organization's information, and the co-operation between business functions within an organization, are increasing.

When organizations are organized in a decentralized way the structure of the information systems must support this. The by far most common way to create a structure today is just to let the structure appear without any planned strategy. The outcome of this could be a confused structure that no one would really understand. An alternative action is to follow a plan or a *strategy* that prescribes how to structure the information systems to each other and to the business functions (e. g. Zachman, 1978; Earl, 1987). A structure of information systems is, in this paper, called an *information systems architecture*. This concept denotes how information and responsibility are distributed between information systems and between different parts of the organization. A second meaning of the concept is how the communication and interaction are accomplished both between the information systems and between the systems and the rest of the organization. The concept has been further examined by Opdahl and Andersen (1994). Brancheau and Wetherbe (1986) use the expression information architecture to describe a high-level map of the information requirements of an organization.

Within our research program for system development there is a project concerning strategies for the structuring of information systems (e. g. Axelsson, 1995; Pettersson and Goldkuhl, 1993; Pettersson, 1994). The strategies are aiming at structuring the information systems of an organization in a way that will facilitate use of the information systems and future changes in the systems. The structure is built to avoid situations where information systems are difficult to survey, manage, maintain and change without unexpected consequences. The strategies present, however, different means for the realization of this aim.

A common way to create an information systems architecture is to separate the application processing from the data used to support it. The data is then integrated and made consistent in large databases, that can be reached by all users in an organization (Martin, 1989). A result from this *globalization of data* is that the possibility for local influences is drastically reduced. The administration of data must be conducted by a central IS-department, i. e. by a data manager. This can appear to be a serious problem in decentralized organizations, where many decisions are made at a local level. Hence, a centralized structure of the information systems can become a threat to the idea of decentralization.

An alternative to the centralized approach is to create a federation of small information systems that are able to interact with each other when necessary. If information systems can be designed so that an independence regarding the storage and processing of information is achieved, each information system will be more flexible. It will then be easier to change or modify existing information systems, and to implement new systems, without disturbing other information systems of the organization. This situation supports decentralized organizations in an efficient way. An IS-strategy that facilitates this is the subject of the paper. The strategy could be described as an *activity-based strategy* with a functional approach to the structuring of information systems*. It has been formulated and used in Sweden (Hugoson, 1989), but similar thoughts can also be identified in different international approaches (e. g. Davis, 1984; Woolfe, 1989).

* It is difficult to translate the Swedish expression for the strategy into English in a way that preserves the exact original conception. This translation is however as close to the origin as possible.

# CASE STUDIES

Three case studies, conducted in the research project, were made in decentralized organizations and are therefore of interest in this paper. The three companies are all rather large organizations with over 200 employees each. Two of the companies have a divisional organization structure (Mintzberg, 1983) and all three companies have the IS-strategy in common. The realization of the IS-strategy and its consequences have been studied. The paper focuses on both success and failure that can be derived to the IS-strategy realization. A divisional structure seems to be well suited for this decentralized IS-strategy. Such large companies probably derive more advantages from message interaction and autonomy between business functions than smaller ones do. The organizations are made anonymous here; a short description of the companies is presented below.

## Paper mill

The first case study was conducted at a paper mill producing cardboard for pre-packages of provisions. The organization is structured in different business functions, for example purchase, economy, manufacturing. There are around 40 information systems located and used in different functions. Each function is responsible for its own information systems and each system is only used in one function.

## Manufacturing industry

The second case study was conducted in a manufacturing industry producing electronic equipment. The company belongs to a group of companies with factories both in Europe and in the United States. The organization has a divisional structure. Each division includes a number of factories with both local and central information systems. The central information systems are generic systems without any local variations. The systems are functioning to communicate both within and between factories.

## Forestry company

The third case study was conducted at a forestry company, which is part of a large group of companies within different branches of business. The studied company sells paper for magazines, mostly on the basis of customer orders. This organization has a divisional structure and the sales offices at different locations interact through a sales system. The sales system consists of different parts containing information about customer orders, the stock, product distribution and invoices. The system is divided into subsystems and each subsystem supports a specific business function in the organization.

## Data collection and data analysis

The first purpose with the case studies has been to find out *the possibilities to realize the theoretical strategy in real situations.* The case studies have given a reasonably convincing affirmative answer to this question. The second purpose has been to investigate *what*

***consequences the realization of the strategy would have for people in an organization.*** Four different categories of consequences were studied:

- responsibility for information systems;
- functionality of information systems;
- transparency of information systems;
- possibility to change information systems.

The case studies were conducted through a qualitative approach and the main purpose of the studies has been to gain profound knowledge about some selected phenomena (i.e. the four categories above) rather than statistical information about whole organizations. Therefore, the method used for data collection was interviews. The persons in charge of the realization of the information systems architecture in each organization were the first to be interviewed. Then users and system analysts were interviewed. By "user", here, I mean persons who use the information system and the information in some part of their employment, not only the end-users who collect and register the data. Additional interviews with the same persons were conducted when necessary. Each interview lasted about two hours. A total sum of 20 interviews was conducted during the case studies.

The questions were not standardized and the interviews had the character of conversations about some interesting issues, i. e. the interviews were conducted according to the *guided interview principle* (Patton, 1990). The case studies also included investigations of other sources such as data models, tables and other types of documentation from the information system development processes. Furthermore, some of the information systems in the studied organizations were demonstrated and analysed.

The data analysis has been conducted with a grounded theory approach (Strauss and Corbin, 1990). The empirical data has been analyzed to find different concepts and categories. The categories have later been compared in order to find patterns, similarities and differences in the material. On basis of the comparison the categories have been related to each other and a theory has finally been constructed. This is a method for qualitative data analysis, which is suitable for studies where the field is rather unknown when the study starts. The approach is often used in studies where human beings are the objects and the researcher wants to study something without any prejudices. The findings presented in this paper are only a part of the total results from the case studies. The research project is further explained in Pettersson (1994).

## THEORETICAL DESCRIPTION OF AN ACTIVITY-BASED IS-STRATEGY

The IS-strategy accentuates that the information of an organization should be structured in well-defined, activity-based, functional, autonomous systems. The responsibility for systems and information is decentralized and there is an in advance defined interaction between the systems (Hugoson, 1989; Magoulas and Pessi, 1991). Hugoson (1989) defines an autonomous information system:

*"An Autonomous Information System is an Information System that reads and updates its own database, and that may be implemented in a separate computer. It has its own data storage and*

*can run for a period of time when other information systems are not running. An Autonomous Information System serves one and only one area of operations in the enterprise/organisation."*

According to the strategy, responsibility for the information systems is a very important issue. The information system is located, due to the responsibility, in a specific organizational function, where the system conducts information processing tasks. This implies that the person in charge of a business function is the one responsible for the information systems in that function. These *business functions* could be for example purchase, economy or manufacturing. It is important to find the business functions when the IS-strategy is going to be realized. The business functions are not always the same as the departments found in an organization chart. Before the system development process begins the business functions must be defined.

The IS-strategy prescribes an organization with several functional-based information systems instead of one or a few centralized, global systems and databases. The information systems contain all necessary, local information in local databases. The autonomous information systems are, when necessary, able to communicate with each other. The IS-strategy distinguishes between local information and "connective information". Connective information is defined as information that is needed in other business functions and therefore sent as messages to these functions. The communication between autonomous, interacting information systems is conducted through exchange of messages according to defined rules, in contrast to the usage of common databases. The users in a business function can only reach information in the information systems of their function. They are not able to reach information in databases outside their own function. All computerized communication between functions is restricted by contracts established between the communicating functions. Hugoson (1989) states that:

*"It is possible, and advisable, to define the message interaction structure and to describe every single message without knowing the data structure of any information system."*

Each business function is able to decide about changes within its own information systems as long as the systems can still send and receive messages from the other business functions. The business functions are making the decisions but they are not designing the information systems. There can of course be an IS-department with that kind of expert knowledge in the organization.

The responsibility for the total information systems architecture is a task for the managers of the organization, since this responsibility requires a general view of all the business functions, their goals and purposes. This responsibility also includes creation and maintenance of global concepts of the organization, that are necessary for the communication between information systems.

Figure 1 shows a schematic picture of the relationship between different business functions and their information systems.

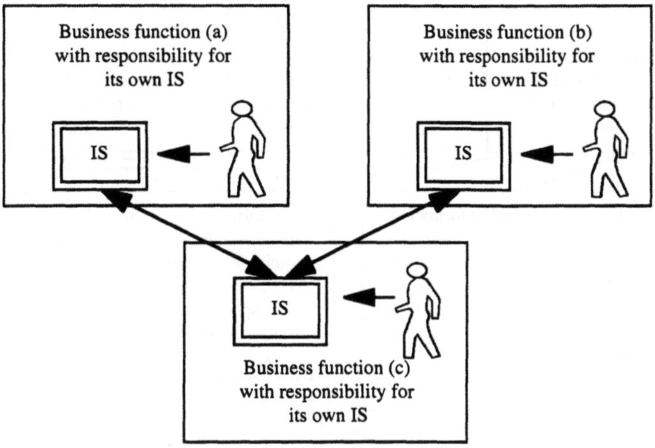


**Figure 1** Information systems in a decentralized structure interacting through messages.

Figure 2 illustrates the relations between different parts of the theory behind the IS-strategy, as it has been described here. By presenting the relations in a graphic form the theory becomes more transparent and communicable. This is more difficult to achieve when writing a linear text, which often hides parts of the theory. The graph follows the description principles presented in Goldkuhl and Röstlinger (1993).

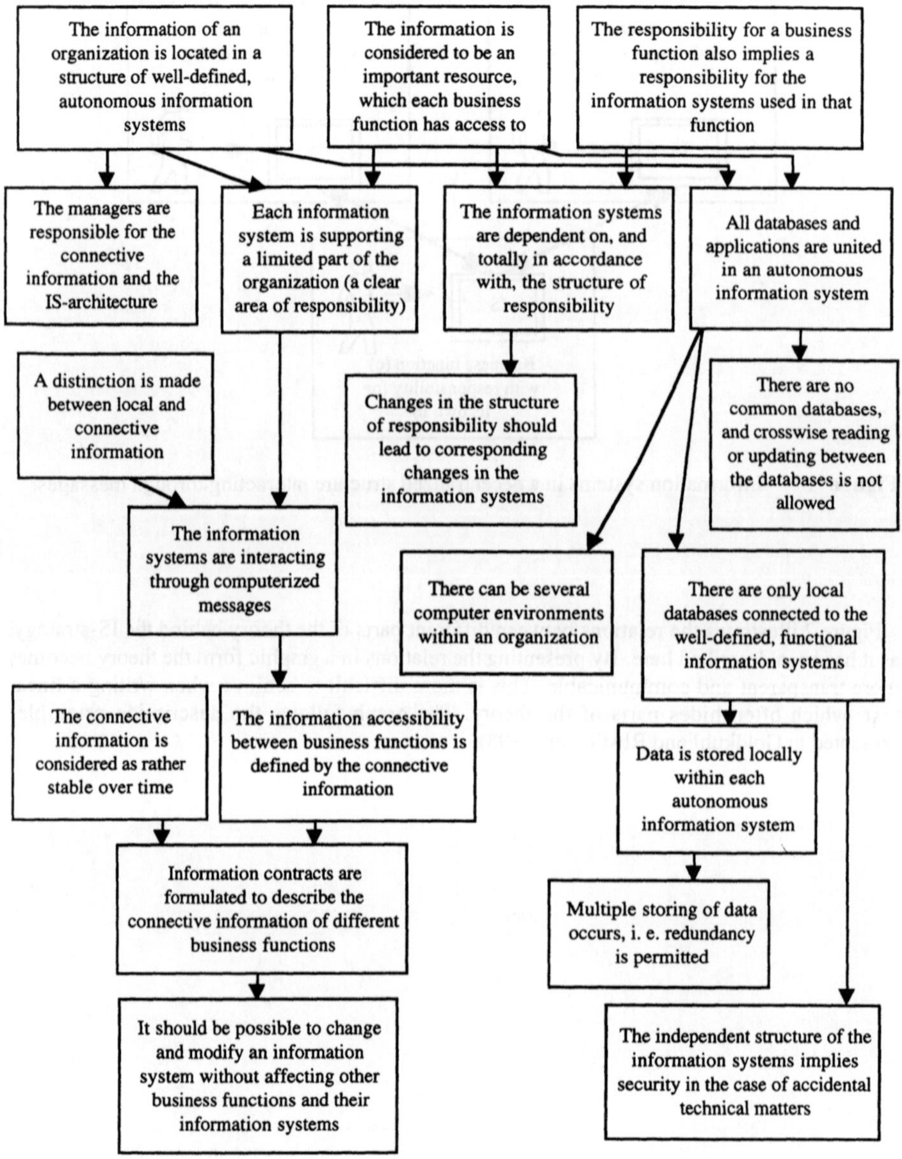


**Figure 2** Relations between different parts of the activity-based IS-strategy.

# SUCCESS OF THE STRATEGY REALIZATION IN THE STUDIED ORGANIZATIONS

In this section, the findings indicating success in the case studies are structured within the categories of consequences, mentioned earlier in the paper. The category of responsibility is omitted since there was no success found in this field.

## Functionality of information systems

When an organization decides to realize an IS-strategy, a process at several levels in the organization starts. The system development process is of course important, but it is not the only one. If the information systems architecture is going to be successfully developed, there are other features beside the information systems that must be considered. The way decisions are made, how responsibility is given and taken, how the managers act and how the users are fulfilling their tasks are a few significant examples. It is of course important to design information systems that support the business functions, but the information systems are not adequate without necessary organizational changes in the same direction. The case studies show that most of the *positive results concerned technical solutions during the system development*, such as implementing the information systems technically and connecting them to each other. The three organizations have all succeeded in developing many interacting information systems in a short time.

## Transparency of information systems

The message interaction between information systems can be realized in different ways; with a separate communication system or file transmissions for example. *The studied organizations have chosen different solutions for the message interaction, but they have all succeeded in accomplishing this technical matter.* The business functions are able to interact and send the information needed in other functions. Thus, the business functions can work in a decentralized way and the IS-strategy has reached its purpose of supporting a decentralized organization.

To be able to interact through messages, contracts over the connective information are established between business functions, as mentioned previously. It takes time and accuracy to get these contracts correct and it is of great importance that the contracts are followed. In the three studied organizations this task has been taken seriously and *there have been contracts made for all messages.* A result from this is organizations with control over the interaction between each business function. This order is not only vital for the message interaction itself, but it also offers everyone a general view of the whole decentralized organization. A high degree of transparency of the information systems facilitates for example the control of goal fulfilment in the organization.

## Possibility to change information systems

Autonomous information systems can be changed and modified without disturbing other information systems. To accomplish such a flexible and independent structure each information system must be well-defined and belong to one business function only. When the studied organizations have managed to find the business functions and develop autonomous information systems, ***the decentralized, flexible structure is a reality.*** The organizations have all succeeded in most of their functions, but no one has done it without setbacks in some function (see section 5). One key to the success of the IS-strategy is that the autonomous information systems of each business function are well-defined and separated from the information systems of other functions. Hence, a lot of time and strength have to be spent on defining the business functions in a correct way.

## FAILURE IN THE STRATEGY REALIZATION IN THE STUDIED ORGANIZATIONS

In this section the findings indicating failure in the case studies are structured within the categories of consequences, mentioned earlier in the paper. The section ends with a discussion about the connections between chosen actions and some of the negative consequences (failures) found in the studied organizations.

### Responsibility for information systems

The responsibility for information, information systems and information systems architecture is a main issue in the IS-strategy. ***The case studies show that the distribution of responsibility within the organizations is a very difficult task to accomplish.*** Most failure and negative consequences found in the case studies originate, directly or indirectly, from different responsibility problems, as these two quotations state:

***"We have total responsibility for the information systems, even though the business functions are supposed to take that responsibility. I would much rather be the one who supplies the business functions with technical knowledge."*** (System developer at the paper mill)

***"It has been very difficult to engage the managers to take the overall responsibility for the realization of the strategy. Someone ought to do this at top level in the company."*** (System developer at the forestry company)

It seems like the importance of responsibility questions has not been taken sufficiently into account during the realization of the strategy, even though the responsibility distribution is fundamental to the existence of decentralized organizations.

When responsibility for the information systems is distributed to each business function, this often means that the manager of the business function becomes the "system owner" of the information systems within his or her function. The capability of these managers differs of course; some take great responsibility for their information systems and some do not. One cause for problems could be that the managers of the business functions do not really use their systems, since they do not have the same tasks as other persons working in their function. The system owners are therefore not always at the right level in the hierarchy of the organization. They are often too high up to be able to see the needs of ordinary users. They do not always possess the knowledge necessary for system owners. Hence, these system owners are more satisfied than the users and do not contact the IS-department as long as the information systems are generating the information, that is needed in the business function. Another cause for these problems is that the system owners sometimes are located far from the users in a geographical sense, for example at the headquarters of the organization. One user in the manufacturing industry complains about this:

*"The system owner is not located in this factory and we have no contact with him. He is not concerned with our needs. Instead, we have to contact the data function at the headquarters by ourselves. We are however too few and unimportant to get our needs satisfied."*

In some of the studied organizations *there is a lack of understanding for what it really means to be a system owner.* System owners have been appointed, but these persons do not have enough information and knowledge about their responsibility. This fact shows the importance of making the strategy known and accepted at all levels in the organization. Otherwise it will never be possible to distribute responsibility and some aspects of the strategy will therefore continue to be unrealized. In absence of responsible system owners the most common solution is that the system developers at the IS-department take the responsibility, even though they would prefer to have another role in the organization.

In the same way as the strategy presupposes active, responsible users in the business functions, it also emphasizes that the total responsibility for the information systems architecture is a strategic task belonging to the managers. This is the way responsibility is supposed to be organized, according to the theoretical description of the strategy. One major problem in the studied organizations has been to achieve this aspect of the strategy. A system developer at the forestry company says:

*"Since the executives have not specified how the work should be done in the future, we have been forced to make decisions of this kind to be able to develop the information systems. We have not the right competence for making these decisions and therefore it should not be our task."*

*Both the users, the middle management (e. g. system owners) and the top managers seem to play very passive roles during the realization of the strategy.* The managers have of course approved of the realization once, but the structuring of information systems is carried out by system analysts and system developers with very little interest from the managers. The low degree of participation from two important groups (users and managers) continues after the realization is completed. The result is instead that the system developers become responsible both for the information systems of the business functions and for the information systems architecture. The main reason for this situation is not that the system developers are unwilling to distribute the responsibility, but that the business functions and the managers are reluctant to take their responsibility.

## Functionality of information systems

A fact, that can cause problems for users, is that large companies sometimes have the same types of business functions at different factories. The managers consider it to be one function for marketing, only geographically divided into a number of places. The users at each factory, on the other hand, consider their business function to be a whole, independent function, not a part of a bigger one. *If the factories are working slightly different in some way, but use instances of the same information systems, this situation can be very problematic for the users.* Their needs for changes in the information systems can not be effectuated unless the users at the other factories also ask for the same changes. A common situation is that a new and unfamiliar language is implemented in the information system, which is difficult to accept for some users. A user at the manufacturing industry says:

*"We have never used the word 'delivery time' in the same way as the other factories have. Though, since we got this generic system we are forced to use it in the same way, whether we like it or not. This leads to a lot of misunderstandings and dissatisfaction."*

The case studies show that this situation gives the organization an easier maintenance of the information systems, but on the other hand decreases the autonomy for each business function. Furthermore, this proves that the way the information systems of an organization are structured sometimes aggravates existing antagonism between groups of personnel as well as creates new conflicts.

## Transparency of information systems

The IS-strategy offers, when it is realized in a successful way, flexibility for the business functions. This is supposed to give the users increased possibilities to influence the system development, changes in the information systems and their total working environment. The strategy makes this desired situation possible, though it does not necessary lead to it. A failure made in the studied organizations was to believe that this would happen without any special effort. It turned out to be many other things that take effect on the users' possibility to influence their situation. *If the common attitude in the organization does not correspond with the intentions of the strategy, then the strategy will not change the climate in the organization.* In spite of the decentralized strategy the decisions can be made by top managers and IS-department without them knowing the users' needs and wishes, as this quotation shows:

*"We are very restrictive when it comes to changes in the information systems required by the users. The fact that users wish something is not enough for us to redesign the system."* (System developer at the manufacturing industry)

A result from such a situation, where no one listens to the users, is often that users start to dislike their information systems. The user acceptance of the systems becomes rather low in the organization. There are many explanations for low degree of user acceptance. One reason, that was obvious in the case studies, is that the system development process was accomplished with no or very little user participation. This happened because of time pressure and a doubtful attitude towards user participation.

## Possibility to change information systems

As mentioned before, the success of the IS-strategy is depending on how well the business functions are defined, since it is crucial that each information system supports only one function. *If the functions are not clearly defined, an information system could be reached by users from different business functions.* In that situation some of the flexibility and autonomy in the business functions are lost, since changes and modifications can not be done independently of the other function, its needs and wishes. This can either be an unconscious action or a deliberate choice to gain some technical advantages, such as faster access to information. A system developer at the paper mill says:

*"I'm very unsatisfied with our two integrated systems. They are a deviation from the IS-strategy. When we developed the systems it seemed as a good idea to integrate them, in order to decrease the amount of transactions between them. Now, I realize that it would be difficult to change or modify one of them."*

Whatever the reason is, it is important to be aware of the loss of autonomy for the business functions, before the decision is made. In the case studies, where this had happened, the effects of the deviation from the theoretical strategy seemed to come as a surprise to most of the involved persons.

In organizations, where managers are rather uninterested in the structuring of information systems, *the system developers are forced to make strategic decisions far outside their formal responsibility and knowledge*. The freedom for each business function to adjust their information systems is then almost complete due to the lack of management control. Problems that occur are for example to decide whether an adjustment should be local or global. During the case studies some complaints about the easiness to reach special solutions for small groups in the organizations were mentioned. These solutions were not always good for the whole organization and they were considered to be the result from a weak central interest in these questions.

## Discussion

Figure 3 shows possible connections between chosen actions and some of the negative consequences found in the studied organizations. The analysis starts with two important questions: the users' influence on system development as well as on changes in the information systems. There are several things that decrease the possibilities of user influence. One factor is the persons who are representing the users during the system development process. If there are no end-users present, the users' influence can be decreased. Two other factors are if the users are getting insufficient information about the consequences of the system development process and the lack of time that often appears in system development projects. Many authors have discussed the importance of user participation (e. g. Mumford, 1984). If the organization has a restrictive attitude towards any kind of changes, this also affects the user influence in a negative way. The lack of user influence can result in a general negative attitude towards the information systems and low user acceptance of the systems, but also unwanted changes in the usage of professional language in the information systems (Goldkuhl and Lyytinen, 1982). This can be a serious problem for the whole organization and give negative consequences for its total effectiveness.

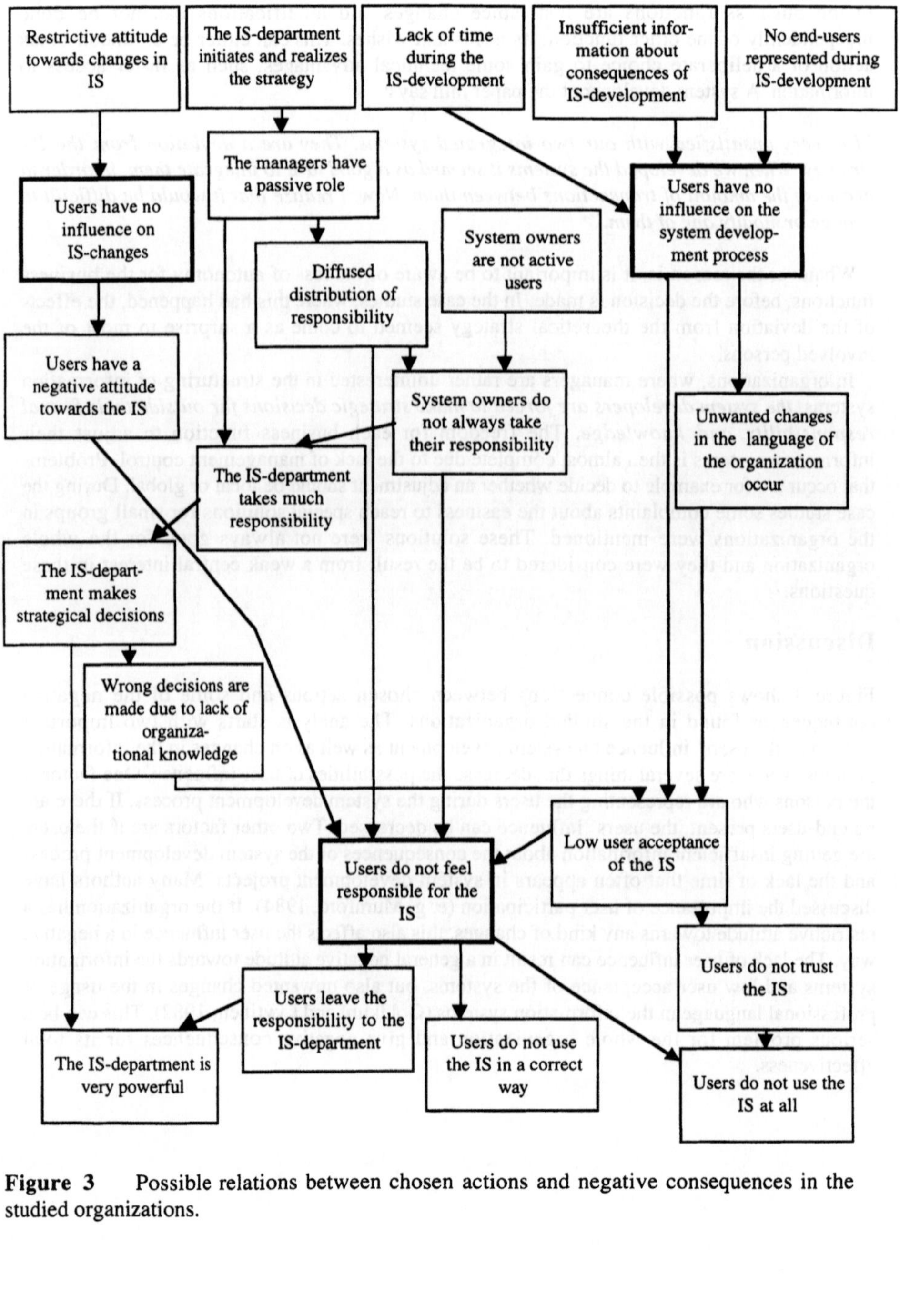


**Figure 3** Possible relations between chosen actions and negative consequences in the studied organizations.

Another problem, which has been observed in many organizational studies over the years (e. g. Davenport, 1993), seems to be that the IS-department often initiates and realizes the strategy with little or no participation from the managers or from the users. This can lead to a diffused distribution of responsibility as well as an IS-department that takes all responsibility. Another cause for this is that the system owners, who, sometimes, are not active system users, do not take their full responsibility for the information systems. If the IS-department has the responsibility it also has to make strategical decisions, which sometimes appears to be wrong due to lack of organizational knowledge. The result from all these problems could at its worst be that the users do not take any responsibility for the information systems and instead leave this to the IS-department. This function will become very powerful in such a situation. When the users have a negative attitude towards the systems and do not trust the information correctness, they might refuse to use them in a correct way or they do not use them at all.

These are results that no one wants to see in their organization. Nevertheless, they can come true if the strategy is realized without influence from the whole organization. A conclusion from this is that the IS-strategy is appropriate in decentralized organizations when the realization is done carefully. The strategy does not, however, give positive contributions to the organization if these issues are not considered seriously. The realization of the IS-strategy must therefore be accomplished at all levels in the organization, with representatives of involved groups.

## CONCLUSIONS

The two previous sections emphasize that the strategy realizations in the studied organizations were successful in some aspects and unsuccessful in others. The organizations seem to be more successful regarding the technical realization of the strategy. When it comes to handling organizational issues problems often emerge. It is important, though, to remember that these consequences are possible consequences. They are not supposed to be seen as inevitable effects occurring in all organizations that choose to realize this specific IS-strategy. The conclusions drawn from the case studies are:

- The organizations succeed in developing several interacting information systems in a short time.
- The message interaction between business functions is successfully accomplished.
- The organizations manage to develop a, to some extent, decentralized, flexible structure of information systems, where changes and adaptations are easily made.
- Users and managers are much too passive during the system development process.
- Users have no or little influence on development or changes in their information systems.
- Difficulties occur when the responsibility for information systems and architecture is going to be distributed within the organization.
- The IS-department take the total responsibility for information systems and message interaction instead of distributing the responsibility to the business functions and the managers.

A final conclusion to be drawn from this material is that the IS-strategy can give a substantial support to decentralized organizations, if only the pitfalls mentioned here are avoided.

## ACKNOWLEDGEMENTS

This research has been performed with financial support from The Swedish Council for Research in the Humanities and Social Sciences and from The Swedish Work Environment Fund. I am also grateful to Helena Bergmann for correcting my English.

## REFERENCES

Axelsson, K. (1995) Centralized or Decentralized Responsibility for Information Systems? - Consequences of two different Strategies. Department of Computer and Information Science, Linköping University.

Brancheau, J.C. and Wetherbe, J.C. (1986) Information Architectures: Methods and Practice. *Information Processing & Management*, vol 22, no 6, pp 453-463.

Davenport, T. (1993) *Process Innovation - Reengineering Work through Information Technology*. Harvard Business School Press, Boston, Massachusetts.

Davis, G.B. and Olson, M. (1984) *Management Information Systems - Conceptual Foundations, Structure and Development.* McGraw-Hill Book Company.

Earl, M. (1987) Information Systems Strategy Formulation, in *Critical Issues in Information Systems Research* (eds. R.J. Jr Boland and R.A. Hirschheim), John Wiley & Sons Ltd, Chichester, pp 157-178.

Goldkuhl, G. and Lyytinen, K. (1982) A language action view of information systems, in *Proceedings of 3rd International Conference on Information Systems* (eds. M. Ginzberg and C. Ross), Ann Arbor, Michigan, Dec 13-15 1982, pp 13-30.

Goldkuhl, G. and Röstlinger, A. (1993) Joint Elicitation of Problems: An Important Aspect of Change Analysis. Presented at IFIP wg 8.2 Working Conference on Information Systems Development: Human, Social and Organizational Aspects, May 17-19 1993, Noordwijkerhout.

Hugoson, M-Å. (1989) A System of Systems. SVING&SVIG Conference, Chalmers University of Technology.

Magoulas, T. and Pessi, K. (1991) En studie om informationssystemarkitekturer. Department of Computer Sciences, Chalmers University of Technology and the University of Göteborg (in Swedish).

Martin, J. (1989) *Information Engineering - Introduction*, Prentice-Hall, New Jersey.

Mintzberg, H. (1983) *Structures in Fives - Designing Effective Organizations*. Prentice-Hall, New Jersey.

Mumford, E. (1984) Participation - From Aristotle to today, in *Beyond productivity: Information systems development for organizational effectiveness* (ed. T. Bemelmans), North-Holland, Amsterdam.

Opdahl, A.L. and Andersen, E.S. (1994) A Metamodel for IS-Architecture Representation (draft paper). University of Bergen.

Patton, M.Q. (1990) *Qualitative Evaluation and Research Methods*. Sage Publications, Newbury Park.

Pettersson*, K. and Goldkuhl, G. (1993) A Comparison between two Strategies for Information Systems Architectures. Presented at Sundsvall 42, 1993, LiTH-IDA-R-94-08, Department of Computer and Information Science, Linköping University.

Pettersson*, K. (1994) Informationssystemstrukturering, ansvarsfördelning och användarinflytande - En komparativ studie med utgångspunkt i två informationssystemstrategier. Licentiate Thesis no FHS 4/94, Department of Computer and Information Science, Linköping University (in Swedish).

Strauss, A. and Corbin, J. (1990) *Basics of Qualitative Research - Grounded Theory Procedures and Techniques*. Sage Publications, Newbury Park.

Woolfe, R. (1989) Managing information systems in a decentralised business. Butler Cox Foundation.

Zachman, J.A. (1978) The Information Systems Management System: A New Framework for Planning. *DATABASE*, Winter 1978.

## BIOGRAPHY

Karin Axelsson holds a licentiate degree in information systems development and has presented a licentiate thesis concerning information systems structuring, responsibility distribution and user participation. She is a Ph.D. candidate at Linköping University, where she is working in the Research group VITS at the department of computer and information science. Her main field of research is in information systems architectures and methods of business redesign. At the moment she is working in an action research project at the Swedish Maritime Administration Hydrographic Department. She is also a member of the board of Swedish Information Processing Society (east chapter).

---

* Married name has changed to Axelsson.

# 11

# A software process model for business reengineering

*A. T. Berztiss*[1,2] *and J. A. Bubenko, jr.*[2,3]

[1] *Department of Computer Science, University of Pittsburgh Pittsburgh, PA 15260, USA;*
*e-mail: alpha@cs.pitt.edu; fax: +412-624-8854*

[2] *SYSLAB, University of Stockholm, Sweden*

[3] *SISU, Stockholm, Sweden*

**Abstract**

A major component of any business reengineering effort is the identification of business processes, and the development of software to support these processes. The development of the software is itself a process, commonly called the software process. One reason for reengineering a business is to decentralize its mode of operation, or to make a decentralized mode more effective. We contend that a properly defined general software process model is essential for the development of support software for a reengineered decentralized enterprise. We have developed a sixteen-step plan for business reengineering, and an enterprise model composed of eight submodels. In this paper we bring together the enterprise model, relevant steps of the business reengineering plan, and the Capability Maturity Model of the Software Engineering Institute to define a software process model for business reengineering.

**Keywords**

Business process, business reengineering, capability maturity model, enterprise model, process model, software process

# 1 INTRODUCTION

A reengineered business is characterized by a set of well-defined business processes that support the goals of the organization (Davenport, 1993; Hammer and Champy, 1993; Johansson *et al*, 1993). The purpose of this paper is to outline a software development process designed for the introduction of software support for the business processes. Although our work is primarily concerned with requirements engineering for so-called information systems, it is relevant to the development of embedded control systems as well. We see in fact no real difference between the two kinds of systems. Both interact with their environments, and the form an interaction takes is nearly always influenced by the contents of an information base. Moreover, advanced information systems, particularly systems that contain expert systems, often exercise autonomous control over key activities of an enterprise. Control is particularly important in information systems for decentralized organizations. It is therefore appropriate to refer to the software systems with which we will be concerned as information-control systems.

In (Berztiss, 1995) we have proposed a sixteen-step process for business reengineering, where the steps do not necessarily follow the sequence given below:

1. Commitment by top management
2. Selection of the executive and operational managers of reengineering
3. Selection of reengineering teams
4. Initial education phase
5. Identification of the processes of the organization
6. Specification of each process
7. Development of alternative implementation plans for each process
8. Cost-benefit study for each plan and selection of an appropriate plan
9. Infrastructure definition based on the selected plans
10. Setting of priorities for implementation of processes and infrastructure
11. Second education phase
12. Pilot implementation of one or two processes
13. Reexamination of the reengineering effort
14. Implementation of the remaining processes
15. Continuing automation of processes
16. Automatic linkages to the environment

Our main concern here will be with Steps 5-9, which will be defined in some detail in Section 2. In (Berztiss, 1995) we point out that the Information Systems Department (ISD) of an organization is well positioned to provide major support for any business reengineering effort - by being outside traditional departments, such as sales, marketing, and personnel, ISD personnel can view their organization with neutral eyes. More importantly, the ISD personnel knows much about the organization, but it must be realized that there is also much it does not know. The missing knowledge has to be supplied by business domain experts. Moreover, the changes to be implemented will be much more radical than the changes the ISD has had to deal with in the past. In fact, in order to deal with these changes, the processes of Information Systems have to be reengineered first of all - many ISDs operate without a properly defined software development process.

In order carry out effectively the support role we envisage for the ISD, it should have reached at least Level 2 of the SEI Software Maturity Model (SMM), which is described in (Humphrey, 1989; Paulk *et al*, 1993; Paulk *et al*, 1993a). The relevance of the model to business reengineering is discussed in Section 3. In particular, the model requires that an organization develop its software by means of a well-understood process that can be subjected to measurements. Our aim here is to arrive at a definition of such a "reengineered" process for business reengineering.

Having the technical competence defined by Level 2 of the SMM is a necessary prerequisite for the effectiveness of an ISD in business reengineering, but it is not sufficient. There also has to be strong cooperation between the technical personnel of the ISD and management representatives. Management has the twofold responsibility of articulating the strategic goals of the business reengineering effort, and of expressing explicitly the business rules by which the organization operates. The need for continuous attunement of the technical aspects of process definition to management views requires a rather complex model of the software development process, based on a model of the enterprise that is being reengineered. In Section 4 we outline the SISU (Swedish Institute of Systems Development) enterprise model, and in Section 5 move from this enterprise model to a software process model. In Section 6 our process models are combined into an abstract process model for business reengineering, and in Section 7 the abstract process model is converted into an operational prototype-based model. In Section 8 we advance some conclusions from this work.

## 2 SOFTWARE SUPPORT FOR BUSINESS REENGINEERING

In this section we shall consider in detail Steps 5-9 of our business reengineering process. The business processes are to be regarded as essentially independent of each other in the sense that each process is supported by its own information base, and the only way a process can change the information base of another process is by sending a message requesting the other process to carry out the change. This is in keeping with the concept of ownership of information by a process (Davenport, 1993), and is essential for effective decentralization. Moreover, unless the total information base is partitioned in such a way, the software modules corresponding to the processes are subject to common coupling, which is an undesirably tight mode of module coupling (Constantine and Yourdon, 1979). Of course, in a centralized system, the individual information bases can be combined into a relational data base, but each table is to be owned by a specific process, and the authority for making changes to the table is to be retained by this process.

*Process identification*

The number of processes with which a company is concerned typically varies between ten and twenty (Davenport, 1993). Conventionally a process is seen as the movement of a piece of work from site to site, where the sites are under control of different departments. Not only is a process defined in terms of a number of sites, but a site may serve more than one process, e.g., a site that checks the credit rating of a customer would normally be used both by order processing and by credit issuance. Therefore the actual identification of processes can be more difficult than it appears.

*Process specification*

In this step a process is separated into component tasks, each task examined to determine whether it is actually needed, unnecessary tasks eliminated, and the remaining tasks restructured. In the restructured process specification there has to be a clear indication of the order in which tasks are to be performed, and which tasks can be performed in parallel. We recommend that specifications be formal, but supplemented with diagrams to help achieve intuitive understanding of the processes. The specification of a process should be sufficiently general to allow a fair degree of implementation freedom. In particular, it should allow a decentralized implementation. Although process identification and process specification are usually regarded as separate steps, taken one after the other, sometimes it helps to consider them as a single amalgamated step. Note that the initial assignment of the activities of an organization to processes may have to be modified once specification of the processes begins.

*Implementation alternatives*

Bridge designers have the standard practice of presenting a client with several preliminary designs, and the designer and client decide which design to carry forward (Spector and Gifford, 1986). The same approach can be used with a business process, but in this step alternative designs are merely listed, with no decision as to which design is to be adopted. It needs to be remembered that any specification, be it expressed as diagrams or text, should leave the implementer with some choice. Thus it can be left open whether a function value is to be obtained by interaction with a sensor, looking up a table, or having a function subprogram compute it. It may also be left open at what site a particular task is to be performed, e.g., is order processing to be done at the main office or at a warehouse.

*Cost-benefit analysis*

The costs for each of the implementation alternatives are established. This is relatively easy, but it is not easy to determine corresponding benefits because of the difficulty of assigning a definite cash value to an intangible benefit such as customer good will. If one of the alternatives is an improvement over another in every aspect, then we know which to choose, but more commonly we have to balance both higher cost and higher intangible benefits of one alternative against both lower cost and lower benefits of another alternative.

*Infrastructure definition*

The infrastructure consists of an information system and a communication system, such as a set of LANs and a WAN. Although a distributed system may present more problems than a centralized system, the concept of information being owned by a process reduces their effect. In this step the infrastructure costs are determined for the total set of processes under the implementation alternative selected for each process. The processes, which we have been considering in isolation, now become integrated. It is possible that a different alternative is now chosen for some of the processes in order to reduce infrastructure costs. One objective is to reduce the volume of data flow - some thoughts on how to achieve this can be found in (Berztiss, 1993).

## 3 THE SEI CAPABILITY MATURITY MODEL

The Software Engineering Institute (SEI) has defined five software process maturity levels. At the initial level (Level 1) there is no process maturity at all - the "process" is characterized by lack of planning. Much software for the support of reengineered processes is being developed by organizations at Level 1, and the unreliability of their services and products is hurting the reputation of business reengineering.

To arrive at the lowest respectable maturity level (Level 2), the software process has to become repeatable. When presented with two development tasks in the same domain, both of the same size and complexity, an organization at Level 1 can be expected to come up with significantly different cost and schedule estimates. At Level 2 the estimates should not differ by much. In order to reach the repeatable level an organization has to maintain extensive statistics relating to its past projects. At Level 3 the process becomes defined. To reach this level, an organization has to be able to transform a generic process structure into a detailed definition of the actual process that is to produce a specific software system.

The next step is to arrive at reliable cost and schedule estimates for all projects. Achievement of this aim makes the process managed. This is Level 4, and reliable cost and schedule estimates are now available for any system development task, even when the organization has not been developing software for the given application domain in the past. In other words, all software development projects can be subjected to adequate management cost controls. The transition to this level is achieved by defining a set of standardized tasks, establishing a costing procedure for each task, and defining the development of a specific software system in terms of the standardized tasks. At the highest level, the software process has become optimized. In order to reach this level, an organization should have automated the collection of process data that are used to improve the software process. For example, these data can indicate that some of the standardized software process tasks are bottlenecks, or that their costs should be reduced.

Each level is characterized by a set of key process areas. For Level 2 there are six such areas: requirements management; software project planning; software project tracking and oversight; software subcontract management; software quality assurance; software configuration management. We claim that an ISD cannot provide effective support for business reengineering unless it has mastered these key areas. It is not easy to isolate all the reasons why many business reengineering initiatives have failed, but the absence of required capabilities in the ISD is often to blame. We shall now elaborate on the key process areas of Level 2.

Requirements management is to achieve a common understanding between a sponsor of a software product and the ISD that the software product will indeed have the properties that the sponsor expects it to have. This means that an agreement is to be reached between the sponsor and the ISD, that the agreement be fully documented, and that changes to the requirements document be made only with the approval of both sponsor and ISD. This agreement is to be the basis for a software project plan. As part of planning, time and resource estimates for the project have to be established, and a schedule of activities has to be drawn up. Sponsors are not to be confused with users. Sponsors view the software as a means of satisfying broad business objectives; users will be interacting with the software on a day-to-day basis.

Software tracking and oversight is then to check that the actual software development process adheres to the plan. Such tracking is to extend to the performance of subcontractors. The activities involved in software subcontractor management consist of selection of subcontractors, specification of contract obligations, and monitoring of the performance of subcontractors.

Software quality assurance activities consist of reviews and audits of software products and of the software process. The aim is to ensure that the products and processes comply with standards and guidelines, and that management is appraised of the results of the reviews and audits. The purpose of software configuration management is to improve software quality by integrity maintenance throughout the development of a software system. It ensures that all representations of the same version are consistent, e.g., that an information-control system is consistent with its functional requirements, or that two different implementations of the same facility are equivalent. As an example of the latter consider a function that returns the sunrise at Trondheim for any given day in the year 1996. This could be implemented as an algorithm that computes the time of sunrise, or as a table with 366 entries. The requirements for a system may stipulate that both implementations be provided, and configuration management must then ensure that substituting one implementation for the other will make no observable difference to a user.

## 4 AN ENTERPRISE MODEL

Here we introduce an enterprise model developed at SISU as part of the ESPRIT Project F3 ("From Fuzzy to Formal") - see Bubenko (1993), and Bubenko *et al* (1993). It emphasizes the separation of concerns during development of information systems, and in this it is related to the modeling of requirements in terms of four modeling "worlds" under the ESPRIT project DAIDA (Jarke *et al*, 1992), and the NATURE project (Jarke *et al*, 1993).

The F3 assumption is that the development of a system requirements specification is helped by a "population" of a number of sub-models. These sub-models describe the kinds of interrelated "documents" (or sub-documents) to be developed. By following a set of "good" sub-models, the risk to develop incomplete or inconsistent specifications can be reduced. By "good sub-models" we mean models that separate concerns in a way that improves clarity, as well as productivity and the quality of work products. Experience has shown that the use of an "objectives-model-driven approach" may lead to improved understanding of the problem domain by decision makers, definers of requirements, system developers, and "end-users". The economic value of improved communication and understanding, and for minimizing rework in later stages of the information systems development process has been observed elsewhere as well (Curtis *et al*, 1988). We propose to structure a requirements specification in an number of "submodels", shown in Figure 1.

In the objectives submodel of a requirements specification we describe, in a structured way, the "why" component of a requirements document. Goals for a particular enterprise or an activity are stated, and their relationships analyzed. This may relate to existing processes that are to be left intact, processes that are to be modified, or new processes that are to be designed. In the formulation of goals reference is made to problems and their causes, opportunities, and development actions. These supporting components explain why certain goals have been formulated, and are therefore important parts of the objectives submodel. The objectives submodel is a graph with the above types of components as nodes, connected by relationships of type "motivates" or "influences". The motivates relationship is here seen as a refinement relationship (e.g. a goal is refined in a number of sub-goals). The influences relationship is a relationship indicating positive or negative influences between components of the objectives submodel. These relationships can be given different levels of "strengths", e.g. low, medium or high.

The concepts submodel is used to define the "ontology" of the "universe of discourse" that concerns us, i.e. the set of object types, relationships, and object properties of the application we are talking about. For developing a functional information systems specification, the concepts submodel will define the "things and relationships" about which information must be represented in the information system, and the rules of behavior of the information system, implemented in the processes of the system. The concept submodel will, moreover, serve as a dictionary of user and customer defined concepts, and conceptual structures to be used to better understand other parts of a requirements specification.

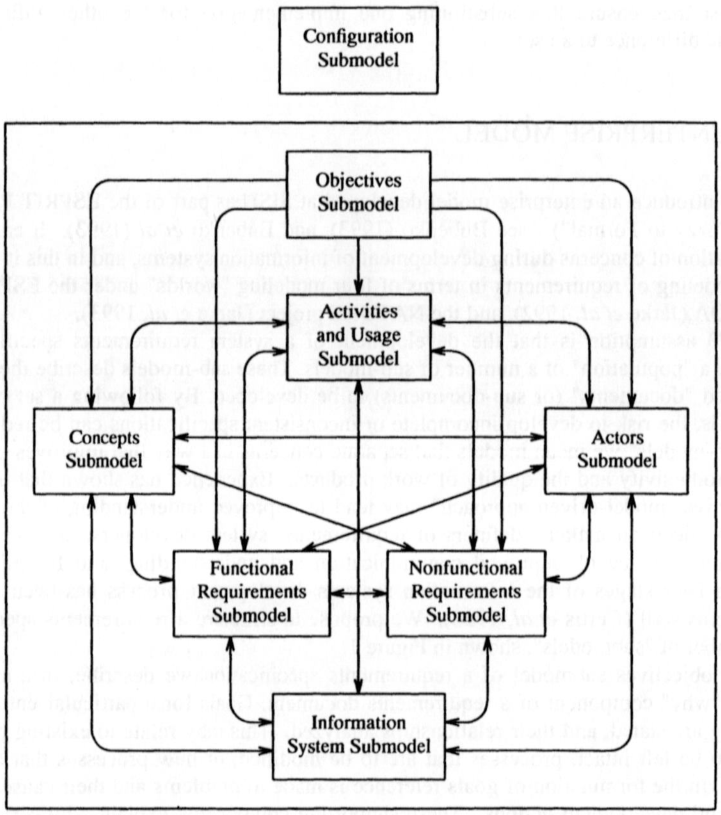


**Figure 1** An enterprise model

The actors submodel is used to define the set of actors of the activity under consideration (individuals, groups, job-roles/positions, organizational units, machines, etc.), and their interrelationships, such as part-of, reports-to, etc. This submodel includes links to the other submodels, e.g., it identifies the "stake-holder" of a particular goal, the actor responsible for managing an activity according to a particular goal, etc.

In the activities and usage submodel, a particular existing process, a process to be modified, or a new process is defined and described from the point of view of activities and tasks, and the information and material flows between them. Describing, for instance, human-computer interaction is part of this submodel. Clearly, components of this submodel are motivated by components of the objectives submodel, they are performed using or referring to components of the concept submodel, and they are typically carried out by components (resources) of the actors submodel. In this submodel we also define business rules, which may be static or dynamic. These rules define permissible system states as well as permissible state changes. Information system requirements, related to the above models, are described by the following two submodels.

The functional requirements submodel elaborates the specific objectives and requirements that are put on the information system to support the activities and objectives defined. Typically it will indicate needs for establishing objects (or relationships, attributes), deleting objects, modifying objects, and the need for checking, querying and browsing objects and relationships.

The non-functional (NF) requirements submodel is primarily related to the activity and usage model, and indirectly to the objectives submodel, as activities normally are motivated by the objectives submodel. NF requirements concern components of the information systems submodel, i.e. information subsystems. NF requirements can be of several different kinds, such as standards for interfacing other systems, restrictions concerning use of hardware and/or software, accuracy of information, timeliness of information, security, access-rights, economic limits of the development project, etc.

The information system is described conceptually by the information systems submodel. By this we mean the complete, formal, functional specification of the information system. It is the task of the IS designer to develop IS designs and descriptions such that designated activities and processes in the activities and usage submodel, as well as the functional and NF-requirements are supported (to a greater or lesser degree).

In order to manage the modeling process and its results, we need the configuration submodel. This is a submodel, orthogonal to the other submodels. The main concepts of this submodel are version and release. We need this dimension for the reason that systems, be they organizational or computer-based, continuously evolve and change. For instance, the concepts submodel, or parts thereof, will change at times. New versions of these submodels will be developed, based on other earlier versions. On the other hand, we cannot disregard such historical information, as some actors may be still using it. Developing a new version of some submodel will most likely also cause needs for change in the other submodels. For instance, a new objectives submodel description will certainly affect and require a reconsideration of all other submodels. To manage "configurations" of descriptions is an important mission of an enterprise modeling facility.

What we have above is basically a set of interrelated descriptions or documents, each constructed with a predefined set of "permitted" types of components and component relationships. Depending on the purpose of the modeling exercise, we may, for a particular modeling job, need only a subset of these submodels. We may think of several other purposes for modeling. One such is the redesign of organizational processes, without assuming any supporting computer system to be developed. Another, quite typical purpose in practical situations, could be to reconsider the organization's goals, objectives, mission, etc., and then study how an existing information system actually supports the new set of goals. This, of course, is part of business reengineering.

# 5 FROM ENTERPRISE MODEL TO PROCESS MODEL

Figure 1 indicates how the seven submodels that comprise the actual enterprise model are interrelated, and clearly shows the special importance of the objectives submodel - this submodel provides the impetus for everything else. We shall now derive a process model from the enterprise model.

In English there are six types of wh- questions - these questions start with why, what, who, which, when, and where. In addition we have questions that start with how. A process model is to provide answers to these questions. In terms of Figure 1, the objectives submodel responds to the why-part, the two requirements submodels relate to the what-part, the actors submodel responds to the who-part, and the information systems submodel to the how-part. The remaining three types of questions all relate to the activities and usage submodel - this submodel includes business rules, and we are concerned with which business rule is to be applied at a given time (when) and place (where).

This leaves the concepts submodel unaccounted for, and rightly so. It does not belong to a process structure. It provides a vocabulary and static structure that indicates how the terms of the vocabulary are related. Also, answering some of the how-part and all of the who-part can be delayed. We note again that at an abstract level it makes no difference how a value is obtained - it could be looked up in a table, computed by an algorithm, indicated by a sensor, or supplied by a user. Generalizing this somewhat, a process step may start out as a manual activity, become partially supported by a computer-based decision support system, and then become fully automated as an expert system. To take a concrete example, the processing of a purchase order may be initially performed by a number of employees in several departments, then, as process structure replaces departmental structure, by several employees belonging to the same process team, then by a single member of the process team, and ultimately by a software system operating on its own. These transitions may take place long after the initial process model for order processing has been formulated. Thus the actors submodel is not of primary importance in setting up an abstract process model. This view is supported by case studies in (Davenport, 1993; Hammer and Champy, 1993; Johansson *et al*, 1993), and case studies reported in *Computerworld* suggest that the failures of some business reengineering initiatives may be attributed to a preoccupation with information technology and role assignments rather than with analysis of the essence of business processes. However, in some contexts, early emphasis may have to be put precisely on the actors (Yu and Mylopoulos, 1994). Note that the distribution of tasks to different decentralized sites belongs to the activities and usage submodel.

Figure 2 shows a process model based on the enterprise model of Figure 1, but the process model takes into account the remarks made above. Two of the labels have been changed: we have generalized the model to information-control systems, and it has been made explicit that configuration control is to deal with both configurations and versions. The actual process is defined as a sequence of five submodels: an objectives submodel feeds an activities and usage submodel in the sense that the enterprise objectives motivate and determine activities and usage within the enterprise, the latter suggest functional and nonfunctional requirements for an enterprise information-control system, and the actual system is based on these requirements. This sequence is the core of the process. Although Figure 2 presents the submodels as an ordered sequence, there is much feedback and backtracking while the submodels are being developed. First, even when an orderly phased development plan is aimed for, it may be found that the initial objectives are unrealistic. Second, concurrent engineering encourages parallel development of the submodels. Some discussion of concurrent engineering of information-control systems can be found in (Berztiss, 1993a).

The core submodels depend on the two submodels that we have put outside the core. As mentioned above, the concepts submodel provides a vocabulary for use by the core submodels, and the actors submodel allocates roles to different operators within the enterprise. Briefly expressed, actors relate to a process, and concepts to the product of the process, but they do not have to be made part of a process while the process is still in an abstract specification stage.

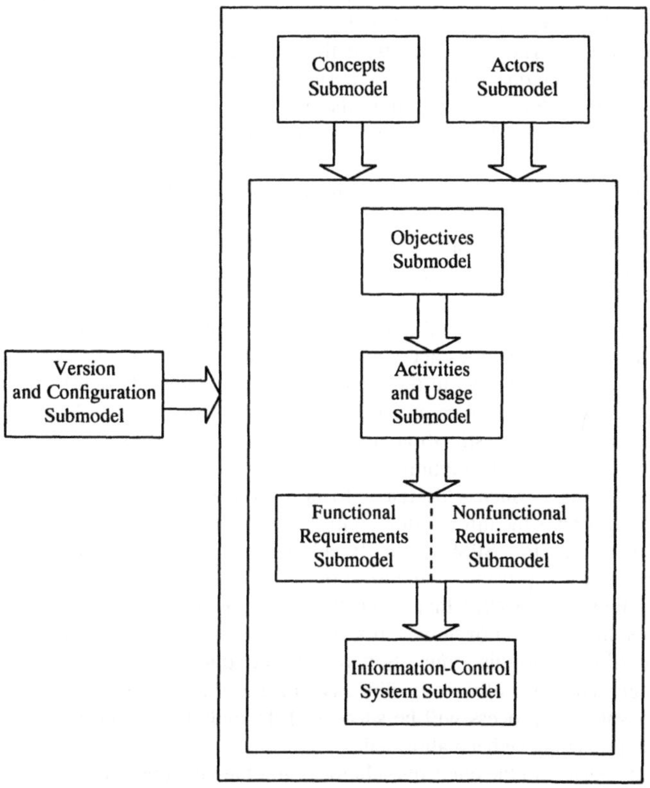


**Figure 2** An abstract software system development model

We have to keep in mind that that we are dealing with three types of processes. The first is an enterprise analysis process that determines which of the operations of the enterprise are to be handled by software, and where they are to be handled. The second is a software process that is to develop information-control software systems. These information-control systems are processes of the third kind, and each such process is a product of the software process. All the information-control systems of an enterprise constitute the software support base for this enterprise.

## 6 A SOFTWARE PROCESS MODEL FOR BUSINESS REENGINEERING

We now bring together our three threads: the software process model (SPM), the business reengineering plan (BRP), and the key process areas for Level 2 of the CMM (CMM2). We propose four activity groups - a WHY-group, a WHAT-group, a HOW-group, and a WHO-group. Submodels of SPM, activities of BRP, and key process areas of CMM2 are to be allocated to these groups. The contributions of the three approaches to modeling the software process for business reengineering are shown in Figure 3.

WHY-group. We allocate to this group the objectives submodel of SPM and the process identification step of BRP. The CMM is not concerned with enterprise objectives at any of its levels.

WHAT-group. Requirements management of CMM2 belongs to this group, and so does process specification of BRP. We noted in Section 5 that the activities and usage submodel indicates when and where particular business rules are to be applied. This is elaborated into requirements, so that the activities and usage submodel and both the requirements submodels of SPM belong to this group.

HOW-group. Under BRP several implementation alternatives are proposed and evaluated in the implementation alternatives and cost-benefit analysis steps. Both these steps belong to the how-group because they lead to the selection of a particular alternative for actual implementation. We noted that software project planning is part of CMM2. This key process area deals with time and resource estimation, and a schedule of activities. For accurate estimation of the time and resource consumption by the project, and also by the product, there has to exist a software design. Such a design is to be produced as part of software planning of CMM2 and this design is the information-control system submodel of SPM.

WHO-group. Only the SPM explicitly addresses the actors issue. Under the other software development approaches the allocation of tasks to actors is postponed, but there are some parts of these approaches that relate to actors. Thus, under BRP, the infrastructure definition gives an indication of how actors are to communicate. Three key process areas of CMM2 can be allocated to this group. Software project tracking and oversight, software subcontract management, and software quality assurance all relate to the performance of actors, and whether a software process will be successful depends in a given instance on how well the tasks of the process have been allocated.

This still leaves us with the concepts submodel and the versions and configurations submodel of SPM, and software configuration management under CMM2. It is important to realize that a conceptual framework is an essential part of software development, although it does not belong to the software process as such. The management of versions and configurations is also outside the software process, but this may change as this topic keeps gaining in importance, particularly when configuration management is coupled to the maintenance of a software reuse library.

| | BRP | SPM | CMM2 |
|---|---|---|---|
| WHY? | Process Identification | Objectives Submodel | |
| WHAT? | Process Specification | Activities and Usage Submodel + Functional Requirements Submodel + Nonfunctional Requirements Submodel | Requirements Management |
| HOW? | Implementation Alternatives + Cost-Benefit Analysis | Information-Control System Submodel | Software Project Planning |
| WHO? | Infrastructure Definition | Actors Submodel | Software Project Tracking and Oversight + Software Subcontract Management + Software Quality Assurance |
| OTHER | | Version and Configuration Submodel + Concepts Submodel | Software Configuration Management |

**Figure 3** Contributions to a software process model

It is interesting to note that CMM2 pays no attention to the determination of the objectives of an enterprise. The closest it comes to it is in Level 3. There the key area Integrated Software Management refers to the integration of management activities with software engineering methods into a coherent generic software process. Then, in adopting the generic process to a specific project reference needs to be made to the business environment.

## 7 PROTOTYPE-BASED PROCESS MODEL

We call software systems "sponsor-defined" when the requirements for such software are for the most part provided by business domain experts outside the ISD. All process software systems are in this category, and they cannot be frozen while the understanding of the business aspects of the enterprise by the ISD continues to be corrected by business domain experts. This is particularly important for business reengineering. In terms of Figure 3, the WHY-part is wholly the province of business experts or sponsors, the HOW-part wholly the province of information systems experts, and the two groups of experts have to define the WHAT-part in close cooperation.

Three major problems that beset development of sponsor-defined systems have been identified (Curtis *et al*, 1988). Besides the inadequate application domain knowledge by developers, there is the related problem that requirements keep fluctuating or contain contradictions. The third problem is that software developers are often victims of communication and coordination breakdowns. All three problems are amplified when radical business reengineering of a decentralized organization is being undertaken. The harmful effects of the three problems can be reduced by prototyping. Although exceptional designers are quite good at acquiring domain knowledge in other ways, even they would be helped by a user-developer dialogue supported by a prototype. The information from users is particularly useful when it is in the form of scenarios of system use. Such interaction between users and developers reduces external communication barriers, and thus helps stabilize requirements, but internal barriers too are lowered when all members of the development team have the same prototype system to refer to.

Briefly, the main purpose of a prototype process system is to allow users to establish that the developers have reached a conceptually sound understanding of the process, and to allow developers to determine that user expectations have been met. To this end a prototype is to provide a user interface and main system components in preliminary versions. We suggest that a prototype be built early, that it be adapted to user needs, and that the suitably modified prototype be converted into an efficient implementation, preferably by automatic transformations. Figure 4 is an idealized and grossly simplified overview of this approach.

In Figure 4 the "Function allocation" box represents the assignment of process functions to people, software, and hardware. One result of the allocation is an informal software requirements statement that is formalized and structured in the "Requirements documentation" box. The initial input to the "Function allocation" box is from the environment, which is a collective term for various sources of information, including the system sponsors. Some changes to requirements also originate in the environment, and lead to a changed requirements document. Such changes differ from changes suggested by users as part of the prototype test. Let us emphasize again that while sponsors view the software as as a means of satisfying broad business objectives, users will be interacting with the software on a day-to-day basis. Sponsor participation in the tests is recommended. Such participation is recognized by the arrow leading back to the "Environment" box from the two tests - this emphasizes that the prototyping process may lead to a modification of initial business objectives - the better understanding of business processes that prototyping provides can influence basic business strategy.

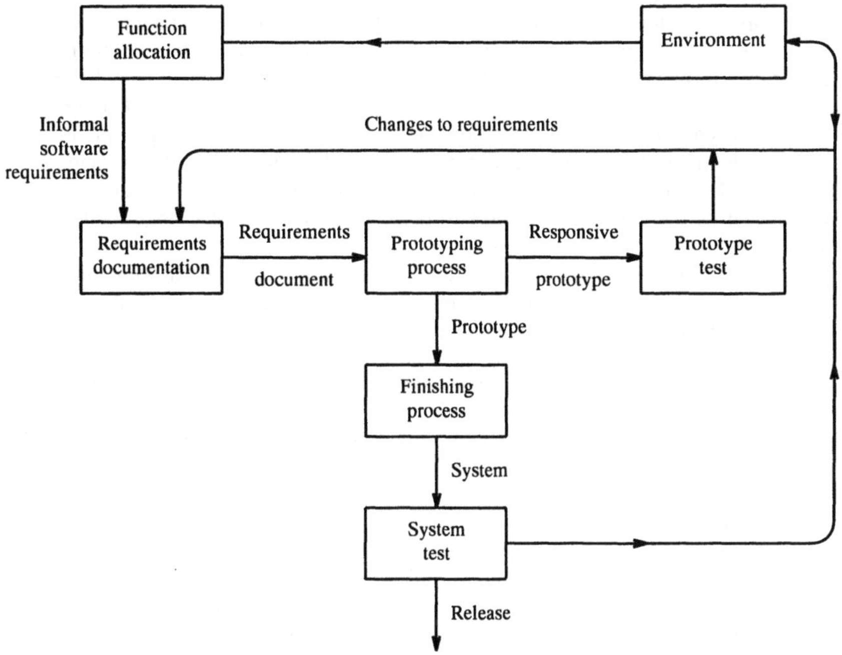


**Figure 4** Prototyping-based software process

Referring from Figure 4 back to Figure 3, we note that the "Environment" box of Figure 4 stands for the WHY-part of Figure 3, the "Requirements documentation" box for the WHAT-part, "Function allocation" for the WHO-part, and the rest of the process for the HOW-part. However, when function allocation is related to the actors submodel, an inconsistency appears to arise between Figures 2 and 4. In Figure 2 the actors submodel is placed outside the core of the process, and with reference to the model of Figure 2 it was suggested that allocation of roles to actors can be delayed. In Figure 4 the "Function allocation" box starts off the process. The apparent inconsistency arises because Figure 2 represents an abstract model, but Figure 4 relates to a concrete software process. While actors need not be of primary concern in the abstract model, a concrete implementation cannot begin before the roles assigned to software have been fixed. Roles can be reassigned at a later stage, but an initial assignment as in Figure 4 is essential. Figure 4 can be regarded as an elaboration of Figure 2 - the objectives and the activities and usage submodels of Figure 2 have become the "Environment" box in Figure 4, the actors submodel has become the "Function allocation" box, and the rest of Figure 4 deals essentially with the conversion of requirements into an information-control system, first as a prototype, and then as a released system.

The requirements document is submitted to a prototyping process, a prototype emerges from this process, and the prototype is tested. There can be great variability in what the

"Prototyping process" and the "Prototype test" boxes contain, and how the two are related. For example, the "Requirements document" may contain an executable specification, i.e., a computer program, in which case there is no need for a separate prototyping process. In some software development processes the prototype test would be prototype execution with user participation. In others, certain properties of the software system could actually be proven. The "Requirements documentation" - "Prototyping process" - "Prototype test" loop is iterated until the prototype passes an acceptance review, which we regard to be a part of "Prototyping process". Testing exposes errors and some oversights, and this leads to changes in the requirements document. Requirements may also undergo modifications because of real world changes, such as the elimination of certain tax deductions. These changes originate in the "Environment" box.

The accepted prototype moves through the "Finishing process" box in which the prototype is turned into a deliverable system. This may mean the integration of prototypes of several subsystems into a composite system, and addition of ancillary features, such as a help system. We assume that another technical review is part of this process. The composite system is then put through a system test. An alternative is to start with the prototype of a kernel subsystem, perform system tests on this subsystem, and then add prototypes of other subsystems, performing system tests after each addition. In any case, the full transition from the WHAT to the HOW of Section 6 is completed in the "Finishing process" box. At this point the WHO-questions need to be fully answered as well.

An important characteristic of prototypes of real-time systems, particularly in a decentralized environment, is that they rarely provide reliable time estimates. This means that a system that has passed its prototype tests may still fail in the field because its responses are too slow. If the "System test" of Figure 4 detects this, then there are three options. First, faster hardware can be introduced. Second, the "Finishing process" can be tuned to improve the program it produces. Third, the specifications can be modified to sacrifice some other properties in favor of improved response times. We hope, though, that early application of performance engineering techniques - see, e.g., (Smith, 1990) - will have given an accurate estimate of the performance of the system as part of "Requirements documentation".

The prototyping-based development plan of Figure 4 is at best a generic scheme. Much detail has to be added to define the development plan for a particular software system. The ability to accept a planned process at all, to adapt a generic process structure to actual needs, and to continue to improve the mechanics of how the adaptation is done defines the process maturity level of an organization, as discussed in Section 3.

# 8 CONCLUSIONS

The comparison of three process views as carried out in Section 6 has shown incompleteness in all three views. At no level is the CMM concerned with the objectives that cause an organization to introduce a new process or reengineer a business process. Neither BRP nor SPM pay much attention to how the software process is to be managed, although Step 2 of the BRP is concerned with the selection of managers for the reengineering initiative. The BRP contains no explicit steps in which actors would be allocated to tasks. Although the detailed outline of the CMM (Paulk *et al*, 1993a) does discuss software configuration management in terms of a software repository, there is no explicit consideration of the repository as a source of software for reuse. Reuse is not considered in SPM either, and BRP does not even consider version and configuration management. These omissions illustrate the benefits that derive from a systematic comparison of several approaches that have the same objective.

Omission of a step need not be a deficiency, but may indicate differences in philosophy. Systematic comparison makes sure that an omission is not an oversight, but a deliberate decision. For example, while under SPM the actor submodel is defined early, the high level of abstraction at which BRP is kept for as long as possible implies that role assignment to actors is delayed until process implementation.

This suggests that the business reengineering process is to be highly flexible. The differences in basic philosophy are not arbitrary, but depend on the organizational culture of the enterprise being reengineered, particularly in the effect this culture has on reengineering teams. There is no single right approach. In some instances management has to select the teams, set an agenda for each team, and closely supervise the teams. In such a situation actor selection is an important early step, but actor selection need not be emphasized as a separate step when the teams are self-selecting and self-managing units comprising both management and technical personnel. To take another example, reuse of existing software is not particularly important when radical business reengineering takes place - after all, the purpose of business reengineering is to bring about significant changes in both business practices and in the software that supports the practices. When an organization already operates according to the principles that business reengineering aims to introduce, the reengineering of a particular business process may necessitate only minor changes, and maximal reuse of the existing software is then a worthwhile objective.

We note again that the composite process model we have considered is very general. Thus it applies equally well to the introduction of a new process, redesign of an existing process, or the radical reorganization of all the activities of an enterprise that business reengineering brings about. The main principle of business reengineering is to keep asking why a particular task is to be performed. This question needs to be put whenever software is being developed.

Moreover, we emphasize abstraction, which means that in early stages of system development it need not make any difference whether a system will be used in a centralized or a decentralized setting. Even the prototype of a process system that is ultimately to be distributed over several geographically separated sites can be developed at a single site. Partly this independence of the implementation mode has been brought about by technology - the transfer of a file between the United States and Norway does not take much longer than the transfer of the file between two users in the same building. Our design methodology also contributes to the independence - careful consideration of how the business processes are defined, and the association of each process with its own information base effectively decouple the processes from each other.

## 9 REFERENCES

Berztiss, A.T. (1993) Information transfer for decision support in distributed administrative systems, in *Decision Support in Public Administration* (eds. P.W.G. Bots, H.G. Sol, R.Traunmuller), North-Holland, 3-15.

Berztiss, A. (1993a) Concurrent engineering of information systems, in *Proc. IFIP WG8.1 Working Conf. on Information System Development Processes* (eds. N. Prakash, C.

Rolland, B. Pernici), North-Holland, 311-324.

Berztiss, A.T. (1995) *Software methods for business reengineering*. Springer-Verlag.

Bubenko, J.A. (1993) Extending the scope of information modelling, in *Proc. Fourth International Workshop on the Deductive Approach to Information Systems and Databases* (ed. A. Olive), Departament de Llenguatges i Sistemes Informatics of the Universitat Politecnica de Catalunya, Barcelona, 73-97.

Bubenko, J.A., Rolland, C., Loucopoulos, P., and DeAntonellis, V. (1994) Facilitating "fuzzy to formal" requirements modelling, in *Proc. IEEE Internat. Conf. on Requirements Eng.*.

Constantine, L.L., and Yourdon, E. (1979) *Structured design*. Prentice-Hall.

Curtis, B., Krasner, H., and Iscoe, N. (1988) A field study of the software design process for large systems. *Communications of the ACM*, **31**, 1268-1287.

Davenport, T.H. (1993) *Process innovation: reengineering work through information technology*. Harvard Business School Press.

Hammer, M., and Champy, J. (1993) *Reengineering the corporation: a manifesto for business revolution*. Harper Business.

Humphrey, W.S. (1989) *Managing the software process*. Addison-Wesley.

Jarke, M., Mylopoulos, J., Schmidt, J.W., and Vassiliou, Y. (1992) DAIDA: an environment for evolving information systems. *ACM Transactions on Information Systems*, **10**, 1-50.

Jarke, M., Bubenko, J.A., Rolland, C., Sutcliffe, A., and Vassiliou, Y. (1993) Theories underlying requirements engineering: an overview of NATURE at genesis, in *Proc. IEEE Symposium on Requirements Engineering, RE'93*.

Johansson, H.J., McHugh, P., Pendlebury, A.J., and Wheeler, W.A. (1993) *Business Process Reengineering: Breakpoint Strategies for Reengineering*. Wiley.

Paulk, M.C., Curtis, B., Chrissis, M.B., and Weber, C.V. (1993), Capability Maturity Model, Version 1.1. *IEEE Software*, **10** (4), 18-27.

Paulk, M.C., Weber, C., Garcia, S., Chrissis, M.B., and Bush, M. (1993a), Key practices of the Capability Maturity Model Version 1.1. SEI Report CMU/SEI-93-TR-25, Software Engineering Institute of Carnegie-Mellon University.

Smith, C.U. (1990) *Performance Engineering of Software Systems*. Addison-Wesley.

Spector, A., and Gifford, D. (1986) A computer science perspective on bridge design. *Communications of the ACM*, **29**, 268-283.

Yu, E. and Mylopoulos, J. (1994) From E-R to "A-R" - modelling strategic actor relationships for business process reengineering, in *Proc. 13th Internat. Conference Entity-Relationship Approach* (LNCS No. 881, ed. P. Loucopoulos), Springer-Verlag, 548-565.

12

# Coupling Process Models and Business Rules

*Peter McBrien*
*King's College London*
*Strand, London WC2R 2LS, UK*
*Tel: +44 171 873 2469, email:* pjm@dcs.kcl.ac.uk

*Anne Helga Seltveit*
*The Norwegian Institute for Technology*
*Trondheim N-7034, Norway*
*Tel: +47 73593677, email:* ahs@idt.unit.no

**Abstract**

Two techniques commonly used in the conceptual modelling of information systems are **process modelling** and **business rule modelling**. In this paper we propose a technique for associating certain types business rules with structures in a process modelling language. This **coupling** of the two models allows them to be used as complimentary languages in conceptual modelling; the process language being suitable when modelling how activities interact, whilst the business rule model is suitable when we need to make precise statements about a certain activity. The ability to model certain aspects of business rules within the process model is particularly important in distributed organisations, where the process model may be used as a means of communication between different parts of the organisation. The coupling also serves (1) to make apparent what effect **re-engineering** of one model has on the structure of the other model, and (2) indicate how the process model may be used to drive the creation of business rules.

**Keywords**

Conceptual modelling, Process modelling, Business rule modelling, Business process re-engineering.

## 1 INTRODUCTION

Process modelling is frequently used in the conceptual modelling of information systems, and allows the description of the dynamic nature of the **universe of discourse** (UoD), usually in the form of some variant of the **data flow diagram** (DFD) of (Gane and Sarson 1978) or (deMarco 1978). Although useful for describing a general picture of how the domain functions in terms of activities (processes) and exchanges of information between the activities (dataflows), the semantics of process models are not precise in their statement of facts about the domain. In particular it is not possible to generate any application code from a DFD model.

In part as an answer to the lack of semantic richness in process models, **business rule** modelling has received growing attention over the past few years, one research project TEMPORA (Loucopoulos, McBrien, Schumacker, Theodoulidis, Kopanas and Wangler 1991) being of interest to this paper, and commercial products using them being exemplified by UNIFACE 6. Business rules are usually expressed in a formal language, which allows precise statements to be made about the domain, and which contain sufficient information such that application code may be automatically generated.

A disadvantage of business rules is that they suffer from a lack of structuring mechanisms — the **rule base** is an essentially flat structure, and in large information systems this can become difficult to manage, test and maintain (Xiaofeng 1991). This will become more apparent in distributed organisations, where the flat rule structure must be mapped onto some structure in the organisation. By contrast, the ability to provide different levels of abstraction and to structure the model as communicating activities can be seen as advantages of process modelling, In particular, process modelling supports the notion of interaction between different parts of a distributed organisation.

In (Krogstie, McBrien, Owens and Seltveit 1991) it was proposed that the two models could be coupled, by defining how certain constructs in one model would indicate the presence of constructs in the other model. Rules were viewed as having the general structure

**when** ⟨trigger⟩ **if** ⟨condition⟩ **then** ⟨consequence⟩

where ⟨trigger⟩, ⟨condition⟩ and ⟨consequence⟩ are logical expressions which may contain several flow names. Such rules would imply the existence of a process which has triggering input (the flows contained in ⟨trigger⟩), non-triggering input (the flows contained in ⟨condition⟩), and output (the flows contained in ⟨consequence⟩).

In this paper we elaborate upon the approach in (Krogstie et al. 1991) to define how the structure of the rules may be more precisely defined within the process model. This tighter coupling facilitates the following activities:

- **rule capture** by the ability to express certain logical constructs within the process model.
- **process re-engineering** being carried out in the process model, since the consequences of such changes in the rule model are made apparent immediately.
- **business rule re-engineering** being carried out in the rule model, since the consequences of such changes in the process model made apparent immediately.
- **communication of business rules** between parts of a distributed organisation, since the relationship of rules to processes means that business rules can be located within a structural framework of the organisation as represented by the process model.

The remainder of this paper is structured as follows. Section 2 briefly describes the TEMPORA process and rule modelling languages. Section 3 describes how the two models may be coupled. Section 4 describes the rule capture process. Section 5 describes the use of the coupling mechanism in information systems re-engineering.

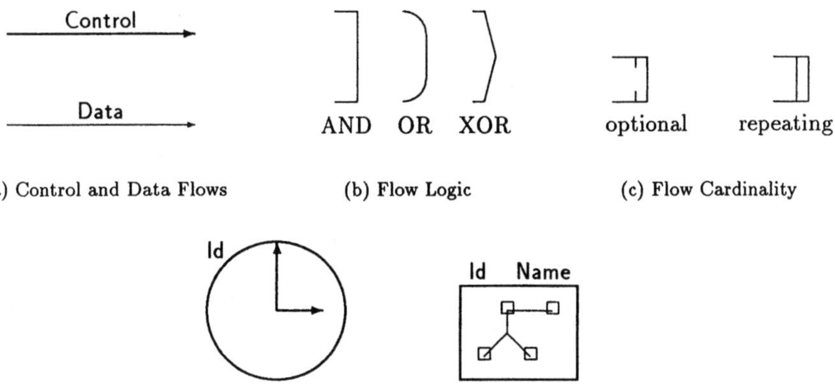


(a) Control and Data Flows (b) Flow Logic (c) Flow Cardinality

(d) Timers (e) ERT View

**Figure 1** Enhancements on DFD found in the PID.

# 2 THE TEMPORA PROCESS AND RULE MODELS

In TEMPORA the capture of a conceptual model is made using three modelling languages:

- An entity-relationship model called the ERT (McBrien, Seltveit and Wangler 1992), containing various extensions to the ER model of (Chen 1976), including the ability model valid-time data model (Jensen *et al* 1984).
- A process modelling language called the PID (Krogstie et al. 1991), containing extensions to DFD modelling which we detail below, and based on the PPP modelling language (Gulla, Lindland and Willumsen 1991).
- A rule modelling language called the ERL (McBrien, Niezette, Pantazis, Thedoulidis, Tziallas, Seltveit, Sundin and Wohed 1991), which allows the specification of rules as logical constraints on the static ERT and dynamic PID models. The ERL uses as its basis the temporal **US logic** (Gabbay 1989), allowing the querying of the valid-time data model in the ERT. The use of the ERL as a mechanism for specifying logical constraints on the PID is the subject of Section 3.

So as to make this paper self contained, we detail a few key aspects of the PID and ERL in the following subsections.

## 2.1 An Enhanced Process Modelling Language: PID

The key differences between the PID model and the DFD model as proposed by (Gane and Sarson 1978) are itemised below, and the new constructs introduced in the PID are illustrated in Figure 1.

- The PID distinguishes between control and data flows. A **triggering flow** is drawn with a thick line. Each occurrence of a triggering flow causes the processes at which it ends to be *considered* for execution. A **non-triggering flow** is drawn with a thin line, and may only be used by a process that is already executing.
- A triggering flow only leads to a process being considered for execution. It will only *actually* execute if the **flow logic** is satisfied. The logic is specified using a combination of **AND ports, OR ports** and **XOR ports**. This indicates what logical combinations of input flows must be present in order for the process to execute.
- The **flow cardinality** is the number of instances of a flow that must be present for a valid process execution. By default it is assumed that one instance of each input flow is used in a process execution, and that one instance of each output flow is generated by the execution. The fact that there may be a lower bound of zero is indicated by a **conditional port**, and an upper bound of many is indicated by a **repeating port**.
- The notion that clock events may be generated at specified intervals is represented by the concept of a **timer**.
- The fact that data stores are views on an entity-relationship model leads to a new syntax for the object, which is called an **ERT view**.

## 2.2 A Rule Modelling Language: ERL

The ERL is intended to allow the semantic modelling of logical statements about the static model captured in the ERT, and the dynamic view in the PID. In conceptual modelling, we may interpret all rules as stating logical constraints on the models they are associated to, and all rules are based on a single structure:

**when** ⟨trigger⟩ **if** ⟨condition⟩ **then** ⟨consequence⟩

A rule holds when its ⟨trigger⟩ has just begun to hold (i.e. an event has occurred which makes ⟨trigger⟩ true), and its ⟨condition⟩ holds. If a rule holds then its ⟨consequence⟩ must also hold, and if this cannot be made the case then an exception should be raised. If either the ⟨trigger⟩ or ⟨condition⟩ part is omitted then that part is assumed to hold. Since trigger events must be modelled in the PID, a rule with a non-empty ⟨trigger⟩ must be associated to some process in the PID, in a manner we will detail in Section 3.

The ⟨trigger⟩, ⟨condition⟩ and ⟨consequence⟩ all have the syntax of an ⟨ERL expression⟩. The ⟨ERL expression⟩ can contain ⟨flows⟩, ⟨ERT access expressions⟩, ⟨logical connectives⟩, ⟨temporal connectives⟩, or ⟨aggregates⟩ (i.e. sets).

- ⟨ERT access expressions⟩ are ERL constructs which select data from an ERT model, where the classes are named, and relationships are used to restrict the selection of instances from classes in some way.
- ⟨flows⟩ name tuples of data (single or aggregates) selected from the ERT. They allow information to be shared between rules, and model the flows in the PID model.
- ⟨logical connectives⟩ are the usual first order logical connectives, together with an $n$-ary exclusive or. We list the connectives in Table 1, where $e_1, e_2, \ldots$ are instances of ⟨ERL expression⟩
- ⟨temporal connectives⟩ are temporal logic counterparts to the first order connectives, and for the purposes of this paper need not be detailed further. However, it should be

**Table 1** Logical propositions and connectives.

| *ERL expression* | *Semantics* |
|---|---|
| true | Always true |
| false | Always false |
| $e_1$ and $e_2$ | Both $e_1$ and $e_2$ hold for some set of variable substitutions. |
| $e_1$ or $e_2$ | Either $e_1$ or $e_2$ holds for some set of variable substitutions. |
| not $e_1$ | $e_1$ does not hold for the set of variable substitutions applied to the expression which the connective is part of. |
| only_one_of($e_1, e_2, \ldots$) | Holds if exactly one of $e_1, e_2, \ldots$ holds. |

noted that their presence, together with the coupling between ERL and PID, give the process model temporal semantics.

- ⟨aggregates⟩ of the variables $v_1, v_2, \ldots$ may be formed by the expression:

$$\{v_1, v_2, \ldots \text{ for\_which } \langle\text{ERL expression}\rangle\}$$

The semantics of rules lead to the following requirements on what must be placed in each part of a rule:

- In the ⟨trigger⟩ part of the rule, we describe what must have just become true for the rule to be true. The trigger should contain the events which must have just occurred if the rule is relevant. The use of ⟨ERT access expressions⟩ or ⟨flow⟩ in the ⟨trigger⟩ will manifest themselves as triggering input flows in the PID.
- In the ⟨condition⟩ part of the rule, we describe what needs to be true for the rule to be considered. The condition should contain statements which must be true (and may have been true for some time) if the rule is relevant. If the condition is false, then the rule does not hold, no action or effect will result. The use of ⟨ERT access expressions⟩ or ⟨flow⟩ in the ⟨condition⟩ will manifest themselves as non-triggering input flows in the PID.
- In the ⟨consequence⟩ part of the rule, we state what must be true if the condition is true. The execution of a TEMPORA specification will attempt to ensure that the consequence is made true if the condition is true. If for any reason this can not be achieved, an error will raised in the runtime system. The use of ⟨ERT access expressions⟩ or ⟨flow⟩ in the ⟨consequence⟩ will manifest themselves as output flows in the PID.

## 3 COUPLING THE RULE AND PROCESS LANGUAGES

This section details how the connection between the ERL and the PID at the conceptual level can be made, using the semantics of the PID and the ERL as a basis.

Both the ERL and the PID can be used to describe the dynamics of a system, and thus there is clearly a degree of overlap in what the languages model in the domain. This motivates us to consider what precisely is to be contained in each model, and the manner in which concepts shared between the models cause one model to define what must appear in the other. We refer to this interaction as a **coupling** between rule and process modelling languages.

## 3.1 Defining the Basic Coupling

As already mentioned in Section 2.2, different parts of an ERL rule correspond to the use of flows in a PID model. We say that the rule is **associated** to the process which has as input and output the flows which the rule uses. The basic relationship is depicted in Figure 2 and can be described as follows:

- The *trigger* part of the process structure, i.e. the triggering flow $\alpha$ entering a process corresponds to the ⟨trigger⟩ part of an ERL rule.
- The *conditional* part of the process structure, i.e. non-triggering flow $\beta$ entering a process, corresponds to the ⟨condition⟩ part of an ERL rule. The process logic $\gamma$ should also be included in the ⟨condition⟩ part. Since the ERL expressions are logical formulae, they can be rewritten to **disjunctive normal form** (DNF), where an ⟨ERL expression⟩ $e$ may be regarded as taking the form:

  $$e = (e_{11} \text{ and } e_{12} \ldots) \text{ or } (e_{21} \text{ and } e_{22} \ldots) \ldots$$

  Thus a condition $c$ has a DNF $c_1$ or $c_2$ or ... where each of $c_1, c_2, \ldots$ can be divided into an input part $c_{1,\beta}$ and a processing part $c_{1,\gamma}$, giving $c$ the form:

  $$(c_{1,\beta} \text{ and } c_{1,\gamma}) \text{ or } (c_{2,\beta} \text{ and } c_{2,\gamma}) \text{ or } \ldots$$

  The input part $c_{1,\beta}$ may contain a flow or name ERT objects in an ERT access expression, and the processing part $c_{1,\gamma}$ may contain ERL expressions excluding flows and ERT objects, such as arithmetic expressions.
- The *action* part of the process structure, i.e. the output flows, corresponds to the then part of an ERL rule. The action part may contain both triggering flows $\delta_1$ and non-triggering flows $\delta_2$.

We have now presented the basic connection between the ERL and the PID by describing the way in which ⟨trigger⟩, ⟨condition⟩, and ⟨consequence⟩ fields are reflected in the PID and vice versa. We now elaborate how the various constructs of the PID detailed in Section 2.1 may be associated to parts of an ERL rule.

### *Processes*

A process requires information from its surroundings, that is, it interacts with other processes, ERT views, timers, and external agents via flows. A process may have one or more input flows and one or more output flows. A process' combinations of flows (input flows or output flows) is expressed using the concept of *ports* and control aspects are expressed using *triggering flows.* Triggering flows and ports make it possible:

- To represent permitted combinations of input/output flows for each process, i.e. the way the various elements of the ⟨trigger⟩, ⟨condition⟩, and ⟨consequence⟩ fields are logically related.

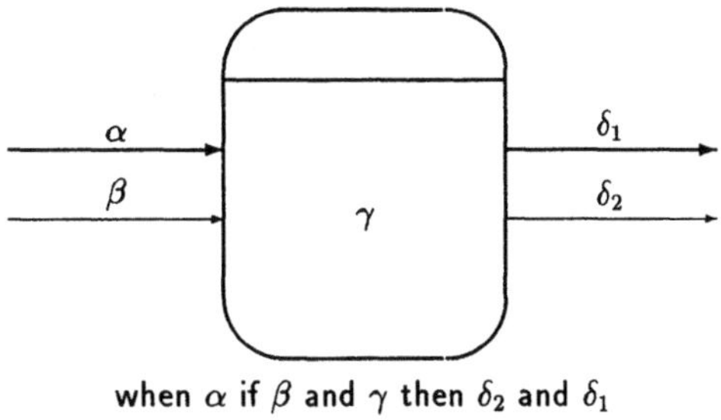


**Figure 2** Relationship between the PID and the ERL.

- To express knowledge about the sequencing of processes.
- To express which flows a process may only optionally use or produce, and which flows may be used or produced a multiple number of times.

For the moment, we will describe only how a process including ports may be described by a *single* rule expressed using the ERL. In the Figures 3 to 7, each construct of the diagram syntax of a PID process including ports is shown together with its logical semantics expressed in the ERL. The details of port construction in the PID are described in (Yang 1993).

The equivalences between AND ports and the ERL **and** logical connective are intuitive. However for OR, we have used a meta predicate $\phi$ with the following definition:

$$\phi(A, B) \equiv (A \text{ and not } B) \text{ or } (\text{not } A \text{ and } B) \text{ or } (A \text{ and } B)$$

This is necessary since if a logical disjunction is executed using SLD resolution (Hogger 1990) (such as in Prolog execution), then the disjunction holds twice when both its disjuncts hold, whilst the semantics of OR are that it holds once when either or both its disjuncts hold. It is the XOR port which corresponds to logical disjunction executed using SLD resolution, i.e. the execution occurs once for each connective, but not together as a single execution.

## *Flows*

A flow in the PID is described by a predicate notation in the ERL called ERL flow. For example, a flow new_part carrying parameters n and p is written as new_part(n,p). It may link rules described by two processes, a process and an ERT view, a process and an external agent, or a process and a timer.

## *ERT views*

An ERT view is defined in terms of an ERT access expression in the ERL. This selection constitutes a part of the ERT and is a structural representation of the contents of the ERT view. A process may read from an ERT view (corresponding to a flow from an ERT view to the process) or a process may write to an ERT view (corresponding to a flow from

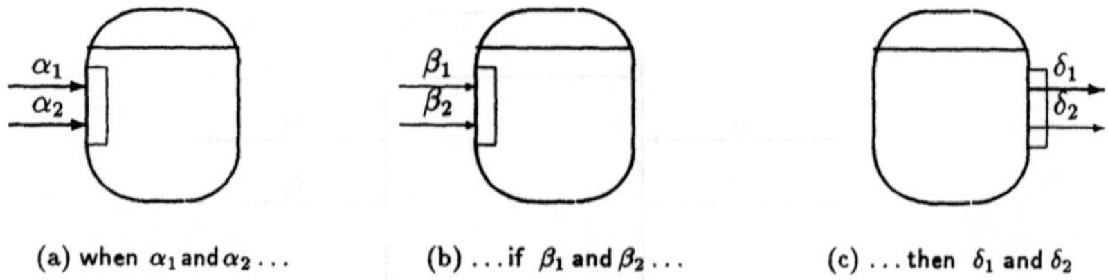


**Figure 3** The semantics of AND ports expressed using the ERL.

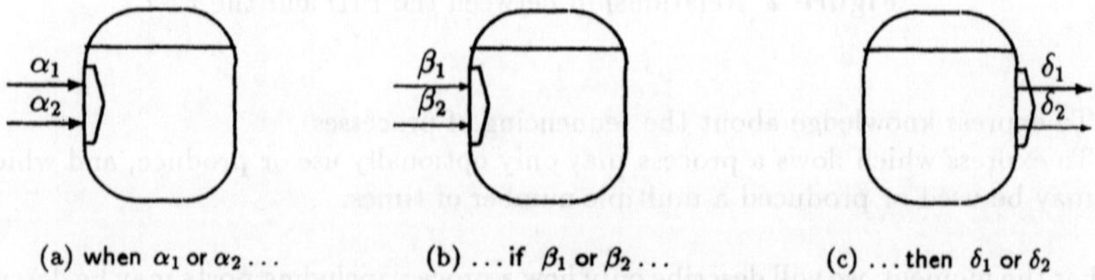


**Figure 4** The semantics of XOR ports expressed using the ERL.

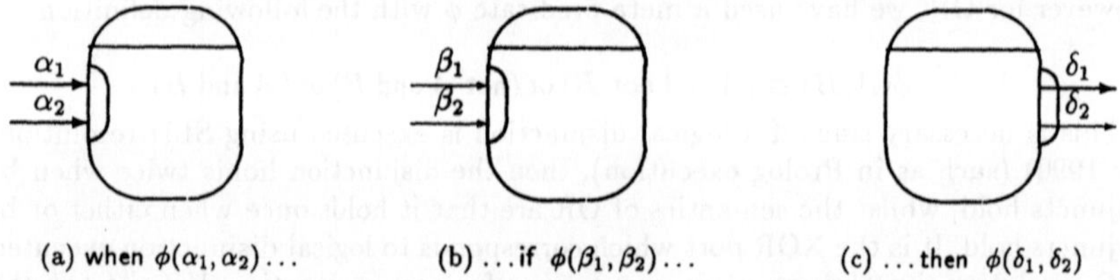


**Figure 5** The semantics of OR ports expressed using the ERL.

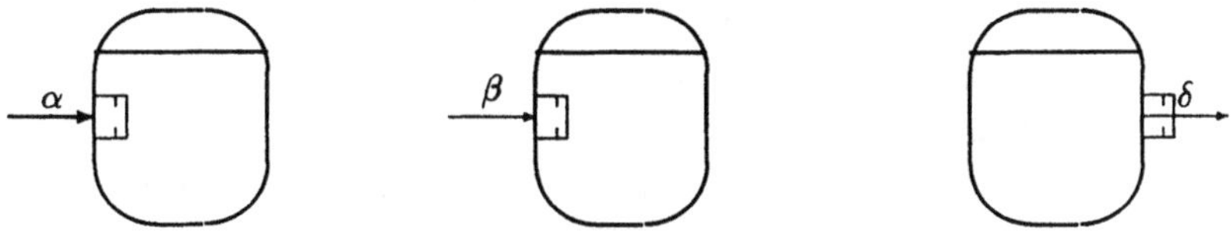


(a) Illegal structure (b) ... if $\beta$ or true ... (c) ... then $\delta$ or true

**Figure 6** The semantics of the conditional ports expressed using the ERL.

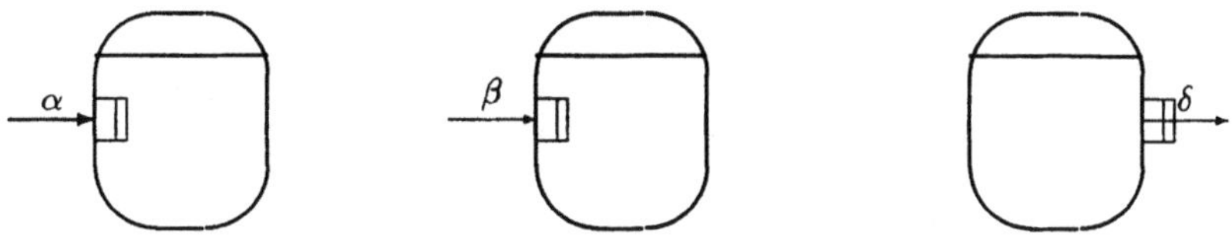


(a) Illegal structure (b) ... if $\{\beta\}$ ... (c) ... then $\delta$member_of ...

**Figure 7** The semantics of the repeating ports expressed using the ERL.

the process to an ERT view). This may be expressed by ⟨ERT access expressions⟩ in the ERL:

- From ERT view via triggering flow: **when** ⟨ERT access expression⟩ ...
- From ERT view via non-triggering flow: ... **if** ⟨ERT access expression⟩ ...
- To ERT view: ... **then** ⟨ERT access expression⟩

### *External Agents*

An external agent may be represented by an ERL rule describing the objects which are passed from/to it in terms of ERT objects. These are expressed by ERL flows, and thus the coupling defined in Figures 3 to 7 apply to flows from external agents.

### *Timers*

The details of timers can be expressed using temporal constructs in the ERL. The temporal constructs may contain temporal connectives such as **sometime_in_past** and **just_before**, references to time points through predicates such as **time_is** and references to time intervals through functions such as **today** and **this_week**. Details of the temporal constructs provided by the ERL may be found in (McBrien et al. 1991).

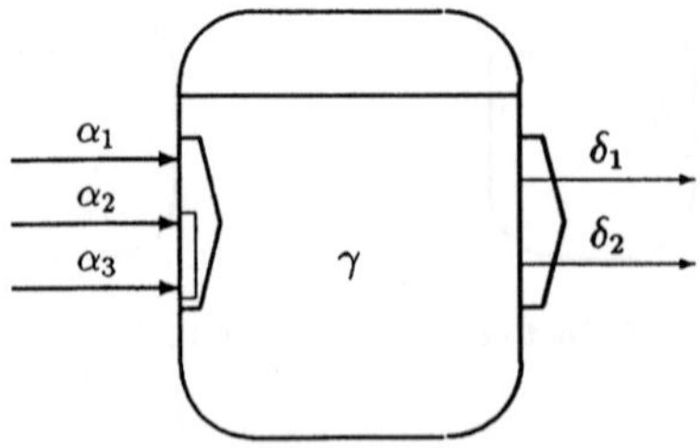


when $\alpha_1$ or $\alpha_2$ and $\alpha_3$
if $\gamma$
then $\delta_1$ or $\delta_2$

(a) PID process and ports (b) ERL rule

**Figure 8** Nesting of ports.

# 4 RULE CONSTRUCTION FROM A PID SPECIFICATION

Having defined the basis of how a PID process can be described by a single rule expressed using the ERL, it should be clear that we can use the process model as a basis for rule capture. If the port structures in the PID are simple in nature, this will lead to rules which also have a simple logical structure. Again if ports of processes are nested in a complex structure, the resulting rule structure will also become complex. For practical purposes we need some method to reduce this complexity. Furthermore, we must deal with various levels of cooperating processes, that is, how rules are related to processes at various levels of decomposition. There are three issues we have to deal with when constructing rules from a PID specification:

1. How do nested input and output ports affect the rule construction.
2. How does the relationship between input flows and output flows affect rule construction.
3. How does rule construction vary when dealing with decomposed or non-decomposed processes.

## 4.1 Nested input ports and nested output ports

A process including nested input ports together with the resulting rules is shown in Figure 8. To construct the rules associated with this process, the ⟨trigger⟩, ⟨condition⟩, and ⟨consequence⟩ fields of a basic ERL rule are extracted from the process structure according to the definitions of the coupling in Figures 3 to 7. The rules are applied to the innermost ports first, being used to generate a 'flow' in the form of an ⟨ERL expression⟩ to be used in the construction for the next port moving outwards. For the example, the two triggering flows $\alpha_2$ and $\alpha_3$ use the rule in Figure 3(a) to yield $\alpha_2$ and $\alpha_3$, then we use this as input to use the rule in Figure 4(a) to get the ERL rule shown in Figure 8.

Clearly, the greater the depth of the nesting, the more complicated the resulting rule. However, we may simplify the situation by instead generating multiple rules. As already detailed in Figure 4(a), a process with two input flows to an XOR port may be modelled

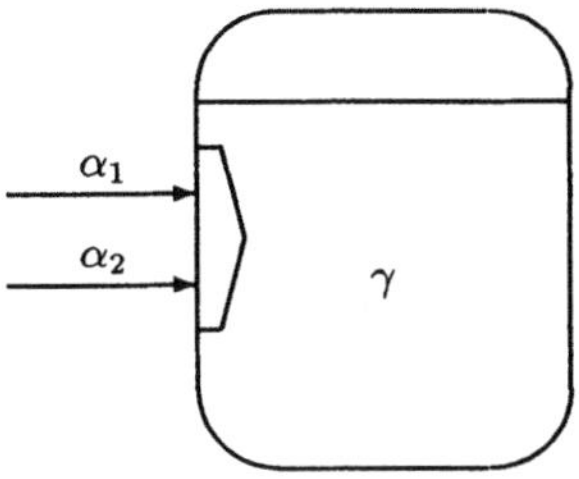


(a) PID process and ports

when $\alpha_1$
if $\gamma_1$
then ...

when $\alpha_2$
if $\gamma_2$
then ...

(b) ERL rules

**Figure 9** Generating multiple rules from an XOR port.

as a rule with a logical disjunction in the trigger part when $\alpha_1$ or $\alpha_2$.... As is the case in standard Prolog, this disjunction may be replaced by two separate rules as shown in Figure 9(b), each of which has as its trigger one of the triggers of the XOR port. This in practice will tend to be the more natural representation of the specification described by PID model in Figure 9(a).

If disjunctions appear between non-triggering flows (corresponding to the ⟨condition⟩ part of a rule) or between output flows (corresponds to the ⟨trigger⟩ part of rule), a composite rule can be split into simpler rules in the manner illustrated in Figure 9.

The process model shown in Figure 10(a) would lead to a trigger of the form when ($\alpha_1$and $\beta_1$) or ($\alpha_2$ and $\beta_2$).... Again the technique of using separate rules for a logical disjunction we would get the rules shown in Figure 10(b). We could also split the action part of each of the rules shown, giving a total of four rules. However, this ignores what the process internals might indicate as far as the rules to be generated, which we will now consider.

## 4.2 Relationship between input flows and output flows

It should be noted that so far we have not taken the internals (i.e. $\gamma$) of the process into consideration. Thus, there is a certain ambiguity in the rules generated — i.e. there is part of the domain which the process model does not capture, and which must be specified in the rule language.

From what we have already described, for a process model such as that shown in Figure 10(a), the output $\delta_1$ or $\delta_2$ will be in the ⟨consequence⟩ part of both rules. However, it is quite probable that $\delta_1$ is associated to only $\alpha_1$ and that $\delta_2$ is associated to only $\alpha_2$, which would mean that the rules in Figure 10(c) would be a correct interpretation of the process model.

To decide which of $\delta_1$ or $\delta_2$, $\delta_1$, or $\delta_2$ should be in the ⟨consequence⟩, the relationship between the inputs and outputs must be considered. We may represent the way inputs and outputs of a process are related to each other in a decomposition of the process. In

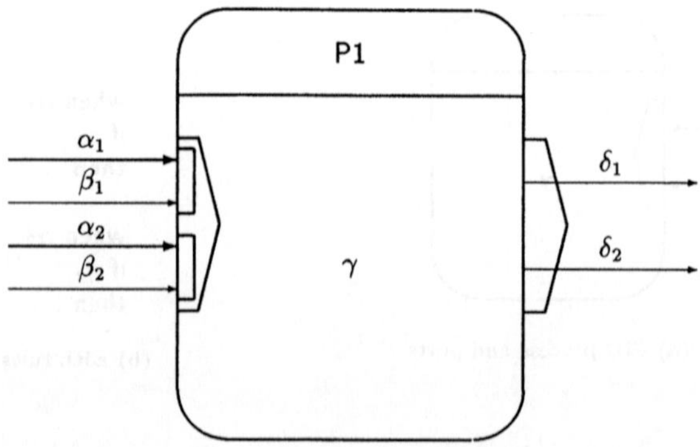


(a) PID process and ports

**when** $\alpha_1$ **and** $\beta_1$
**if** $\gamma_1$
**then** $\delta_1$ **or** $\delta_2$

**when** $\alpha_2$ **and** $\beta_2$
**if** $\gamma_2$
**then** $\delta_1$ **or** $\delta_2$

(b) ERL rules

**when** $\alpha_1$ **and** $\beta_1$
**if** $\gamma_1$
**then** $\delta_1$

**when** $\alpha_2$ **and** $\beta_2$
**if** $\gamma_2$
**then** $\delta_2$

(c) Alternative ERL rules

**Figure 10** Multiple rules and nested ports.

Figure 11 the internals of the process in Figure 10 are taken into account. By doing this, the ambiguity in the two ERL rules as described above is removed.

In Figure 12(a), we give a simple example of our method applied in a practical situation. We have modelled a process **staff_payments** which handles all payments made to staff, and have discovered that payments are based on **salary** or **expenses** records, and are triggered by a command from a clerk or the temporal event of it being midnight. The basic coupling between processes and rules would give the rule illustrated in Figure 12(b). This might seem over complex, and thus we may use the disjunction elimination to produce the four rules shown in Figure 12(c). At this point, the various possible behaviours of the process are made more apparent, and our analysis can check that all the rules produced correspond to the domain. It might be the case, for example, that we never produce salary cheques on the command of the clerk, and thus the rule

**when pay_staff_no(...) if** ⟨ERT access expression⟩$_{\textsf{salary}}$ **then give_cheque(...)**

may be eliminated — a restriction on the process logic specified in Figure 12(a) which

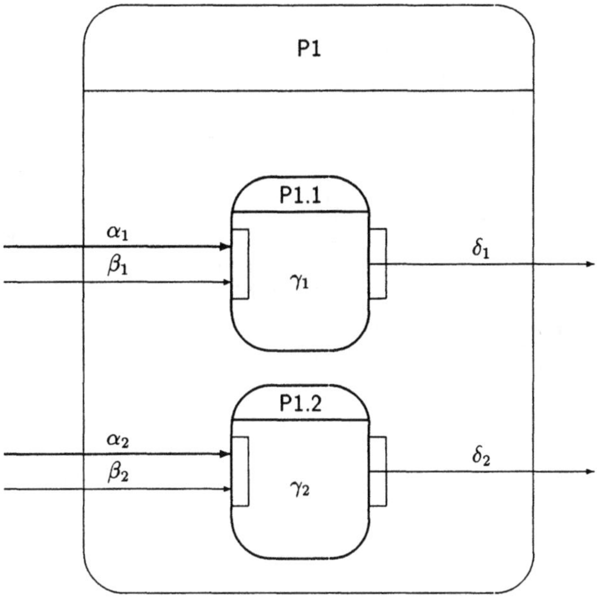


**Figure 11** Example of a decomposed process and its corresponding ERL rules.

we may specify in the process model by decomposition or modifying the port structure. Once we are satisfied that we have a set of rules which correctly reflect the domain, we may proceed to specify the details of the process logic by expanding the condition part of the ERL rules.

## 4.3 Decomposed versus non-decomposed processes

Each non-decomposed process should have an associated set of ERL rules describing the behaviour of the process. In addition, one may optionally specify in rules the behaviour of decomposed processes, these rules being interpreted as constraints on the behaviour of the rules describing the non-decomposed processes. The rules associated with the processes at the lowest level of decomposition constitute the rule base which may be compiled to executable form. Rules associated with decomposed processes may be used as constraints on the execution of the rules of non-decomposed processes.

# 5 RE-ENGINEERING OF PROCESS AND RULE MODELS

The strong coupling between rules and processes described in Section 3 may be used during business process re-engineering to facilitate the modification of models. A particular step

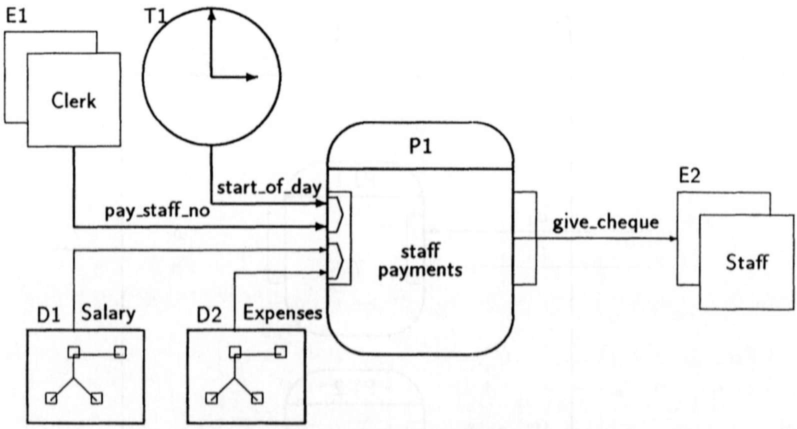


(a) PID model to process payments due to staff

when start_of_day or pay_staff_no(...)
if ⟨ERT access expression⟩$_{\text{salary}}$ or ⟨ERT access expression⟩$_{\text{expenses}}$
then give_cheque(...)

(b) P1 represented as a single rule

when start_of_day
if ⟨ERT access expression⟩$_{\text{salary}}$
then give_cheque(...)

when pay_staff_no(...)
if ⟨ERT access expression⟩$_{\text{salary}}$
then give_cheque(...)

when start_of_day
if ⟨ERT access expression⟩$_{\text{expenses}}$
then give_cheque(...)

when pay_staff_no(...)
if ⟨ERT access expression⟩$_{\text{expenses}}$
then give_cheque(...)

(c) Disjunctions removed from the single rule

**Figure 12** Example of ERL and PID Relationships.

in the process of business process re-engineering may involve changing either the process model or the rule model. We now detail how changes in one model reflect on the re-engineering of the other.

## 5.1 Process Model Updates

Modifications in the process model will imply changes be made in the rule model.

- The deletion of a construct in the PID implies the deletion of the construct in the rules associated to the process. The user may view these rules to ensure that the deletion of the PID construct was a correct procedure to follow.
- The addition of a process in the PID implies the creation of a rule in the rule model. The ports used to describe the process may be used to give a structural template of the rule to be created.
- The addition of a port or flow to a process in the PID implies the alteration of the logic used in the rules used to implement then process. The user may be prompted with the rules that need modification.

For example, if we decided in Figure 12(a) that payments to staff will now only be triggered by a direct command from the clerk, and not by a temporal event, then the two rules in Figure 12(c) that begin **when start_of_day** must be removed, and any details we have added to the condition part in the form of process logic must be incorporated in the two remaining rules.

## 5.2 Rule Model Updates

Modifications in the rule model will imply changes be made in the process model.

- The deletion of a rule which is associated to a PID process, and for which some construct of the process no longer has a rule associated to it, implies that construct should be revised. Either a replacement rule needs to be created, or the construct deleted.
- The alteration of the logic used in a rule implies the alteration of any associated process logic.
- The creation of a rule which includes a ⟨trigger⟩ component implies that the rule be associated to some process in the PID. This process may already exist, or it may be required that some modelling activity must proceed in order to produce a new process.

For example, if we decided in Figure 12(c) that payments to staff which exceeded a certain amount would be made by multiple cheques, then we would need to alter the process model to make the output from **P1** a repeating port.

# 6 SUMMARY & CONCLUSIONS

The motivation for the coupling between the process based and rule based approaches was to reduce the fragmentation of specifications when multiple languages are used for conceptual modelling. In achieving this, we utilises each language's strengths and used them as complementary languages for information systems modelling. Three particular areas where the strengths of one language served to enrich the other were:

- The process model gives a flexible representation and presentation of the rule model. This allows us to have both a form based representation (in the ERL) and a graphical representation of rules (in the PID). The form based representation uses a formal language, allowing the precise statement of the domain, and suited to the use of automated application generation. The graphical representation of rules uses a less formal language, but allows the structure of specifications to be made readily apparent.
- The ERL language has temporal connectives for the querying and update of a valid-time data model. With the ERL-PID coupling in place, this serves to give the process model temporal semantics.
- The rule model serves to define the process logic of the process model, and hence turns it into an executable specification. We may use the rules as a basis for animating the model, as well as generating application code.

Thus, in combining the process based and rule based approaches we exploit the *user-friendliness* and the *structural properties* of a process model and the *expressive power* and *formality* of a rule model. We thus allow development and maintenance to take place at the correct level of detail. The use of rule modelling in distributed environments is supported by the structuring capabilities of the process model. Re-engineering precise statements about activities is made on rules, and the process model altered to reflect the changes to rules. Re-engineering of how activities interact takes place in the process model, and the rule model then altered to reflect those changes.

## 7 ACKNOWLEDGEMENTS

The work reported in this paper was partly funded by the Commission of the European Communities under the ESPRIT R&D programme. The TEMPORA project (number E2469) was a collaborative project between: BIM, Belgium; Hitec, Greece; Imperial College, UK; LPA, UK; SINTEF, Norway; SISU, Sweden; University of Liège, Belgium and UMIST, UK.

## REFERENCES

Chen, P. P. S.: 1976, The Entity-Relationship model: Toward a unified view of data, *ACM TODS, vol. 1, no. 1.*

deMarco, T.: 1978, *Structured Analysis and System Specification*, Yourdon Press.

Gabbay, D.: 1989, The declarative past and executable future, *Temporal Logic in Specification: Altrincham Workshop 1987*, LNCS, Springer-Verlag, pp. 409–448.

Gane, C. and Sarson, T.: 1978, *Structured Systems Analysis: Tools and Techniques*, Prentice-Hall.

Gulla, J., Lindland, O. and Willumsen, G.: 1991, PPP an integrated CASE environment, *Proceedings of the Third Nordic Conference on Advanced Information Systems Engineering*, Vol. 498 of *LNCS*, Springer-Verlag.

Hogger, C.: 1990, *Essentials of Logic Programming*, Vol. 1 of *Graduate Texts in Computer Science*, OUP.

Jensen *et al*, C.: 1984, A consensus glossary of temporal database concepts, *SIGMOD Record*.

Krogstie, J., McBrien, P., Owens, R. and Seltveit, A.: 1991, Information systems development using a combination of process and rule-based approaches, *Proceedings of the Third Nordic Conference on Advanced Information Systems Engineering*, Vol. 498 of *LNCS*, Springer-Verlag.

Loucopoulos, P., McBrien, P., Schumacker, F., Theodoulidis, B., Kopanas, V. and Wangler, B.: 1991, Integrating database technology, rule-based systems and temporal reasoning for effective software: the TEMPORA paradigm, *Journal of Information Systems*.

McBrien, P., Niezette, M., Pantazis, S., Thedoulidis, B., Tziallas, G., Seltveit, A., Sundin, U. and Wohed, R.: 1991, The TEMPORA external rule language, *Proceedings of the Third Nordic Conference on Advanced Information Systems Engineering*, Vol. 498 of *LNCS*, Springer-Verlag.

McBrien, P., Seltveit, A. and Wangler, B.: 1992, An entity-relationship model extended to describe historical information, *Proceedings of CISMOD '92*, Bangalore, India.

Xiaofeng, L.: 1991, What is so bad about rule-based programming?, *IEEE Software* 8(5), 103–105.

Yang, M.: 1993, *COMIS - A Conceptual Model for Information Systems*, PhD thesis, IDT, NTH, Trondheim, Norway.

## BIOGRAPHIES

Peter McBrien received a B.A. in Engineering and Computer Science from Cambridge University in 1986. After working at Racal and ICL, he joined Imperial College as a Research Associate in 1989, where he obtained his PhD in 1992. Leaving Imperial College in January 1994, he spent two months working at The Norwegian Institute of Technology (NTH) as a visiting academic before joining the Department of Computer Science at King's College London as a lecturer in April 1994. His research activities at present cover the area of temporal databases, rule based programming, algebras to support conceptual modelling, and modelling techniques for temporal and rule based systems.

Anne Helga Seltveit obtained her siv.ing. (MSc) degree from NTH in 1987. She then worked as a research assistant in the Informations Systems Group lead by Prof. Sølvberg. She obtained her dr.ing. (PhD) degree in January 1995. In 1988 she had seven months study leave, working with Andersen Consulting in Chicago. Her research activities include work on the process, rule and temporal database modelling languages.

# 13

# Discussants comments on the ten main papers

# Exotica/FMQM: A Persistent Message-Based Architecture for Distributed Workflow Management - Discussion -

*Stef Joosten and Sjaak Brinkkemper*
*Centre for Telematics and Information Technology*
*University of Twente*
*P.O. Box 217, NL-7500 AE Enschede the Netherlands*
*E-mail: {joosten | brinkkemper} @cs.utwente.nl*

SUMMARY

This paper argues that most workflow management support systems are vulnerable due to the single database architecture upon which they are based. Furthermore, the single server architecture creates a performance bottleneck when large quantities of workflows are being managed.

To overcome this problem, the authors propose to store the knowledge in a distributed manner by means of persistent messages. The idea is that a message sent is never lost until it is received. In the proposed architecture, a node holds only the information needed to perform its part of the workflow. Every node holds a queue for each process that makes use of that particular node. These queues are implemented in stable store, thus providing the persistent functionality of messages. Each node maintains a process table for every process, based on its invocation by a process definition node. The process definition node may distribute a process over a number of nodes, each of which makes its own process tables. The process is kept together by a process thread. Instances are started, maintained and stopped by means of activity threads. An activity thread is started by a process thread. A nice feature is that instance tables need not be kept in stable store, because a crashed instance can always be recovered on the basis of the process tables (which are in stable store) and the current state of the queues.

PERSPECTIVE

This is the first detailed exposition of the distribution problems that are involved with workflow enactment. Most authors ignore the integrity problems associated with workflow, simply because they are handled by a single database implementation. The authors argue convincingly that this conventional workflow architecture will not stand up to the needs of large scale workflow systems.

The idea to use persistent stores at the individual nodes is new. The paper is well written and clearly understandable by researchers with a little knowledge of workflow in general and FlowMark in particular.

## CRITIQUE

There is no evidence as yet that the proposed architecture works. So far, only the ideas have been described.

This work has many similarities with the design of the Job Transfer and Manipulation protocol (JTM; see l'Anson & Pell, Understanding OSI Applications, Prentice Hall, Englewood Cliffs, 1993. chapter 13). However, the relation with JTM is not mentioned.

The use of the reference model of the Workflow Management Coalition is rather obvious. That model is superficial enough to accommodate any serious workflow architecture.

The work leads to so many different consequences that all need research, that the section on future work is unreasonably shallow.

## QUESTIONS

Is it possible to prove the stability of the workflow system, based on the assumption that node/process queues and process tables are persistent? Has this proof been done?

The removal of messages from queues implies that copies of messages are made in case different activities share a message. Does this lead to redundancy? Performance loss?

How is the aggregation of managerial information and statistical data of running workflow applications at runtime nodes being supported in the sketched architecture? The distribution architecture seems to require extensive querying of all runtime nodes.

# The Systems Integration Architecture: An Agile Information Infrastructure - Discussion -

*John Krogstie*
*IDT, NTH*
*N-7034 Trondheim*
*Email: johnkrog@idt.unit.no*

## DISCUSSANT'S SYNOPSIS

The Systems Integration Architecture (SIA) project claim to take a fresh approach to integration with special emphasis on supporting Agile, Virtual enterprises and special need for reconfigurable, de-centralized information systems. Agile Manufacturing is an approach in which manufacturers must be able to rapidly respond to unanticipated market demands, producing new products with resources outside of their immediate company in so-called Virtual Corporations. In these, complementary core competencies from diverse companies including suppliers and customers, are combined temporarily into a new, decentralized company existing only to fulfill that market demand and dissolving when the demand is satisfied. Even if a company is not ready to become Agile, to survive in today's competitive world, it must be continually seeking to improve itself. Such continuous improvement requires change, often rapid change.

To address this situation, the authors propose a workflow modeling and enactment system based on the IPO (Input-process-output) approach. Processes can be manual, computer aided, or automated. In the two first cases one also indicate the human actor of the process. The input and output from processes have a type, a data format, a file structure, and an access type. Control flow is also possible to indicate. Around this partly traditional language, the system integration architecture is built up, providing services in data management, control, and communications. SIA uses the concept of processes to allow the user to define a workflow by checking for the appropriate format for the tool integration through a special user-interface. SIA also keeps track of the information interfaces through a data management system via a communication kernel based on CORBA. SIA is currently being implemented in C++ on a several UNIX-platforms.

## POINTS FOR DISCUSSION

We will below raise some points for discussion based on our own background.

- Generally, we feel that more references to literature within conceptual modeling and comparisons with this kind of work could be provided. Reading the paper, I see a clear connection to work within many different perspectives in the conceptual modeling field, e.g. the structural (data) perspective, the functional (process) perspective e.g. Ward/PPP, the behavioral perspective, the organizational(actor/agent/role) perspective e.g ALBERT and the communicational (speech acts) perspective e.g Action Workflow.

- Within workflow modeling, it is usual to differentiate between two main approaches, the IPO approach, which the article present, and the language action approach. The IPO approach is usually proposed for use in stable environments whereas the language action approach is proposed for use within changing environments. The article proposes an IPO approach for rapidly changing environments. Have you looked upon the language action approach?
- The matching mechanisms that are proposed support matching on a syntactic level by matching types and modalities, but not on a semantic level. When having a fully automated process being "a rule based design system which transforms a set of specifications into a full design according to the rules embedded in it" there is a need for a semantic matching being also based on the content and meaning of the data. As far as I can see, there is no support for this in the framework, an area which will be especially problematic when putting together virtual organizations based on parts of organizations which inevitably will have a different culture, use partly different terminology etc. Here one might find inspiration within work on view integration and reuse of conceptual models (see e.g. Francalanci and Shanks for an overview of these fields).
- The article refer t oan implementation effort of the framework How far has the implementation come?
- Do you have any experiences with the practical use of the framework?

# Message flow control - Discussion -

*Atika Laribi and Michel Leonard*
*Centre Universitaire d'Informatique, Universitat de Geneve*
*24, rue du General-Dufour, CH-1211 GENEVE 4*
*Switzerland*
*Email: {laribi | leonard}@cui.unige.ch*

This paper presents a framework for the development of a message control system, an issue which is at the heart of Decentralized Information Systems implementation. Even though the major IS concept of business transaction is presented as being the cornerstone of the system, it is not thoroughly explored. The authors stay at a rather technical level and fail to fully explain the implications of their approach on Decentralized Information Systems. However, by staying at this level, the authors are able to bring to our attention a fundamental issue namely the control of message exchanges. The paper therefore, changes its focus from business transactions to transaction protocol handler. This handler coordinates the exchange of messages between actors. One has to be careful with terminology here, as actor is defined in a purely technical context and does not necessarily refer to the usual Information System actor. For the benefit of the DBMS community, a quick analogy is made with database transactions. Even though business transactions have all the ACID properties, one way they differ significantly from their database counterpart is the fact that they may be carried out by humans. Although database transactions management has been extensively studied, a model specific to business transactions is required to cater for the differences. Business transactions can have a superior and subordinates. A given transaction T1 can be both the subordinate of a transaction T2 and the superior of a transaction T3. ExSpect (Executable Specification Tool) is used to implement the transaction state transition diagram representing the system architecture. The paper lays the ground for the development of a useful analysis tool for Information Systems managers. The prototype presented can be directly used to simulate the interactions between a given transaction and the transactions it needs to cooperate with to complete a given activity. The coordination revolves around the control of the message flow between the different cooperating transactions. This is indeed an important feature of the prototype since the only way business transactions communicate is through messages.

# A light weight name service and its use within a collaborative editor - Discussion -

*Patrizia Asirelli*
*Instituto di Elaborazione dell'Informazione del C.N.R., Via S. Maria, 46- 56126 Pisa, Italy.-*
*Tel. +39-50-593477*
*Email: asirelli@iei.pi.cnr.it*

**Abstract**

In this short discussion on [LUPA95] I shall point out a tendency in the evolution of an area of research that suggests interesting, in my opinion, extensions to the ideas presented in that paper. Furthermore, I am going to suggest the exploitation of the Light Weight Name Service, eventually extended, within the framework the World Wide Web.

## INTRODUCTION

First I shall introduce few notions of Software Configuration Management (SCM for short) that immediately suggest which extensions could be made to the LWNS proposal and why those extensions would be useful. Then I shall briefly point out other similarities with the World Wide Web that I am certain the authors have considered and point out which advantages the LWNS, eventually extended, would bring into that area.

## SOFTWARE CONFIGURATION MANAGEMENT AND ITS RELATION TO THE COLLABORATIVE EDITING PROBLEM

As the author says in [LUPA95] their LWNS proposal has the basis for further extensions and, in my opinion, the trend in the Software Configuration Management (SCM for short) area [WSVCC88], [WSCM91], [ESEC87],[ICS95] [FEL79] [TRENDS94] should be considered. The reason for this is the similarities it shows with the DUPLEX environment for which LWNS was designed while, on the other hand, I believe the SCM area could take advantage and suggestions to deal with "distributedness". Configuration Management refers to the activity that controls software evolution. The basic idea is that a software system is built up by putting together pieces (modules) of software that are developed by different programmers, may be at different time. At present, given the "distributedness" of many of the environments on which we work, the developers of a module may be resident on a different site and he/she may be also using a different tool and computer. Still, the development of the system is an activity that is collaborative, thus there must be a manager. Thus, the SCM activity basically deals with two main concepts: the system model that describes the architecture of the software system and the software components (objects) or system family. Software components themselves are objects that may be obtained by collecting together objects and so on. Everything becomes even more complex when considering "reuse" and multiple "versions" of objects. Versions may be "variants" (different implementation of the same "specified function") or "revisions" (evolution of an object) that may be plug into the system to lead to a different version of the system itself. The configured system is a collection of all the software components. Thus to build a configuration it means to assemble objects with certain characteristics. Characteristics are properties of objects for which one version is chosen rather than the other, e.g. the modification date [FEL79], etc. Summarizing, SCM environments need:

- a file system where objects can be found;
- strategies to choose the objects in the file system.

The actual trend in SCM is that configurations can become very sophisticated and the process of building a system version can become more powerful if more knowledge on the objects is put into the file system, thus, for example it could be possible to build configurations not only with objects that have a certain creation/modification date[FEL79], but also on the basis of the "author's name/group" or whatever else one might think it necessary and possible to say on objects. This trend is thus asking for evolution of the simple file system to be a database[TICHY85, TICHY88, ESTUB86, ESTUB94], and not just a relational one but, for example, Object-Oriented[ATKI89, DEUX91, ESTUB94], Deductive [ZAN90, ASI87a, ASI87b, ASI88, AQUI91, AQUI92] or a knowledge base in general. Thus the tendency is to give more structure to the information on the objects and on strategies and inference rules; on deductive capabilities in general so to be able to make some form of reasoning The similarities with the collaborative editing environment (DUPLEX), suggest that a name server for it should grow towards the above kind of knowledge base. Thus the suggestion is to investigate into an evolution of the LWNS towards a more flexible structure for the object references. that would permit to say more than just: 1) the address of the service; 2) the access protocol;3) the object's local name. This probably would also mean that all the LWNS should have to be reconsidered e.g. the prefix table should become a database etc..The efficiency of such an approach should be evaluated to find a fair compromise between fast responses and complexity of the query to find objects in the collaboration (or in the Web, see next section).

## LWNS WITHIN WWW?

The World Wide Web is overwhelming every one of us and this Conference certainly sees an interested and competent audience. Although not all of us may be directly involved in working for the Web, in the sense of producing documents to be put on it or producing tools for it, I am fairly certain that every one of us is, by now, aware of how things work and how to navigate within WWW. It is from this very little and naive experience that while reading the paper [LUPA95] a question naturally emerges: such a naming service could be adopted as the name service within WWW. Again, I would like to point out the similarities between the environments for which the LWNS was designed and the WWW. There is collaboration among users connected trough Internet, as in WWW. Long distance between users. Users that work on the same documents or use documents produced by other users. There is also the same kind of approach in constituting a collaboration. Users may be added, deleted and their reference modified. There must be a manager of the collaboration (the Web node: ftp, http, etc.). Thus there seems to be no reason why one should not investigate into the use of such a name service within WWW. The advantage for the WWW community would be, in my opinion, that there would be more flexibility in the creation/modification/deletion of objects and more powerful retrieval operations could be performed on the net. On the other hand, extending the LWNS in the direction mentioned in the previous section, and then integrating it into the Web, would bring into it some form of reasoning with all the advantages previously mentioned.

## CONCLUSION

I would like to conclude this discussion mentioning that, from the documentation I have found on the Web [WWW,URL], I see a tendency to extend the actual UR system towards the direction discussed here. That is, as far as I can see, the evolution proposed for LWNS considering the trend in the Software Configuration Management, and the integration (or use of it) within the WWW, would exactly be coherent with the tendency shown in the extension of the actual naming system of the WWW [URL]. Now a question arises: the UR system can be extended and made soon freely available. This is a fear expectation considering how fast this area has grown in very little time, then: wouldn't the LWNS become quickly obsolete? I am sure that the authors of [LUPA95] had already made the considerations I have made in this discussion and will present their own opinion on the matter.

## ACKNOWLEDGMENTS

I would like to thank Keith Jeffery, Arne Sølvberg and the organizers of the ISDO'95, for giving me the opportunity to learn something new and to write this paper. I also thank my colleague Dr. Franco Mazzanti for all the useful and stimulating discussion on these ideas.

## REFERENCES

[ASI87a] P. Asirelli, P. Inverardi - Enhancing Configuration Facilities in Software Development: A Logic Approach, Proc. of ESEC - 1st European Software Engineering Conference , Strasburg, 8-11 Sept., 1987, Lecture Notes in Computer Science, No. 289, Springer-Verlag 1987.

[ASI87b] P. Asirelli, P. Inverardi - A Logic Database to Support Configuration Management in Ada, Proc. Ada Europe International Conference, Ada Components: libraries and tools, Stockholm, 26-28 May, S. Tafvelin (ed.), The Ada Companion Series,Cambridge Univ. Press, 1987.

[ASI88] P. Asirelli, P. Inverardi - EDBLOG: a kernel for configuration environments, Proc. Int. Workshop on Software Version and Configuration Control, J.F.H. Winkler (ed), Grassau, B.G. Teubner Stuttgart, 1988, pp. 422-425.

[ATKI89] Atkinson M.P., Bancilhon F., DeWitt D., Dittrich K., Maier D. and Zdonik S., The Object-Oriented Database System manifesto, Proc. DOOD 1989, Kyoto, Japan, pp. 40-57.

[AQUI91], D. Aquilino, P.Asirelli, P. Inverardi, P. Malara - Supporting Reuse and Configuration: A port based SCM model; Proc. of the 3rd Int. Workshop on Software Configuration Management, J. Feiler Ed. , 12-14 June1991,Trondheim - Norway, ACM Press.

[AQUI92] D. Aquilino, P.Asirelli, P. Inverardi - Maintaining Knowledge in System Development-Abstract to be presented at the Fourteenth International Conference On Software Engineering (ICSE14) -Melbourne, Australia, May 11-15, 1992.

[DEUX91] Deux O. et al., The O2 System, Communication of the ACM, Vol. 34, N. 10, pp34-48.

[ESEC87] Proc. of ESEC - 1st European Software Engineering Conference , Strasburg, 8-11 Sept., 1987, in LNCS 289, Springer-Verlag 1987.

[ESTUB86] Estublier, J. Adele: a data base of programs. Presentation manual, Laboratoire de Genie Informatique, France, June 1986.

[ESTUB94] Estublier, J., Casallas, R., The Adele Configuration Manager, Adele: a data base of programs. Presentation manual, Laboratoire de Genie Informatique, France, June 1986.

[FEL79] S.I. Feldman, "MAKE - A Program for Maintaining Computer Programs", Software Practice and Experience 9, pp. 255-265 (April 1979).

[ICS95] Workshop on Configuration management of the 17th ICSE, International Conference on Software Engineering.

[LUPA95]J.-C. Lugeon and F. Pacull, A Light Weight Name Service and its use within a collaborative editor. In Proc. of the IFIP WG8.1 Working Conference on Information System Development for Decentralised Organisations-ISDO'95, Chapman & Hall, 1995.

[TICHY85] Tichy, W., RCS- A System for Version Control, Software Practice and Experience 15,7 (July 1985), 637-654.

[TICHY88] Tichy, W., Tools for Configuration Management, Proc. Int. Workshop on Software Version and Configuration Control, J.F.H. Winkler (ed), Grassau, B.G. Teubner Stuttgart, 1988.

[TRENDS94] Trends in Software: Configuration Management, W. Tichy Ed., John Wiley& Sons, 1994.

[URL] http://www.ncsa.uiuc.edu/demoweb/url-primer.html
or http://www.w3.org/hypertext/WWW/Addressing/Addressing.html

[WSCM91] Proc. of the 3rd Int. Workshop on Software Configuration Management, J. Feiler Ed. , 12-14 June1991,Trondheim - Norway, ACM Press.

[WSVCC88] Proc. Int. Workshop on Software Version and Configuration Control, J.F.H. Winkler Ed., Grassau, B.G. Teubner Stuttgart, 1988.

[WWW] http://www.w3.org/hypertext/WWW/TheProject.html

[ZAN90] Zaniolo C., Deductive Databases: Theroy Meets Practice,(Invited Paper) Proc. EDBT'90, Lecture Notes in Computer Science, No. 416, Springer-Verlag, pp. 1-15.

# Organizational management system in a heterogeneous environment: A WWW case study - Discussion -

*Martin Bever*
*IBM Deutschland Informationssysteme GmbH*
*European Networking Center*
*Vangerowstrasse 18*
*D-69115 Heidelberg, Germany*
*Email: mbever@vnet.ibm.com*

## INTRODUCTION

Since the introduction of the World Wide Web, this technology has experienced an unforeseen growth. A significant portion of the overall traffic found within the Internet now is due to WWW, and it is still heavily growing. This clearly indicates WWW is solving a problem users have all around the world, namely having easy access to all the informations present within different places.

On the other hand, one also can see the proliferation of new problems arising from this approach, namely how to find the right information in reasonable time, and how to ensure what one gets is still up to date (no way to deduce this from WWW pages).

## THE REPORT

The paper written by Silva, Borbinha and Delgado reports about using the WWW technology to give users easy access to a multitude of data management systems (e.g. file systems or data base systems), storing informations in a variety of formats often different from HTML. A gateway is used to map both the format of the content to the HTML format exchanged within WWW, and the functionality provided by the data base to HTTP In this way, it becomes possible to read documents in multiple formats using a WWW client. Since these clients are available on many platforms, this approach conveniently provides access to all informations within a heterogeneous environment.

However, since each data base uses a specialized format and access technique, a corresponding specialized gateway process is required. This clearly makes sense if lots of documents that have to be kept in a special format shall be made available to WWW users. If, however, an information service about an organization has to be developed from scratch, why not writing these pages directly in HTML? Extending these considerations, one might ask the question whether HTML is the solution to the problem how to describe the contents of a sheet. We have seen other approaches (like ODA) in the past, and new ones still are evolving (like e.g. the Portable Document Format, PDF). Open issues are e.g. the extension of HTTP to allow real-time access to multimedia data. Finally, finding the right information in time would become much easier if a rich search function were available in HTTP, like e.g. in the Document Filing and Retrieval (DFR) protocol.

## IMPACT OF VVWW TO TELECOOPERATION

Extending the scope of the paper, large organizations have to find solutions how their different sites (mostly located all around the world) can efficiently interact among themselves and with their customers. It is the goal of telecooperation to increase the efficiency of any collaboration between parties located at different geographical sites even across country borders.

Making information available in the appropriate form to a multitude of users clearly is one important aspect in this area. The paper restricts itself on accessing documents in an off-line mode, i.e. retrieving it page by page from a repository and reading it within a WWW client. However, a perhaps even more important scenario is the synchronous interaction among groups of people within a desktop conference.

Here, the cooperative viewing of documents is a topic of main interest. It should be possible to view the document in a synchronous manner, to add annotations to it and so on. A final question that is worth further discussion is about the impact the WWW technology can have on telecooperation, and the perspective of the technology in this rapidly growing, highly interesting area.

# A federated information system for quality management processes - Discussion -

*Jan l. G. Dietz*
*Delft University of Technology,*
*Faculty of Technical Mathematics and Informatics*
*Information Systems Group*
*P.O. Box 356, 2600 AJ Delft, The Netherlands*
*E-mail: dietz@is.twi.tudelft.nl*

## DISCUSSANT'S SYNOPSIS

A key question for the field of information systems in the context of business process (re)engineering, which leads to networks of working groups integrated by material and information flows, is whether the latter imposes new practices for the (re)design and (re)engineering of the information systems supporting the business processes, and if so, which ones. The authors address this question by contending that a new information systems architecture is needed in order to fulfill the requirements imposed by a continuously changing and flexible business environment. This new architecture then should be repository-based and federated.

Although the basic technology (computer networks, repositories and access mechanisms) to implement such an architecture is available, there are a number of problems still to be solved. Three of these problems are indicated and discussed in the paper:

- The conceptual distance between different working groups.
- The task-oriented access to and availability of information.
- The management of change of an installed information system.

According to the authors these problems can be solved adequately if information systems are based on the Trader architecture, which is the outcome of the WibQuS project on the integration of quality management methods in which all of the authors have participated.

The problem of the conceptual distance is addressed by the hierarchical layering of the conceptual schema in the Trader architecture, based on a common repository meta model. The architecture allows for distinguishing between global schemas and private schemas.

The problem of information access and availability is addressed by the design of an abstract request language. A request is formulated by a predicate and an argument list. This is transformed automatically to SQL-statements appropriate for the DBMS that controls the information base containing the information searched for. In addition, a task and view oriented information system browser is proposed in order to meet the need to explore the (federated) repositories. This kind of queries are formulated in a graphical way.

In order to address the problem of management of change, the authors propose to use the Trader functionality itself to conceptualize changes and eventually adjust databases. This proposal is not elaborated however.

## DISCUSSANT'S CRITICISM

Although the paper is clearly structured, I found it rather hard to read for two reasons. One of them is that conceptual issues (specification) and technical issues (implementation) are mixed up, especially in section 3. The other one is that the figures are badly explained, and next to that contain errors. A serious error is contained in figure 1. If I understood the accompanying text well, then there are not three but two levels of abstraction: both QFD and DACAPO are instances of the type Method. At best DACAPO could said to be included by QFD (a relation type that is defined at the meta level), but DACAPO definitely cannot be an instance of QFD. A minor, but nasty error is contained in figure 3. To my knowledge, the last line of the query template should read: "{1}{1}MR.{1}M = {1}M.ID".

Although the paper draws heavily on the notion of task and its relationship to information need and information production, this attention appears to be nothing more than lip service, because the notion is not defined. It is the discussant's conviction that as long as notions like business process, task, communication and information remain not exactly interrelated, more or less axiomatic, notions, one cannot expect much progress in the field of information systems design & engineering, whether or not in the context of business reengineering. In this respect I like to bring to the authors' attention recent work that is rather successful in providing a profound and integrated understanding of these notions (see references below).

## BIBLIOGRAPHY

[1] Medina-Mora, R., Winograd, T., Flores, R., Flores, F., The Action Workflow approach to workflow management technology, in: Turner, J., Kraut, R. (eds.) Proceedings of the 4th Conference on Computer-Supported Cooperative Work, ACM, 31 october- 4 november, Toronto, 1992.

[2] Taylor, J.R., Rethinking the theory of Organizational Communication, Ablex Publishing, Norwood, N.J., 1993.

[3] Dietz, J.L.G., Busines Modelling for Business Redesign, Proceedings of the 27th Hawaii International Conference on System Sciences, IEEE Press, 1994.

[4] Dietz, J.L.G., Modelling business processes for the purpose of redesign, in: IFIP Transactions A-54 Business process Re-engineering, Information Systems Opportunities and Challenges, North-Holland, 1994.

# Modelling business relationships in a non-centralized systems environment - Discussion -

*Panos Constatopoulos*
*Institute of Computer Science FORTH*
*Science and Technology Park PoB. Box 138*
*GR-71110 Heraklion, Crete,Greece*
*Email: panos@ics.forth.gr*

In this paper Macdonald and Veryard present a methodology for modelling business relationships to support information system development in a decentralized, eventually federated, open setting.

Federation and openness are viewed from three prespectives : technical, organizational/ managerial and market/entrepreneurial. The authors discuss the issues involved in designing and implementing open, federated systems. In particular they address organizational issues, such as incremental development; systems and information crossing organizational boundaries; the effects of interaction distance on resource sharing, communication between agents and coordination between activities; determining requirements in view of multiple requirements ownership and organizational learning; and connections among organizational, technical and commercial aspects.

On the premise that openness essentially concerns federated computing accross organizational boundaries, the authors adopt organizational structure and boundaries as the perspective from which to model business relationships. In view of the organizational issues examined, this can offer useful support to the development of an open information system.

Although intuitively quite clear and well illustrated by the case study, the proposed methodology lacks formality and completeness. Underlying the four zones of organizational intervention (fig. 5) and the eight methodology tasks (fig. 6) there are a number of basic concepts (e.g. agent, interaction, activity, task, perspective) as well as a set of related axioms and rules concerning the construction of models. Some degree of formalization, providing precise semantics, would be necessary for the applicability of the methodology and eventual incorporation in computer-supported development environments. Furthermore, it will be very interesting to see a complete definition of the methodology including the implementation and learning zones. Implementation refers to organizational implementation. The authors view this as a process of change and introduce a vague notion of "problem solving engine" to address implementation and delivery problems.

Instrumental in the proposed methodology is the notion of 'interaction distance'. An intuitive notion, clearly illustrated in the case study, yet hard to make operational. They key to this effect would be the precise definition of interaction distance as a distance measure in an appropriate space, along with a procedure for computing it. Until such a definition becomes available , only illustrative use of the notion will be possible.

The applicability of the methodology to the development of federated systems relies on the explicit consideration of boundaries. It will further be interesting to investigate the nature of federated development of systems and the applicability of the business relationship modelling methodology in that case.

# Realization of a decentralized IS-strategy - Discussion -

*Rudolf Andersen*
*IDT, NTH*
*N-7034 Trondheim*
*Norway*
*Email: rudolf@idt.unit.no*

The paper presents a theory of an IS-strategy which focus on facilitating operation and co-operation of decentralised, function oriented and autonomous information systems designed to support independent business functions. This is a topic of great importance to contemporary businesses. Current trends are towards reengineering the business into independent profit centres and organising the work into lean work processes. Together with an increasing rate of change in the environment, the need for flexible information systems support to provide cost-effective solutions has not been reduced. The survivers in this climate are the businesses which manage to maintain adequate information systems support through the storms of organisational reshuffling. An important part of this is to maintain an information systems architecture which is modification friendly, and which supports rather than constrains the core business of the organisation.

The paper presents a theory which focus on autonomy of information systems. A strong link between responsibility of business functions and responsibility of information systems is emphasised. And the information resources of value to the whole business, are provided to the business functions through a functionally oriented information system. The theory is presented and discussed in an informal way. The IS-stategy theory presented includes several concepts/phenomena which have been heavily investigated in the IS literature, e.g., user involvement, management involvement, and user attitudes towards IS. Thus, one would expect to find more extensive references to the literature.

The analysis of the theory is supported by a case study of three different organisations employing alternative strategies for decentralising their information systems. This empirical approach potentially provides for very interesting results. The fact that this is a real life case study, means that the findings and conclusions have an interest to a number of organisations. However, we are told very little about the case study method. The organisations taking part in the case and the actual findings of the case are also described in very little detail. This means that the analysis of the theory presented and the conclusions drawn from the findings in the case study have limited credibility and value to the reader. In this respect it would have been better not to abstract so much, but rather give actual statements from the interviews.

# A software process model for business reengineering
# - Discussion -

*T. William Olle*
*T. William Olle Associates LTD*
*2 Ashley Park Road*
*KT12 1JU Walton-on-Thames, Surrey, United Kingdom*
*Email: 100010.3176@compuserve.com*

## OVERVIEW

The main aim of this paper appears to be to attempts to "bring together" earlier pieces of work from different sources namely

- SPM, the software process model by the authors
- BRP, the business re-engineering plan
- CMM2, level 2 of Capability Maturity Model by SEI

The aim of the bringing together appears to be more for comparative analysis rather than synthesis.

## BUSINESS RE-ENGINEERING

The frequent use in the paper of the term "business re-engineering" is somewhat misleading as the main thrust of the paper is towards a "software process model", in other words a model of the software process which should be used to develop the software to support the business processes. Business re-engineering is surely aimed at improving in the way the business processes are performed, this improvement being based on the availability of a computerized information system (which the paper persistently refers to as "software").

## PARTS OF ENTERPRISE MODELLING

One has to look at Figure 3 to realize that the SPM and the SISU Enterprise Model are extremely close. One of the more useful features of the paper is the description of the SISU enterprise model although, as described, it would be better referred to as an "enterprise modelling facility" (a term used once in the text. The term "enterprise model" should be restricted to its more frequent and more intuitive use for referring to a model of an enterprise and not for referring to " a way of modelling enterprises".

Nevertheless, the breakdown of enterprise modelling (in Figure 1) identifies the following parts: 1) configuration, 2) objectives, 3) activities and usage, 3) concepts, 4) actors, 5) functional requirements, 6) non-functional requirements, 7) information system, is quite useful, although it is not clear why everything has to be called a "sub-model" when it is clear it is a modelling facility . It is also not clear why the information system has to be positioned as part of enterprise modelling. Surely enterprise modelling is about developing an analytic model of the enterprise. On the basis of this analytic model, the computerized information system can be designed and the design can be regarded as prescriptive model.

One must also question whether non-functional requirements (as described in the paper) are actually part of enterprise modelling. They should preferably be positioned as part of the prescriptive statement about the computerized information system.

Another quibble concerns the interpretation of the "concepts sub-model". As described in terms of object types, relationships and object properties, it seems to be restricted to nothing more than good old fashioned data structuring (sometimes referred to as information structuring).

## CONFIGURATION MANAGEMENT AND TRACEABILITY

It is good to see configuration management and version control mentioned albeit only in the context of enterprise modelling. The orthogonality of configuration management to other parts of enterprise modelling is unquestioned. However, the all important concept of traceability should have been mentioned in this context as it is one of the more important reasons for needing configuration management.

In simple terms, it is necessary to be able to trace the capabilities provided in a computerized information system back to the requirements established in the model of the enterprise and to be able to trace the requirements established in the model of the enterprise forward to the capabilities provided in the computerized system.

## CONCLUSIONS

It would be surprising if a conclusion of this paper were that the three pieces of work compared in the paper were other than incomplete and disparate. Each of the three has a different perspective on the overall information systems life cycle. One can also argue that problems related to project management, important though they are, can usefully be separated from the essentially technique work being performed in a technical project.

Nevertheless there must exist a set of fundamental concepts and it might be helpful for teaching and for practice if researchers could achieve some consensus one what these concepts are.

# Coupling process models and business rules - Discussion -

*Colette Rolland*
*U.F.R. 06 - Gestion Universite de Paris 1, Pantheon Sorbonne*
*17, Rue de la Sorbonne*
*F-75231 Paris Cedex 5, France*
*Email: rolland@masi.ibp.fr*

The paper presents a nice, simple technique for relating a process model to a rule model. The process model is an extension of the Gane& Sarson's data flow diagramming technique which distinguishes between control and data flows and introduces the notion of AND, OR and XOR ports. The rule modeling language (ERL) allows to express rules in the form when (trigger) if (condition) then (consequence) to constraint static or dynamic aspects of the conceptual schema. Both models have been developed within the ESPRIT project TEMPORA. The paper clearly shows the correspondences between the process model and the rule model and show how change in one model can affect the other. Rules have been demonstrated to be an important aspect of conceptual modeling. However little effort has been paid to the methodological dimension of rule elucidation and formalization. By introducing the idea to derive business rules from data flow diagrams, the authors of the paper contribute significantly to this field. Moreover, the careful study of the impact of change in one model to another is a useful contribution to system evolution and reengineering. However it is not stated whether the models have been used in practice for business reengineering even though it is claimed that this is the purpose. The acceptance of the models in a professional arena and their actual usefulness have not been validated. The appropriateness of the approach in a distributed context remains to be demonstrated. But the paper presents a solid piece of work and an interesting and good mapping between a process model and a rule model.

# 14

# Panel Description: The future of business meetings - possibilities and problems of computer support in virtual organisations

*Panel Chair:*
*J. M. Haake, GMD-IPSI*

*Panel Participants:*
*M. Bever, IBM-ENC*
*J. Bumiller, Daimler-Benz Research*
*D. Martin, SMART Technologies*

Due to globalisation of markets, business processes of today are characterized by a change from individual work to team work as well as by a shift from single, independently acting corporations to virtual organisations operating as dynamic networks. On the other hand, trends emerging in this context are joint ventures and outsourcing - trends which result in an increased complexity and frequency of communication, co-ordination and co-operation within companies as well as across organisational boundaries. As a consequence, meetings at all levels have become more frequently over the past decade. This development calls for improved and enhanced communication facilities at an internal level, e.g., between various teams of a company, and at an external level, e.g., between a corporation and its suppliers or customers.

So far, efforts to electronically support synchronous communication (e.g., meetings by video-conferencing systems) have mostly been limited in terms of integration. The main reasons for insufficient progress - or even failure - of most current meeting support systems are their lack of flexibility and their insufficient integration with asynchronous modes of co-operation and related applications (e.g., workflow management systems, multimedia collaboration teleservices). Problems arising from this deficit are manyfold: Documents of a meeting participant are unusable since their format is incompatible to the electronic meeting support system; data are unaccessable due to missing interconnectivity; particular expertise required during a session is not available since there is no support for immediate electronic consultation of absent group members or external experts - or even more important, the only person who is authorised to make a crucial decision at some point of a negotiation can not be consulted.

Such deficits lead to incompensatory delays, decrease "speed to market" or reduce the quality of strategic managerial decisions. Moreover, they inevitably cause considerable costs for the intense communication and cooperation activities typically required in virtual organisations.

This financial overhead could be drastically reduced if integrated, flexible meeting support systems based on powerful telecommunication services and communication channels were in place which accounted for the particular requirements of virtual organisations.

There are a number of technologies available for implementing meeting support, such as: the integration of the computer and the phone, radio-linked notepads, desktop teleconferencing, video conferencing rooms, distributed coupled meeting rooms, etc.

The integration of the PC (and computers in general) with the telephone is what is driving a lot of the possibilities for having virtual meetings with our co-workers. Up to now, the ubiqitous availability of the telephone, the fact that everyone knows how to make a telephone work, and the inexpensive cost of acquisition and operation has focused electronic meetings through the telephone network.

But as the cost of being connected via video, audio, and data conferencing technologies comes down dramatically, as the 55 million people that buy new PC's this year get more familiar with the inherent technologies, and bandwidth becomes cheaper and more availability, there is likely to be a wide-spread adoption in the use of computer based telecommunications for the sharing of information.

There is likely to be some significant variation in how well organizations do in adopting and using this technology based upon the types of meetings that they conduct, the availability of cross-platform solutions, the ease of use of these technologies, the bridging of same time data access to different time information tools, the provision of means for integrating information, etc. Similarily, different kinds of meetings and situations may require different support thus leading to different kinds of meeting support (each with the potential of using different technology).

All of the problems are not solved, but the impetus is there for a whole new generation of tools to be accepted by workers in the world community. We have solved significant problems in getting people to accept new ways of conducting meetings at a distance and in the same meeting room. This will result in broader acceptance of the enabling software technologies that provide for more productive meetings in the coming months and years.

The goal of this panel was to discuss the requirements, potential solutions and problems of meeting support in virtual organisations.

## THE PANELISTS

**Joerg M. Haake** is a department manager at the Integrated Information and Publication Systems Institute of GMD - German National Research Center for Information Technology where he is leading research in hypermedia-based collaboration support systems.

**Dr. Martin Bever** is manager of Telecooperation IBM Deutschland Informationssysteme GmbH. He is managing a research department at the IBM European Networking Center. His main research interest is in distributed telecooperation applications.

**Dr. Johannes Bumiller** is a rearcher at Daimler-Benz Research Information Technology. His main interests are in Computer Supported Cooperative Work.

**David Martin**, President of SMART Technologies Inc. of Calgary, Alberta, Canada. Since 1987 he has led the Company to develop hardware and software products that allow the interconnection of people in electronic meetings. The Company is at the forefront of the integration of computers with the telephone through its alliance with Intel Corporation.

# 15

# Panel Description: Are the Organisations' IT competence the LIMITING factor ?

*Panel Chair:*

*Nils Høeg, Corporate Staff for Information Systems*
*Norsk Hydro a.s, Oslo, Norway*

*Panel Participants:*
*Dr. Espen Andersen, Foundation Research Program CSC*
*Research and Advisory Services, Cambridge, Mass., USA.*

## POSITION STATEMENT FROM PANEL CHAIR

With due respect to IFIP and it's name, from a pragmatic user industry point of view, it is only the last five to ten years that the computers have evolved into "information machines". The advent and proliferation of the PC, and the merging with the gradually deregulated communication world, has really given new meaning to the concept and realisation of "information systems". In numbers, the networked PCs are racing to catch up with that other info-machine, the telephone, of which there are about 1000 millions worldwide. Just as the telephone had significant organisational effects, so will the PC/IT-networks, with information machines that are potentially 10-100 times as powerful.

As we all know, the telephones (or most of them) are very easy to operate and use. Gradually, over several decades, the telephone services have become better and cheaper, and available to practically everyone working in organisations with information or communication needs. Managers and workers of practically all categories understand the potential function and role of the telephone, in day to day operation, in new approaches to e.g. marketing, and as an obvious resource when organising activities, whether locally, nationally or across the world.

Not so with the PC/networked info-machines. They have been thrust upon individuals and organisations at an unprecedented pace during half a decade, often by vendors and other pushers who don't understand the vital processes they are influencing. The hype is scoring even at the highest offices, and investments in individual HW and SW tools are passing all previous records.

While the present hype is vast, so are the potential benefits of the wired organisation and society. We who pretend to understand at least part of the larger picture should ask ourselves:

Which are the critical success factors for the realisation of these benefits, and the utilisation of the enormous material and human resources involved ?

Of the many factors that constitute today's and tomorrow's information architectures, it seems that most of the focus is on the material end: information highways, bandwidths, ISDN, faster/better/cheaper hardware, better/smarter/cheaper software and methods, etc. These are all objects of investments and ROI, sales and profits, and grants and funds for research and development. These are all healthy drivers in our marketdriven economies, which function very well in the information industries and markets. We certainly want deregulated and non-dominated markets, and we are almost there. Thus, I don't see any truly limiting factors ind the material IT-arena. Some countries and regions may have competitive disadvantages, but in the large, world (IFIP-type) picture : We have and will have more than enough of material IT-resources available.

BUT, will we have the human resources available, with the knowledge, understanding and skills (=3D competence) to utilise the vast offerings of= IT ? Or are we forced to drink from a fire hydrant ?

The simple and plain position of mine is that IT-competence is the limiting factor for our utilisation and application of IT. This applies to practically all organisations, and particularly to decentralised organisations, where many more individuals and organisational units will influence and further develop the information systems.

The lack of IT-competence is not within the IT-communities. The overwhelming challenge is to provide all influencing participants in the present and future workforce with the necessary IT-competence (knowledge, understanding and skills). Influencing participants are those employees which in a large or small way influence the way in which organisations are organised. Traditionally strictly in the realm of managers, in the (near) future organisations all participants should understand the objectives and processes, and influence by contributing to improvements as part of the job. The necessary IT-competence to do this will of course vary with organisational position and role, but I venture to state that all employees in future, successful organisations need to have a considerable IT-competence compared with today, in order to function well and to be comfortable in their work environment.

## SUGGESTED ISSUES FOR PANEL DISCUSSION

Can we (quickly) agree that IT-competence, among the users, could be a limiting factor, or at least one of a few critical factors, for the successful development, use and improving of distributed information systems ?

If so, could we discuss the role of the IT- professionals in alleviating this situation (e.g. by understanding more about what goes on in business and other=20 organisations).

We should also present and discuss approaches to defining and realising the necessary IT-competence levels for the users, at the base level (like the Finnish Computer Driving Licence), at the management level, and for other professions.

## INDEX OF CONTRIBUTORS


Aerts, A.T.M. 51
Agrawal, D. 1
Alonso, G. 1
Axelsson, K. 168

Berztiss, A.T. 184
Borbinha, J. 84
Bubenko, J.A. 184

Delgardo, J. 84

El-Abbadi, A. 1
Elmasri, R. 35

Fijma, D. 118

Gunthor, R. 1

Hofman, W. 51

Jarke, M. 100
Jeusfeld, M. 100
Juopperi, J. 19

Kanmath, M. 1
Khan, K 35

Lehtola, A. 19
Lugeon, J.-C. 67

Macdonald, I.G. 133
McBrien, P. 201
Mijers, G.M. 118
Mills, J.J. 35
Miriyala, S. 35
Mohan. C. 1

Pacull, F. 67
Peters, P. 100
Pihlajamaa, O. 19

Seltveit, A.H. 201
Silva, A. 84
Sladek, A. 19
Somers, L.J. 51
Subramanian, K. 35
Szczurko, P. 100

Veijnalainen, J. 19
Verhoef, T.F. 118
Veryard, R.A. 133

# KEYWORD INDEX


Business
  process 184
  process re-engineering 19, 201
  re-engineering 184
  relationship modelling 133
  rule modelling 201
  transactions 51

Capability maturity model 184
Case studies 168
CGI gateways 84
Client-server computation 84
Computer supported cooperative work 19
Conceptual modelling 201
CSCW 67

Databases 84
Decentralisation 118, 168
Distributed Systems 1

EDI 51
Enterprise
  model 184
  modelling 133

Federated information system architecture 100

Information
  access mechanisms 100
  distribution 118
Information systems 84, 168
  architecture 168
  strategy 168

Internet 84

Large scale distributed systems 67

Naming 67

Open distributed processing 133

Petri nets 51
Process
  model 184
  modelling 201

Quality management processes 100

Reliability 1
Repositories 100
Responsibility 168
Reuse 118

Scalability 1
Simulation 51
Software process 184
Systems documentation 118

Transaction protocol 51

User participation 168

Workflow 19
  Management Systems 1
  tools 19
WWW 84

MIX
Papier aus verantwortungsvollen Quellen
Paper from responsible sources
FSC® C105338

If you have any concerns about our products,
you can contact us on
**ProductSafety@springernature.com**

In case Publisher is established outside the EU,
the EU authorized representative is:
**Springer Nature Customer Service Center GmbH**
**Europaplatz 3, 69115 Heidelberg, Germany**

Printed by Libri Plureos GmbH
in Hamburg, Germany